About the Author

JULIE GREER JOHNSON is Associate Professor of Spanish in the Department of Romance Languages at the University of Georgia. She has contributed articles to *Celestinesca, Hispania, Hispanófila, Kentucky Romance Quarterly, Latin American Literary Review, Hispanic Journal*, and *South Atlantic Bulletin*.

Women in Colonial Spanish American Literature

Women in Colonial Spanish American Literature

Literary Images

JULIE GREER JOHNSON

Contributions in Women's Studies, Number 43

GREENWOOD PRESS
Westport, Connecticut • London, England

Library of Congress Cataloging in Publication Data

Johnson, Julie Greer.
    Women in colonial Spanish American literature.

    (Contributions in women's studies, ISSN 0147-104X;
no. 43)
    Bibliography: p.
    Includes index.
    1. Spanish American literature—To 1800—History
and criticism. 2. Women in literature. I. Title.
II. Series.
PQ7081.J54   1983   860'.9'9287   83-1500
ISBN 0-313-23681-X (lib. bdg.)

Library of Congress Catalog Card Number: 83-1500
ISBN: 0-313-23681-X
ISSN: 0147-104X

First published in 1983

Greenwood Press
A division of Congressional Information Service, Inc.
88 Post Road West
Westport, Connecticut 06881

Printed in the United States of America

10 9 8 7 6 5 4 3 2 1

In memory of Frances Greer Johnson

CONTENTS

ACKNOWLEDGMENTS

I wish to express my gratitude to Professor Merle E. Simmons whose excellence as a teacher and scholar has enriched my life and shaped my professional career. His friendship and guidance during and since my days as a student at Indiana University have meant a great deal to me personally and have served to inspire all of my scholarly works including the present volume. I would also like to thank Professor Raquel Chang-Rodríguez of The City College of the City University of New York and Professor M. Ruth Lundelius of the University of Georgia for reading the final manuscript of this book and for making valuable suggestions for its improvement.

This project was generously funded by research grants that I received from the University of Georgia over a three-year period. I am especially indebted to Dean John C. Dowling of the Graduate School, to the late Professor Charles H. Douglas, Assistant Vice President for Research, to Professor Jean-Pierre Piriou, Head of the Department of Romance Languages, and to Professor Leroy Ervin and the members of the Sarah Moss Fellowship Committee. In addition to its financial support, I am grateful to the university for the leave of absence that permitted me to consult resources essential to my research and thank the staffs of the Nettie Lee Benson Collection of the University of Texas at Austin and the Bancroft Library of the University of California at Berkeley for their cooperation.

Throughout the text of this book, I have included a number of quotations from the primary sources used in my study, and I have had those excerpts that have not appeared in previous English works translated. For the translations of the descriptions of women in chapters 1 and 2, I wish to recognize Professor Joaquín Ponce of the Virginia Military Institute and Raquel Elizondo and Professor Miriam Balboa Echeverría, both of the University of Texas at Austin, for those in the remaining three chapters.

Women in
Colonial
Spanish
American
Literature

INTRODUCTION

The study of women in colonial Spanish American literature has focused primarily over the years upon the works of the Mexican poet and intellectual, Sor Juana Inés de la Cruz and the portrayal of female characters in *La Araucana* by the Spanish epic poet, Alonso de Ercilla. While the literary production of the period's greatest writer and the most artistically rendered descriptions of women by a single author are important elements to such an investigation, they represent only two sources of information on colonial woman's literary image. The material dealing with women is not concentrated in any one genre of colonial writing but is scattered throughout the prose, poetry, and drama produced over the three hundred years of Spanish domination in the New World. A compilation of these references reveals to some extent the vision men had of women and their attitude toward them and the perception women had of themselves and their place in society. Although the image of women is taken from a literary context, it often provides information concerning their role in history and their participation in the development of the arts.

Women who appear in colonial literature represent a wide variety of social, racial, cultural, and economic backgrounds, and they come from many areas of Spain's American possessions. These factors, however, do not entirely determine the treatment they receive. The portrayal of women was also shaped by the stereotypes found in Peninsular literature of the late Medieval period and the Golden Age which represented traditional attitudes of Spanish society toward women. Once these images were transferred to the New World, they inspired other writers to follow them and ordered to some degree social patterns in the colonies. Colonial authors, however, did not usually incorporate previous literary models indiscriminately or directly into their works but carefully selected those which suited their present circumstances and their purpose for writing. By placing them in a new situation and endowing them with different dress, manners, customs, and names, they artistically transformed these Spanish characters into residents of the Indies. The literary techniques used by colonial writers to delineate a female character include the author's commentary about her, the narration of her actions, the incorporation of speeches made by her, and conversations between her and other important characters who appear in the work. While the imprint of Spain's literature on colonial letters has been widely recognized by scholars and extensively studied in general, few of them have applied this concept directly to the portrayal of women.

Two outstanding women, Sor Juana Inés de la Cruz and Madre Francisca Castillo, dominate the small group of female writers during the colonial period, and their works have attracted the attention of literary scholars both past and present. Even though interest in women's studies and feminism has increased the amount of recent research done on the period's principal literary figure, Sor Juana Inés de la Cruz, she has been a perennial subject for many decades. Some of the most important criticism regarding her own image or the one she presents of other women are: Ermilo Abreu Gómez' prologue to *Poesías de Juana Inés de la Cruz*; Anita Arroyo's *Razón y pasión de Sor Juana*; Ezequiel A. Chávez's *Ensayo de psicología de Sor Juana Inés de la Cruz;* Julio Jiménez Rueda's *Sor Juana Inés de la Cruz en su época*; Irving A. Leonard's "A Baroque Poetess" in his *Baroque Times in Old Mexico*; Alfonso Méndez Plancarte's prologue to his edition of her complete works; Amado Nervo's *Juana de Asbaje*; and Ludwig Pfandl's *Sor Juana Inés de la Cruz, La décima musa de México: Su vida, su poesía, su psique.* Two comprehensive views of Madre Castillo's writings are contained in Darío Achury Valenzuela's edition of her works and María Teresa Morales Borrero's *La Madre Castillo, su espiritualidad y su estilo.*

Among male writers whose descriptions of women have been previously examined by scholars are Alonso de Ercilla and Juan del Valle y Caviedes. Ercilla's portrayal of women has been a recurrent theme in articles dealing with his epic poem *La Araucana*. From José Toribio Medina's view of Ercilla's Araucanian women in his article "Las mujeres de *La Araucana*" to that of Lía Schwartz Lerner in her "Tradición literaria y heroínas indias en *La Araucana*," the interpretation of these female characters has changed considerably as sources of the poem have come to light. Once perceived as historical figures, Ercilla's women are now thought to be primarily literary. Although Caviedes' literary treatment of women is not the most important aspect of his works, it has drawn the attention of scholars who have studied his poetry. Assessments of his views on women are contained in Daniel R. Reedy's *The Poetic Art of Juan del Valle Caviedes* and Glen L. Kolb's *Juan del Valle y Caviedes: A Study of the Life, Times and Poetry of a Spanish Colonial Satirist.*

Supplementing these important studies are several papers on or related to the topic of women that I have published. They include: "Feminine Satire in Concolorcorvo's *El lazarillo de ciegos caminantes*" [*South Atlantic Bulletin* 45, no. 1 (1980)], "Three Celestinesque Figures of Colonial Spanish American Literature" [*Celestinesca* 5, no. 1 (1981)], "Three Dramatic Works by Juan del Valle y Caviedes" [*Hispanic Journal* 3, no. 1 (1982)], "A Caricature of Spanish Women in the New World by the Inca Garcilaso de la Vega" [*Latin American Literary Review* 9, no. 18 (1981)], and "Bernal Díaz and the Women of the Conquest" [*Hispanófila* 82 (1984)]. These articles in revised form have been incorporated into this book and appear with the permission of their editors.

Given the small number of publications dealing with the topic of women in colonial literature and their limited approach, it is clear that many aspects of this subject have remained virtually untouched by scholars. The purpose of this study is to present a general overview of the literary images of women created by the main historians, poets, satirists, and dramatists writing in Spanish between 1492 and 1800, including not only men's vision of women but also women's view of themselves. In examining the portraits of women, attention is given to their sources in Spanish literature, their adaptation to a New World context, and their relevance to colonial Spanish American society. The descriptions appearing in this study come from major colonial Spanish American writings. They were composed in America and treat American themes. Besides these sources, however, a limited number of Spanish works containing exceptional portraits of the New World's female residents is reviewed.

In categorizing the numerous and diverse images of women, I have considered the writer's sex, the attitude of the writer toward women and possible causal factors for it, and the genre and purpose of the work in which they appear, and have chronologically organized each unit of my study in the following manner.

The first two chapters contain idealized visions of women by males, and the attitude of these authors toward their subjects is a remnant of the age of chivalry. Chapter 1 deals with historical prose and poetry designed to glorify the deeds of the New World's men. Female characters who appear in these works are generally strong and courageous and possess the qualities of the epic hero or the legendary Amazon. The second chapter provides a profile of women in lyric poetry written specifically to pay tribute to them. Woman's image in these pieces is that of perfect beauty and impeccable virtue and follows the poetic descriptions of Petrarch, Garcilaso de la Vega, and Quevedo.

The portraits of women examined in chapter 3 are again creations of men; however, in this section dealing with colonial satire, they are presented from a negative point of view. Women are portrayed as evil, ugly, and immoral, their characterization having been influenced by Rojas' *La Celestina*, Quevedo's scathing descriptions of female figures, and the unsavory women of the picaresque novel.

Chapter 4 treats women and female characters in colonial drama. Because of the diverse reasons for writing and presenting dramatic works in the New World, the attitudes and imagery regarding women are quite varied. The plays considered in this segment of the book range from the catechistic skit, in which Eve's role in man's fall is emphasized, to the sophisticated *comedias*, in which ladies become involved in numerous love entanglements. Several of Sor Juana's pieces are discussed in this chapter, since they represent the highest level of excellence attained by a colonial playwright writing in the colonies.

The views women writers present of themselves are contained in the fifth and last chapter. Because females were denied a formal education in colonial Spanish America, few possessed the skills with which to record their reactions and responses to the New World's environment. Of those who did compose literary works, however, only two authors, Sor Juana Inés de la Cruz and Madre Francisca Castillo, have left detailed autobiographical accounts. Like their male counterparts, they too depended upon previous literary images. Even though Sor Juana found herself pioneering a new role for women, she was unable to state this openly in her writings and was forced to adopt the vision Church officials had of her as a nun. Madre Castillo, on the other hand, chose to emulate Saint Teresa of Jesus and to portray herself as the Spanish mystic had done earlier in her autobiography.

From my analytical review of the portraits of women presented in these designated areas of colonial Spanish American literature, a pattern of reality interwoven with fantasy unfolds. The combination of these two elements reveals not only the adaptability of Spanish literary tradition, that is types, characters, themes, and so forth to the new social milieu of Spain's empire in America but also divulges the desires, dreams, preferences, and prejudices that men had throughout the period with regard to women and shows to some extent the impact that these images had on the way women viewed themselves.

CHAPTER 1

WOMEN IN EARLY HISTORICAL WRITINGS

Historical works of literary merit, which document the Spaniards' exploration, conquest, religious conversion, and settlement of the New World, offer the first view of women in America and outline their involvement in these early endeavors. A number of women, many of whom were the relatives or consorts of principal male participants in these historical events, were recognized individually by colonial writers for successfully meeting the challenges posed by the harsh environment and hostile conditions of the New World. The female population in general is presented as a major factor in the establishment of the socioeconomic foundations for a stable society, although it suffered considerably during this tumultuous time. Colonial works also reflect the regulation of both Spanish and Indian women by church and state and record the progressive emigration of Spanish women to the New World, the importance of marriage and remarriage in solidifying control over new territories, and the function of women in the transmission of cultural tradition.

The previous portrayal of female characters in Spanish literature, however, especially in novels of chivalry, often determined both the attitude of early Spanish American authors toward their female subjects and their vision of women in the New World. This confluence of historical and literary currents in colonial writing begins with the discovery of the Indies, which offered the Spaniards a real-life opportunity for adventures only imagined by writers of chivalric novels.[1] These fantastic romances, which enjoyed their greatest popularity during the first half of the sixteenth century and were avidly read on both sides of the Atlantic,[2] molded the new arrivals' perception of America and set standards of behavior to be observed in Spain's newly acquired territories. Ambitious soldiers of fortune, who assumed the role of the heroic knight errant in exotic lands, obeyed prescribed rules of chivalric decorum. They served God and king, aided the downtrodden, and honored and protected women.[3] Their vision of the opposite sex was an idealized one, based upon a lady's beauty and virtue, but it was also influenced by the Spaniards' love of strength and their glorification of war. The perfect woman, according to these men, was one who demonstrated certain admirable masculine traits, since some feminine characteristics were associated with cowardice and weakness. The artistic portrayal of women as brave and armed was not inappropriate for their sex but constituted a tribute to their powers and abilities.[4] Because of the appearance of warring women in creative narratives written in Spain, the Spaniards were not surprised to see women in the New World engage in warlike activities and demonstrate considerable prowess, and they often projected this image upon other women whose accomplishments were meritorious.

Many adventurers who came to the New World, however, did not follow these chivalric canons of conduct, and they were severely criticized for their behavior by some colonial writers. The abuse of women was condemned as ungentlemanly and a sign of moral turpitude. Women as well did not always restrict themselves to the acquisition of respected manly characteristics, and they too were maligned for their display of unwarranted boldness, cruelty, and promiscuity and were occasionally associated with previously held images of evil. Whether praising men for their heroic deeds or admonishing them for their failure to comply with acceptable standards of behavior, explorers, conquerors, missionaries, and men of letters portrayed women in their works to a limited extent, and the influence of Spain's light literature may be traced throughout their characterizations.

The search for such marvelous wonders of the world as the Fountain of Youth, El Dorado, the Seven Cities of Cibola, and Utopia obsessed Spanish fortune hunters who came to the New World and whetted their appetites for inconceivable wealth and fame. The most tantalizing myth, however, and one which promised both of these rewards, was that of the Amazon women. This belief in their existence drove the Spaniards onward in the exploration of two continents and directly influenced some of their first written impressions of native American women.[5] Since the time of the ancient Greeks, rumors of a tribe of female warriors, who lived apart from men and who fought with solid gold weaponry, had circulated widely in western Europe, and during the Medieval period, this legend was kept alive by travelers' reports from all parts of the world. Columbus was the first of many explorers to suggest that these famous *viragos* were inhabitants of his newly discovered lands, and he notes in his journal that they lived in caves on the island of Matinino. He was unable to confirm his hypothesis, however, because unfavorable sailing conditions thwarted his attempts to reach its shore.[6]

Apart from the historical documentation of alleged Amazon settlements, this fascinating legend was enhanced by the publication of Garci-Rodríguez de Montalvo's *Sergas de Esplandián*, the sequel to *Amadís de Gaula*, which includes an encounter between Amadís' son and the Amazon Queen Calafia. The following excerpt taken from these exploits establishes the possibility that the kingdom of the Amazons might lie within the Spaniards' recently discovered territories and provides a description of this race of women warriors:

You should know that to the right of the Indies there was an island called California, very close to Earthly Paradise, which was populated by black women, without a single male among them, whose style of living was almost like that of the Amazons. These [women] had striking physiques and courageous and passionate spirits and great strength.[7]

Sergas de Esplandián enjoyed tremendous popularity as the heir to the first and best chivalric novel, and its appearance at the outset of the sixteenth century made it readily available to soldiers departing for the Indies.

In 1518 Juan Díaz, a member of the Grijalva expedition sent to Yucatan, reported the presence of a colony settled exclusively by women.[8] Rumors such as this one further raised expectations that the Amazons were within reach and led to the proliferation of geographical designations using the words *mujeres* [women] or *amazonas* [Amazons]. In his *Historia general y natural de las Indias [General and Natural History of the Indies]*, Gonzalo Fernández de Oviedo points out that the Spaniards mistakenly assigned such toponyms to areas where they found groups of armed females and not women with only one breast as the original Greek term "Amazon" indicates.[9] Although the place name "Punta de las Mujeres" ["Cape of the Women"][10] given to the location mentioned by Grijalva is inappropriate, it prompted the Cuban governor, Diego Velázquez, to warn Cortés of the dangers posed by this tribe in orders dated October 23, 1518.[11] While the conqueror did not encounter these elusive women, he states in his fourth letter to Charles V that his lieutenant, Cristóbal de Olid, had proof of their existence in western New Spain. Encouraged by Olid's findings, Cortés commissioned another expedition in 1524. In his instructions to its leader, he refers to the quest for the wealth of these *guerreras* [female warriors] and notes their similarities with the Amazons of "ancient histories."[12]

Efforts to discover the Amazons' stronghold were not limited to mainland Mexico and the Caribbean islands but continued in many parts of the New World. In South America, Francisco de Orellana led an exploratory mission in 1541 and 1542 to penetrate the continent's jungle interior by traveling its mightiest river system. The account of this trip, written by Fray Gaspar de Carvajal, offers a detailed description of the Amazons that they supposedly met and information about their segregated society.[13] Explaining the Spaniards' narrow victory over a band of Indians, Carvajal points to its exceptional female leadership and the extraordinary prowess of its women:

I want it to be known. . . why these Indians defended themselves in this manner. It must be explained that they are the subjects of, and tributaries to, the Amazons, and, our coming having been made known to them, they went to them to ask help, and there came as many as ten or twelve of them, for we ourselves saw these women, who were there fighting in front of all the Indian men as women captains, and these latter fought so courageously that the Indian men did not dare to turn their backs, and anyone who did turn his back they killed with clubs right there before us, and this is the reason why the Indians kept up their defense for so long. These women are very white and tall, and have very long hair braided and wound about the head, and they are very robust and go about naked, [but] with their privy parts covered, with their bows and arrows in their hands, doing as much fighting as ten Indian men, and indeed there was one woman among these who shot an arrow a span deep into one of the brigantines, and others less deep, so that our brigantines looked like porcupines.[14]

If the eyewitness report were not convincing enough, conclusive proof of the existence of Amazons was provided for the Spaniards by an

Indian prisoner's testimony. Carvajal's loose transcription of his interrogation reveals the Spaniards' state of psychological preparedness for such a curious experience and their eagerness to have these warring women correspond closely to their literary predecessors. In addition to locating the riches of the Amazons, they must have been intrigued by the concept of a matriarchal society that contrasted so sharply with their own social patterns and traditions. The captive, who was undoubtedly in no position to disagree with the Spaniards, probably responded very simply to the carefully devised questions of his impressionable captors. According to the Indian, Queen Coroni ruled seventy towns where her female subjects lived in lavish splendor without men. At certain times of the year, however, they engaged in mating rituals with men from neighboring settlements in order to perpetuate their closed society in which the female offspring were raised within the confines of their sovereign domain and the males were disposed of (pp. 104–5).

The Inca Garcilaso de la Vega, who tells the story of Hernando de Soto's expedition based upon the testimony of one of its survivors, hints that these bellicose women also inhabited the North American kingdom known as Florida. He describes the fervor with which the Indian women fought at the battle of Mauvila and mentions that the Spaniards were reluctant to defend themselves once they discovered that their adversaries were females. A little later in his narrative, he indicates, in an episode which takes place in the town of Tula, that the region's women did not always use orthodox methods of attack. In this instance, five Indian women confront Francisco de Reynoso Cabeza de Vaca and subdue him by grabbing hold of his genitals.[15]

Early descriptions of the New World's warring native women made by members of expeditions to Mexico, South America, and Florida established the strong, courageous woman as the dominant American female type. While the quest for everlasting youth and untold wealth and happiness came to a disappointing conclusion at the end of the age of exploration, interest in the Amazons continued throughout the early years of the colonial period. Even when the impossibility of their actual existence was confirmed, their attraction as a literary theme persisted, and they emerged as symbols of feminine strength and independence. In Spain, Lope de Vega and Tirso de Molina incorporated the Amazon legend into their Golden Age *comedias*,[16] and in the colonies, the specific reference to these mythological females or the general allusion to women resembling them may be found in the historical prose and poetry written from the time of the conquest of Mexico to the period of the Spanish campaigns in Chile.

The most extensive and varied testimony about women during the conquest years is contained in the *Historia verdadera de la conquista de Nueva España [The True History of the Conquest of New Spain]* written by Bernal Díaz del Castillo, a soldier in Cortés's army.[17] In his colorful and sensitive account of the dramatic events of the Spaniards' march to Mexico and the city's ultimate capture, he notes the arrival of the first Spanish woman on the coast of Yucatan and the participation of both Spanish and Indian women in the fall of the Aztec empire. He also offers a glimpse into the personal lives of several notable members of the Spanish military by alluding to the wives and female companions of Cortés, Alvarado, and Guerrero. Reflecting the popular culture possessed by Spanish soldiers of the sixteenth century, Bernal Díaz expressed his wonderment at women in the New World and interpreted their actions in accordance with chivalric conventions. He pays homage to the brave female participants in the Mexican conquest and courteously acknowledges the presence and support of others. By using the hero from *Amadís de Gaula* as a literary model, he elevates the role of an Indian woman to that of heroine and endows her with abilities uncommonly attributed to her sex. The canons of courtly love and Fernando de Rojas' *La Celestina* as well were not unknown to him and were incorporated into his history to a lesser extent.

While the precise role of women in the conquest of Mexico has eluded historians since the conclusion of the siege of Tenochtitlán, it is clear that the presence of one woman, Doña Marina, parallels the most important events of this monumental campaign and accounts in no small way for the remarkable success of the Spaniards. A vivid portrait of this exceptional woman, who receives only cursory mention by Cortés in his *Cartas [Letters]*,[18] is provided by Bernal Díaz. The latter's personal knowledge about her and his unaffected style of writing afford the reader a clear yet intensely subjective image of her.

From a historical standpoint, the information offered by Bernal Díaz concerning Marina's part in the campaigns against the Indians is the most complete and accurate record written by an eyewitness, and his avid interest in minor points of concern such as her background, physical appearance, and demeanor vastly enriches his unpretentious account. He first mentions the Indian woman, who was destined to assure the final Spanish victory over the powerful Aztec empire, when she was given to Cortés as a gift from the chiefs of Tabasco.[19] Indian maidens were customarily offered by chieftains to outsiders in order to form new alliances and reaffirm old friendships. Even on this occasion, Bernal Díaz' reference to her as "one very excellent woman" (XXXVI, 58) foreshadows her imminent greatness. As the victim of a cruel deception, Marina had been delivered to a neighboring tribe by her mother and stepfather in order to deny her the right to succession as *cacica* (noble female leader) of her native Painala. When she is awarded to the Spaniards, she is baptized because she is to become the companion of Alonso Hernández Puerto Carrero and receives the title of *Doña* to denote the high station she previously held among her own people.[20] Marina's obvious precocity and refined comportment, as well as her comeliness, gained her immediate recognition from the Spaniards and established her as a prominent and well-respected participant in the conquest. Little light is shed upon her personal relationship with Cortés in Bernal Díaz' account, but her intimate ties with the commander of the expedition are unabashedly disclosed by the revelation that she bore him a son. Later she is married to the Spaniard, Juan Jaramillo (XXXVII, 61–62).

From Cortés's initial advance into the interior of Mexico to his final assault on the capital, Marina is constantly at his side and serves as an interpreter, adviser, messenger, informer, and peacemaker. At Cholula, her timely discovery and disclosure of a conspiracy against the Spaniards saved Cortés and his army from certain annihilation (LXXXIII, 146–47). Her linguistic acumen, invaluable from the beginning of her association with the Spaniards, enabled Cortés to communicate with Moctezuma (LXXXVIII, 161) and aided in the Aztec ruler's peaceful captivity (XCV, 183). Prior to the rebellion in Tenochtitlán, Doña Marina had warned the Spaniards of a possible attack (CVIII, 210), and in 1521, she again served as translator during the Spaniards' last siege of the city (CLIII, 358).

Although Bernal Díaz' depiction of Doña Marina is basically historical, he has carefully selected portions of her life that enhance her stature as a participant in the conquest. His elaboration of these episodes makes her into a true heroine. By comparing or contrasting her to several easily recognizable models from Spanish literary tradition, Bernal Díaz is able to describe the extent of Marina's unusual strength, spirit, and wisdom and her amazing acts of heroism. Like the awesome appearance of the magnificent city of Tenochtitlán, her intelligence, resourcefulness, and courage also proved to be a wonder of the New World for the soldier of fortune from Medina del Campo. Her presence, like many other elements of the American scene, appeared to belong to the world of fantasy. In this vein, Bernal Díaz particularly notes Marina's nonconformity with the traditional concepts of womanhood, which recalls in several respects the life and character of the legendary Amazons. Doña Marina, like these mythical females, lived in a natural state which demanded from her "such manly valor," and he categorically states: "[she] never allowed us to see any sign of fear in her, only a courage passing that of woman" (LXVI, 115).[21] Although she never actually takes up arms, Marina's adeptness at survival and her performance of tasks uncommon for a woman are directly related to warlike activity. As a leader, she is referred to as a "great chieftainess" and a "mistress of vassals" (XXXVI, 59), and her highly visible position as Cortés's interpreter makes her a prominent figure in the eyes of the Indians. Marina's Indian name, Malinche, also meant the companion of Marina, and was frequently used by them in reference to Cortés (LXXIV, 129).[22]

The influence of *Amadís* on the *Historia verdadera* of Bernal Díaz may be seen throughout the work, and it appears to have been a determining factor in the author's decision to present such detailed information about Marina's life. After introducing Doña Marina, Bernal Díaz presents one of his many digressions from the main thread of his historical account. This carefully selected interwoven episode is a succinct compendium of Marina's past along with a future event in her life that will take place after the conquest of Mexico. The purpose of these intercalated occurrences is to establish Marina as a heroine and to set forth evidence of a potential for greatness even during her youth. In several ways, the early happenings in the life of this young Indian woman correspond to events during the childhood and adolescence of the exemplary Christian knight Amadís.[23] Both Doña Marina and Amadís are of noble lineage, and as children, they become victims of efforts to deny them their birthright. After the departure of their fathers—one dies and the other undertakes a journey—their mothers, with the aid of family servants or slaves, abandon them in secret. Amadís and Marina are then reared at some distance from their homes and by people whose culture is different from their own.[24]

Interjecting a personal note, Bernal Díaz mentions that he knew Marina's mother and continues to relate the circumstances of their meeting some years later. The second part of this insertion is reminiscent as well of a similar episode in the life of the young Amadís. After the children are deserted by their kin, members of both families are reunited. The scenes in which their reunions take place are tearful and filled with remorse as the regrettable events of the past loomed over their gatherings. All is forgiven, however, when the warmth and generosity of the hero and heroine assure a sincere reconciliation with their parents.[25] In these two instances, Christian ethics dominate the behavior of Amadís and Marina, and both young people serve as defenders of the faith, Amadís by exemplifying good in his performance of noble deeds and Marina by symbolizing the conversion of an entire race of pagans. They accept without question God's will in determining their destiny, and both exude love, understanding, and respect for their mothers regardless of the offenses deliberately carried out against them.

Although the lack of knowledge about native women led to the glorification of some, as in the case of Doña Marina, it caused suspicions to surround others, especially older women who had remained loyal to their traditional way of life. An example of this may be found in Bernal Díaz' narration of the treacherous plot perpetrated by Moctezuma against the Spaniards and Marina's courageous effort to save them. The Spanish author takes advantage of the drama and suspense of the moment to add more novelistic elements to his account. His additions to this historical event concern the development of the character of an old Indian woman who becomes the focus of attention while attempting to arrange an advantageous marriage for her son. She approaches Marina with her proposition and reveals the Aztec conspiracy in order to protect her future daughter-in-law. Because of her function as a go-between, the old woman is presented in a role similar to that of the Celestina[26] when she comes to visit Melibea for the first time:

There was an old Indian woman, the wife of a Cacique, who knew all about the plot and trap which had been arranged, and she had come secretly to Doña Marina, having noticed that she was young and good looking and rich, and advised her, if she wanted to escape with her life, to come with her to her house, for it was certain that on that night or during the next day we were all going to be killed. . . .and she would there marry her to her son, the brother of a youth who accompanied her. When Doña Marina understood this (as she was always very shrewd) she said to her: "O mother, thank you for what you have told me! I would go with you at once except that I have no one here whom I can trust to carry my clothes and jewels of gold of which I have many; for goodness sake, mother, wait here a little while, you and your son, and tonight we will set out, for now, as you can see, these Teules are on the watch and will hear us." (LXXXIII, 146–47)[27]

The old woman's negative portrayal is a result of her attempt to corrupt a forthright and seemingly unassuming individual, and Bernal Díaz uses this sinister figure to develop further the characterization of his heroine. By placing Marina beside the Celestinesque Cholulan *cacica*, he emphasizes the dissimilitude of the two women, thus enhancing Marina's image as a beneficent person, and represents symbolically the eternal struggle between the forces of good and evil. In his re-creation of this scene, even the dialogue is reminiscent of the repartee between the lovely, young girl and the deceptive and greedy old woman of Rojas' masterpiece, as the Indian matron's ploy is based on flattery and Marina addresses her as "mother," a common appellation for a person of her age.[28] Neither Melibea nor Marina, however, is taken in by the persuasive words of the old women, and both try to deceive them. Melibea feigns opposition to Celestina's proposal in order to conceal her interest in the young Calisto, and Marina pretends to accept the Indian woman's offer but immediately informs Cortés.

Other Indian women who are identified individually in the *Historia verdadera* are usually, like Doña Marina, consorts of noteworthy Spaniards. Gonzalo Guerrero, Pedro de Alvarado, and Bernal Díaz himself were among the many Spaniards awarded daughters of Indian chieftains, and each one of these women is mentioned by the aged conqueror.[29] The most colorful characterization of the three is that of the wife of the stranded Spaniard Guerrero. His description of her, like that of Doña Marina, emphasizes the unusual characteristics of native women, but he notes in this case some of the liberties exercised by them that were not particularly flattering according to his way of thinking. The one sentence of quoted discourse allegedly spoken by the *india* (Indian woman) conveys quite clearly her negative response to Jerónimo de Aguilar's suggestion—that Guerrero join Cortés—as well as her aggressive and arrogant nature. Graphically and concisely it reveals the author's ability to provide immediate insight into the personality of this spirited woman and to disclose his judgment of her indirectly: "And the Indian wife of Gonzalo spoke to Aguilar in her own tongue very angrily and said to him: 'What is this slave coming here for talking to my husband—go off with you, and don't trouble us with any more words'" (XXVII, 44).

Bernal Díaz offers scant information about Spanish women who participated in the conquest because few dared to subject themselves to the rigorous and dangerous day-to-day existence of the mainland.[30] However, he does mention several of the earliest female settlers to come to Mexico and the fate that awaited them there. Unfortunately, the first women to reach the Mexican coast were shipwrecked in 1511. The tragic story of their death at the hands of natives is told by Jerónimo de Aguilar, who was a survivor of that expedition and who later became a soldier in Cortés' army (XXIX, 47). Only one Spanish woman, María de Estrada, is reported by Bernal Díaz to have accompanied Cortés and to have fought with his troops against the Indians (CXXVIII, 258). Others arrived with Pánfilo de Narváez; however, they were killed at Tustepeque during the days following the *noche triste* (CXXVIII, 260–61).[31]

In a courtly manner, Bernal Díaz also mentions Cortés' wife, Catalina Xuárez. Out of deference to his captain and perhaps in defense of the lady, he portrays her as a dutiful wife (XX, 34) and indicates that her marriage to Cortés was a love match (XIX, 31–32). His reference to their relationship may have been devised to counter any rumors that the marriage was arranged, since Catalina's family was closely associated with the governor of Cuba, Diego Velázquez, whose influence had been politically advantageous to Cortés at the outset of his career as a military officer.[32] Although Bernal Díaz hints that problems came between the two in later years, he never mentions the controversy surrounding her demise. Catalina later joined Cortés in New Spain after the conquest. However, as Bernal Díaz reports, the leader was not pleased to see her but concealed his feelings about her unexpected arrival (CLX, 394). Only three months after the couple's reunion, Catalina died, probably of asthma. Rumors circulated at the time that Cortés may have been responsible for her death.[33]

The name of the Virgin is invoked many times throughout Bernal Díaz' lengthy chronicle, and in several instances, she is presented as a living person. His references to her indicate that the Cult of Mary was zealously supported by Spanish soldiers in the New World and underscore her importance in sanctioning political and military advancements. This humanization of a deity not only served as an inspiration to the Spaniards to fight and conquer in the name of Christianity but also was an essential factor in the instruction and subsequent conversion of the Indians. As the "great lady from Castile" (C, 196),[34] her relationship with the men who fought in her behalf appears to be guided by several of the conventions of courtly love. Because of her divinity, the Virgin occupied a position of superiority over the men of the conquest, and in return for their devotion to her, she granted them physical and spiritual powers to enable them to overcome the infidels.

Bernal Díaz' *Historia verdadera* is unequaled by any other chronicle of the colonial period in its presentation of both primary and secondary female characters in a variety of roles. Although their portrayal reflects that of a number of Medieval literary sources, the author's perspective as a member of the military influenced him to depict generally heroic women and to place them in circumstances which reveal positive aspects of the conquest. Bernal Díaz is the only early colonial writer to make a woman a major figure in the historical events unfolding in Spain's American possessions. A different view of early sixteenth-century life, however, is presented in the accounts of the first friars and priests to follow Spanish troops to the New World. These men often characterized women as victims of violence and targets of the devil.

At the outset of the subjugation of the New World's indigenous population, a crusade was launched by religious men in order to protect the conquered Indians from oppressors and to provide for their spiritual salvation. Considering native Americans as human beings with souls, rather than as obstacles to the fulfillment of aspirations as many conquerors had done, religious writers focused upon the Indians' defenselessness and vulnerability and portrayed them as faithful and devoted Christians. This humanitarian approach toward the Indians and the veneration they had for woman as the mother of mankind are important factors in their literary presentation of women.[35] Also, although the Church considered women to be subordinate and generally repressed them, it viewed the female soul as equal to that of a man.[36]

Padre Bartolomé de Las Casas, who ultimately became the Indians' greatest defender in the New World, provides a grim view of the conquest in his *Historia de las Indias* [*History of the Indies*].[37] He also includes a limited account of women who participated in this monumental undertaking such as the Caribbean queen whose tragic death exemplifies the inhumane treatment accorded many native women and several female relatives who aided and accompanied Christopher and Diego Columbus and Pedro Arias de Avila (Pedrarias). Indian women are calculatedly characterized as beneficent, sensitive, and assailable in order to emphasize the heinousness of the crimes committed against them and the dishonor some conquistadors and government officials brought upon Spain by their abuse. European women, on the other hand, are politely and respectfully presented as strong, dutiful supporters of the male members of their families, who were forging a new destiny for the Spanish empire.

The portrayal of Queen Anacaona,[38] the sister of King Behechio of Xaragua, typifies Las Casas' depiction of the Indian in general. She is kind by nature, refined according to her own cultural standards, and needlessly betrayed by the Spaniards. Her story begins with the arrival of a company of Spaniards under the command of Bartholomew Columbus, the admiral's brother, to a community about sixty leagues from Santo Domingo. Described as "a very remarkable woman, very prudent, very graceful and elegant in her speech, manners, and movements, and very friendly to Christians" (I, 442), Anacaona provides an elaborate welcome for the strangers in a setting resembling a court. The king's many sparsely but ornately clothed wives furnish the entertainment for the occasion as they sing, dance, and perform tribal *areitos* (I, 441).[39] Although the Indians could have easily overpowered the small band of soldiers, they are friendly and hospitable and agree to supply the Spaniards with cotton and cassava bread.[40]

This period of good relations between the Indians and the Spaniards changed, however, under the administration of Nicolás de Ovando, Christopher Columbus' successor as governor of Hispaniola, and the Indians suffered greatly. By 1503, Behechio had died, and Anacaona was the sole ruler of the province of Xaragua. Spanish officials again visited her kingdom, and they were greeted cordially and feted by her and her subjects. The Spaniards, nevertheless, were eager to demonstrate their strength to the island's native population and decided that the massacre of a few Indians would serve as a reminder of their superiority.[41] Anacaona's tribe may have been targeted for this show of force because it was a matrilineal society. The Spaniards could have found it hard to deal with a lady chieftain, or they could have thought that her kingdom would be exceptionally vulnerable without the leadership of a man. After reiterating Anacaona's favorable qualities and the generosity she had shown the Spaniards,[42] Las Casas describes the circumstances of her seizure and lynching:

Anacaona starts to scream and everyone begins to cry, asking why she is in such distress. The Spaniards tie her hands in a hurry and isolate Anacaona with her hands bound. They stand at the door of the *caney* or large house and post guards so that no one may leave. They set it on fire; the house burns down; and the unfortunate kings and their subjects are burned alive in their own lands, until everyone, under the burning straw and wood, turns into ashes. . .in deference to her rank, Queen Anacaona was hanged. (II, 237–38)

This act of inhumanity was later deplored by Queen Isabel herself (II, 239).

Although Las Casas focuses upon the Indian throughout much of this three-volume account, his work is a general history of early Spanish America and thus provides information about eminent colonists including their wives and families. While each brief reference to a Peninsular woman mainly offers insight into the personal life of a prominent man, it reveals as well feminine support for the exploration, conquest, and settlement of the New World and female participation in the establishment of a stable society in Spanish America.[43]

Before discovering America, Christopher Columbus had spent considerable time in Portugal where he met and married Felipa Moñiz, the daughter of the Portuguese explorer Bartolomé Moñiz Perestrelo.[44] His mother-in-law gave him many of her late husband's navigational instruments and charts which heightened his interest in the search for new lands. During the first years of their marriage, the couple lived on the island of Porto Santo, and there Felipa gave birth to their son, Diego (I, 35).[45] In 1509, young Diego took his wife, María de Toledo, to live in Santo Domingo where she staged dramatic skits to entertain her guests. These dramatizations are among the first Spanish plays performed in the New World (II, 366–67) and offer some proof of the woman's role in the transfer of Spain's culture to the colonies.[46]

Las Casas also mentions Isabel, the wife of Panama's Governor Pedrarias, and remarks on her daring at leaving the distinguished Spanish court for the wilds of Central America. Because of her assertiveness and bravery, he characterizes her as a "manly matron" (III, 32). After arriving in Panama, Pedrarias betrothed his older daughter, María de Peñalosa, to its first governor, Vasco Núñez de Balboa, and later ordered his beheading (III, 77).[47] The couple's other daughter, Isabel de Bobadilla, although not referred to by Las Casas, became the wife of Hernando de Soto and is described in the Inca's *Florida* as a "woman of the utmost benevolence and discretion." She was later named governor of Cuba in 1539 when her husband left the island to explore the North American continent.[48]

Another work by the Dominican Las Casas, *Brevísima relación de la destrucción de las Indias* [*Brief Account of the Destruction of the Indies*], resembles an abridged history but is actually a political document that presents a survey of Spain's offenses throughout the American colonies.[49] Capitalizing upon the traditional respect Spaniards accorded women and the family unit, Father Las Casas deliberately and systematically enumerates Spanish atrocities against Indian women in order to stir sympathy as well as guilt within the most insensitive reader. He also implies that a woman is the property of her husband and that her virtue has a direct bearing on his honor and reiterates the Church's position against the battery and rape of daughters, wives, and mothers. Few names of the women who are victims are given, since Las Casas depends primarily upon the general allusion to them under such unfortunate circumstances to evoke pity.

According to his account, women were annihilated along with men, but their death was often preceded by greater humiliation. Maidens were raped and maimed, and mothers witnessed the fatal beating of their children. Husbands and wives were separated, and the women who survived were often sold into slavery. After being branded, they were sent to the fields or mines where they died from starvation or exhaustion. On the island of Hispaniola, King Guarioner, ruler of the gold rich province of Cibao, was dishonored when his wife was raped by a Spanish soldier (p. 30), and in Peru, the pregnant wife of a provincial king was tortured and killed to assure the leader's submission as well as that of his subjects to Spanish rule (p. 122). The mass murder of Panamanian women was carried out also, and Las Casas' description of this massacre includes the pathetic cries of their husbands and friends in order to emphasize their surprise and bereavement at such barbarism: "Oh, vile men! Oh, cruel Christians! So you kill women? Killing women is a mark of abominable, cruel, and bestial men."[50]

Las Casas' portrayal of women in his *Brevísima relación de la destrucción de las Indias* is propagandistic rather than informative. Here he calculatedly uses the adverse historical circumstances of Indian women to incite his readers into publicly condemning such outrageous offenses and to gain support for the Indians' legal protection. His insistent presentation of native women in shockingly violent scenes in both the *Historia* and the *Brevísima relación* vividly points up one of the important negative aspects of the conquest and no doubt greatly contributed to the success of his humanitarian campaign. Public outcry resulted in the passage of the New Laws, which went into effect in 1542, and this legislation halted, at least for a time, the continuation and growth of the *encomienda* system of Indian labor in the Indies.[51] However, Las Casas' bold accusations against the Spanish conquerors diminished Spain's position within the European community and initiated the so-called Black Legend which was propagated by the Crown's foreign enemies.

While Father Las Casas defended the Indians from Spanish oppressors, another religious writer, Fray Toribio de Benavente, sought to protect them from an even greater threat, that of the devil himself. This mendicant friar, who became better known by the Nahuatl word "motolinía" meaning "poor man,"[52] was among the first group of Franciscans to reach New Spain in 1523 and to carry out the baptism of Indians on a massive scale. His account documents the success of the Franciscan Order in their conversion, and on several occasions, he notes the effects of the evangelization upon women. In accordance with Church tradition, he views women as more susceptible to evil than men because of their inherent moral weakness but recognizes their great potential for spirituality and the important role they played in establishing the Christian Church in the New World.

In his *Historia de los indios de la Nueva España [History of the Indians of New Spain]*, Motolinía reports that the Indians of Mexico were easily converted to Christianity, and he presents a number of personal experiences which reveal their devotion and zeal toward their newfound faith. One episode, involving a female convert, dramatizes the spiritual conquest of the New World and the ever present conflict between good and evil and illustrates the obligation women have in the guidance and protection of their families. In the following excerpt, the devil appears in person to challenge a new Christian mother physically:

In Tetzcoco as a baptized woman was going along with an unbaptized child on her back (that being the way they carry children in this country) and passing at night through the courtyard of the *teocallis*, which are the houses of the devil, the devil came out to her and seized the child, trying to take it from the mother, who was terrified because the child was not yet baptized nor signed with the cross. She cried aloud: "Jesus! Jesus!" and the devil at once let go of the child; but as soon as she ceased to speak the name of Jesus the devil tried again to take the infant. This happened three times, until she got out of that fearful place. The very next morning she brought the child to be baptized in order that no such peril might befall him again, and so it was done.[53]

The friar's recollections also include several instances in which newly baptized women are not given time to demonstrate their loyalty to the Church. They find consolation in having received the sacrament, however, and face death bravely as Christians. One woman from Tetzitepec, after being indoctrinated and admitted into the faith, became ill and died before she was able to return to her village with her children and spread the gospel among her neighbors (pp. 258–59). Motolinía's portrayal of female figures as heroic enhances the image of the conversion as a fight between two opposing armies. The strength and courage of these women occurs only after their baptism and is directly attributable to the Catholic faith. Just as women participated in the conquest and advanced the cause of peace, so too they contributed to the final victory of Christianity over paganism in the New World.

With the military conquest of Mexico complete and the evangelization of the Indians underway, the Spaniards looked toward the south for even richer empires to conquer. One of these men, who continued the subjugation and settlement of the New World, was Pedro de Alvarado, whose presence in Peru and Guatemala had important consequences for both colonial literature and the history of women in Spanish America. After the death of the Inca Atahuallpa, Alvarado arrived in Peru to join in the partition of the vast Andean empire. Among the soldiers he brought with him was Sebastián Garcilaso de la Vega Vargas, who was soon to be the father of the Inca Garcilaso de la Vega by his union with the Inca princess Chimpu Ocllo.[54] When the child reached manhood and was well on his way to establishing himself as one of the colonial period's most talented writers, he praises Alvarado for his many accomplishments in his *Historia general del Perú [General History of Peru]* and includes an anecdote concerning Spanish women taken to Central America by the conqueror in 1538.[55] As a *mestizo*, the Inca felt deeply about the disregard of some Spaniards for the welfare of Indian women, and he expresses his resentment in this episode. Here he comes to the defense of native American women by contrasting them to several villainous Spanish women.[56]

Because of concern over *limpieza de sangre* (the purity of bloodlines), a long-standing preoccupation of the Spanish, as well as other social pressures brought to bear by both church and state, marriages with Indian women were discouraged, and women were brought over from the Peninsula under the Crown's supervision to become the legitimate spouses of Spaniards residing in the New World.[57] Although unions between Spanish soldiers and Indian women were quite common in the early years of the conquest because of the scarcity of Spanish women, few men of high social standing actually married natives.[58] Alvarado himself, after fathering several *mestizo* children in Mexico, had returned to Spain to marry and had brought his new bride, Beatriz de la Cueva, to Guatemala to begin life together there.[59] The other Spanish women who sailed with them were to become the wives of Alvarado's many comrades who had been victorious in the conquest. It is the presence of these women in the New World and their reaction to the unusual surroundings that provide the basis for the Inca's story. His view of them and of what happened upon their arrival is highly subjective and quite imaginative and serves as a warning to wealthy, prominent old men who contemplate taking a young bride.

The return of Pedro de Alvarado and his new wife to Guatemala was certainly an occasion for great celebration, and all of his old friends as well as the new arrivals were in attendance. With the festivities well underway, the young Spanish women gaze out across the hall at their future husbands. From a location concealed to the men, the women express their shock at the broken down condition of the old soldiers, but they are consoled by the fact that their husbands' advanced age and previous injuries will prevent them from having a long life. Thus they, as widows, can enjoy success and prosperity and marry anyone they please after the old gentlemen's demise. Much to the amazement of the ladies, however, their conversation is overheard by one of the conquerors. After chastising the women for their outspokenness and after informing his companions of what had transpired, he withdraws from the scene and immediately marries an Indian woman. Although the Inca provides a rare glimpse of some aging war heroes, it is his characterization of several of the first Spanish women in the New World, designed to present them in a negative light, that makes his anecdote so unique.

Although the only descriptive statement made by the Inca concerning the new arrivals is that they are ''noblewomen'' (III, 81), the initially favorable impression it creates is quickly dashed by his narration of their actions and the inclusion of a crucial portion of their dialogue.

The surreptitious meeting as well as the traitorous tenor of their exchange in the home of one of Spain's great heroes demonstrate a surprising boldness, lust for life, and outright greed on the part of the women. Ironically, they resemble the conquerors in their youth, who came to America to seek adventure and to acquire riches. The language used by the women is a significant feature of their characterization, since it portrays them as being both rude and cruel. Speaking of these brave men now past their prime, one woman says: "They can go to the devil: they are in such a state that they look as if they had escaped from hell," and another callously likens marriage to a second, younger husband to exchanging "an old broken pan for a new whole one" (III, 81). This conversation is not only invented by the Inca but slanted as well to unmask the maliciousness of the women whose portrait of the conquerors dwells upon their decrepitude and disfiguration. Labeling them as "broken down old creatures," the women proceed to enumerate their deformities: "Some are lame and some have arms missing, and some ears, and some an eye, and some half their faces, and the best-looking of them has got one or two or three scars across his face" (III, 81). The mocking tone of these disclosures is grotesquely humorous, but in view of what follows it is pathetic. Considering the personal sacrifices that these men have made and the intent of the women to deprive them of any happiness in life, the Inca encourages sympathy toward the men and contributes to the further detriment of the women.

The old conqueror's response to the deplorable conduct of these female fortune hunters is rational rather than emotional, which emphasizes still more the differences between the sexes, and his carefully measured words to his fellow soldiers reflect a clear understanding of the disparaging remarks spoken in haste by the women. Although his announcement to his comrades is delivered with complete self-control, it is laden with sarcasm: "You marry these ladies, for they fully intend to repay you for the honor" (III, 81). After citing the succinct statement of the old veteran, the Inca continues to reveal the man's character by mentioning how devoted and faithful he was to his Indian wife and two children and how determined he was to assure their future. At the conclusion of the Inca's brief story, the reader takes much satisfaction in knowing that the old fighter was not deceived by such base creatures; however, the Inca immediately shatters this optimistic view of what transpired by saying that in Peru few men in this situation possessed such wisdom and foresight. As a result of their imprudence and gull-ibility, they often observed strangers enjoying the benefits of their siz-able estates while they themselves were confined to hospital beds.

While the astute, old conqueror appears to be the hero of the story, he actually shares this distinction with the ideal Indian woman who, together with the Spaniard, symbolizes the beginning of a new and noble race of Spanish Americans. This tribute to native American women is intentionally obscured in the beginning of the Inca's account by historical details, but it quickly emerges as his principal aim and pro-vides additional contrast to the already maligned Peninsular women. By praising Indian women and their families, he appeals to the reader's sense of justice in sanctioning marriages between Spanish men and Indian women and in condemning any interference, especially by the government, which directly affected these partnerships and the lives of their *mestizo* offspring. The Inca's underlying purpose in presenting this episode and in relating it to events in Peru is, of course, to justify his own personal existence, since his father, a captain in the royal army, chose to marry a Spanish woman rather than his mother, a direct de-scendant of the Inca dynasty.[60] According to the Inca, the *indias* and their kin contributed significantly to the success of the conquest and so to the expansion of the Spanish empire in America.

In another anecdote about a daughter of Huayna Capac, the Inca again comes to the defense of an Indian woman involved in interracial marriage and demonstrates as well an appreciation of native American culture imparted during his childhood. However, in this case, instead of emphasizing the steadfastness of Indian women, the Inca stresses that their Spanish mates must be worthy of them. The principal figure in this brief intercalation is Doña Beatriz Coya, who is credited with finally persuading the Inca prince Sayri Tupac, heir to the ancestral empire, to come out of hiding and make peace with the Spaniards (IV, 140, 145). Prior to that, however, she was the subject of controversy because at the death of her husband, Pedro de Bustincia, she controlled considerable wealth.[61] Since so many Spaniards had died in the unending civil upheavals and had left rich widows, the governors sought to per-petuate through marriage the allotments of Indians, granted in many cases by the Crown in return for loyal service, among other deserving subjects. Doña Beatriz was a prime target of these officials, and plans were made to join her in wedlock to a Spanish gentleman, Diego Her-nández. An impasse is created, however, when rumors reach the bride that her intended spouse was formerly a tailor. Although his occupation may have been incorrectly circulated, he was not the nobleman that she felt she deserved. The entire story is then centered around the princess Beatriz, who has been betrothed against her wishes to an ordinary Spaniard. The perspective taken by the Inca in the ensuing events is the feminine one, and he espouses the Indian position on the union between Spaniards and native Americans.

The Inca's choice of the princess as his main character is deliberate and significant. While Spanish women were more frequently left alone to manage villages of Indians, he selected a member of the Incan royalty in these circumstances and a close relation to Huayna Capac like his mother.[62] Chimpu Ocllo no doubt faced a similar situation, and the Inca, like the princess, found himself torn between two very distinct cultures and forced to reconcile their differences.

The first problem that Beatriz Coya must contend with is the struggle among the various forces of society. This resultant internal conflict pits her own convictions, fostered by strict discipline and the proud Inca tradition, against the persistant pressures of her family and other interested parties.[63] The situation culminates in her indecision at the wedding ceremony when she responds to the nuptial vows by saying: "Ichach munani, ichach manamunani," which the Inca translates as "Maybe I will, maybe I won't" (IV, 12).[64] Whether her response was deliberate or merely defensive, she clings to her native language under such dire circumstances. Furthermore, she has taken advantage of this formal gathering to make her thoughts known and has done so directly and without warning. The princess's controversial conduct reflects the strength and pride of the Inca dynasty in the face of adversity, and her words and manner of expression synthesize Incan attitudes toward the aggressive Spaniards and voice a reluctance to accept their culture.[65] Although the response of Beatriz Coya is understandable in many respects, she is still a woman speaking out, which was quite objectionable according to sixteenth-century behavioral standards both in Spain and in Peru. As the Inca discloses in the first fourteen chapters of the Fourth Book of his *Comentarios reales,* all women in Incan society were clearly subordinate to men and under their constant supervision, and *coyas, ñustas,* and *pallas,* as the women of royal blood were called, were subjected to even stricter scrutiny. Nowhere else in the *Comentarios* or the *Historia* is such an independent Indian woman as the princess to be found.[66]

The secondary conflict presented by the Inca in this anecdote is the one at the individual level between a man and a woman and results from the princess's defiance of her future husband at the marriage. Although the princess resists the new order of her world until the last moment, the ceremony is successfully concluded, and the union is completed. With this symbolic rite, Beatriz Coya now enters into what was considered to be the very natural and proper state for a woman, that of matrimony, and a wife's duty in both Christian and Incan society is to obey her husband. She has not really lost her fight to preserve her identity but has actually fulfilled her responsibilities and obligations to maintain the dignity of the Incan line; the circumstances have, of course, been altered by the change in her marital status. With the decline of the empire clearly in evidence, the royal ruling class was forced to coexist with the conquering Spaniards. The princess finally submits to the Crown's supremacy over her country as well as the dominance of her Spanish husband over her life. At the close of this episode, the Inca indicates that the marriage solemnized that day was indeed a lasting one, as the couple was still living together when he left Cuzco for Spain.

Although the general tone of his story about the princess is serious because it reflects an important consequence of the conquest, the Inca's narrative is not without humor. To complete the symmetry of his work and yet provide a twist to the outcome of the preceding events, the Inca offers a final comment in which he makes an appropriate observation about human behavior:

Other marriages of this kind took place throughout the empire, and were arranged so as to give allocations of Indians to claimants and reward them with other people's properties. Many, however, were dissatisfied, some because their income was small and others because their wives were ugly: there is no perfect satisfaction in this world. (IV, 12)

The men were not the only ones who were upset with the outcome of these marriages. Women also expressed their discontent, since their second husbands were often considerably older than their first.

In these two anecdotes from the *Historia general*, the Inca reveals that concern over miscegenation was not simply restricted to the conquerors. While Spaniards were often preoccupied with the racial differences of their female companions, Indian women, especially those of noble lineage, scrutinized the social status of their Spanish suitors.

The native Peruvian is also critical of the government for using marriage for political purposes and intimates that the effects of this interference were felt by the next generation and became the source of continual frustration for many *mestizos* like himself.

Although the Inca also alludes to women involved in the bitter power struggle that erupted among Peru's conquerors, another historian, Pedro Gutiérrez de Santa Clara, dramatizes their plight in his *Quinquenarios [History of the Peruvian Civil Wars]*[67] and uses their mistreatment to unmask the immorality of Spaniards in the New World. This Mexican writer, who was an alleged participant in the Peruvian civil wars,[68] employs the theme of abused women in much the same way as Father Las Casas in his *Historia de las Indias*. However, in the *Quinquenarios*, the victims are not Indian but Spanish, and the perpetrators of crimes against them are the rebellion's two principal figures, Gonzalo Pizarro and his commander in chief, Francisco de Carvajal. Women on both the loyalist and rebel sides of the conflict are portrayed by Gutiérrez de Santa Clara, and most of them are the devoted wives of soldiers and officers. Although his descriptions of Spanish women and information about them, like those of Bernal Díaz and Father Las Casas, remain close to historical reality, his inclusion of a popular saying and a humorous folktale add literary elements to several of his characterizations.

While awaiting a crucial confrontation with the Viceroy Blasco Núñez Vela and his forces, Pizarro encouraged the women of Quito to write their husbands and implore them to desert the loyalist army then stationed in Popayán. The wives were deliberately provided with misinformation regarding rebel movements and were promised a reward for their efforts. When the persuasive letters reached the troops, many men left for home leading officials to believe that Pizarro would soon be leaving his camp for Lima. By tricking Quito's female residents into being pawns, the rebel leader caught the diminished loyalist army unaware, and his cunning strategy led to the defeat and death of the viceroy at Añaquito (II, xxviii, 14–18; II, xliv, 29–33).

Because of Pizarro's success in this instance, he attempted the ruse again on the women of Arequipa, whose husbands were under the command of President Pedro de La Gasca. This time, however, the plan failed miserably. After being taken to Cuzco, the women united behind Doña María Calderón and outwitted the rebels by warning their spouses. Unfortunately, when Pizarro found out about this conspiracy, he had her brutally murdered by Carvajal and his henchmen. This episode is clearly used by Gutiérrez de Santa Clara to present Pizarro and his followers as cruel, unprincipled individuals. Not only does the rebel leader order the slaying of a devoted wife and mother by a group of professional killers, but the attack takes place in the woman's bedroom in the presence of her children:

She, . . . not daring to jump out of bed because she was in her nightgown, began to plead and beg the cruel butcher not to touch her and to realize that it was highly improper for a well-bred gentleman such as he to kill weak and helpless women in that manner. (V, xxxii, 130)

The Inca Garcilaso de la Vega, who was cognizant of Carvajal's disregard for women as well, relates that the commander had Doña María's body hung in the window of her house and that passing under it upon leaving, he sarcastically said: "By ——'s life, madam gossip, if that doesn't chasten you, I don't know what to do with you."[69]

While praising María Calderón's opposition to Pizarro, Gutiérrez de Santa Clara also implies that idle talk by the female conspirators may have been responsible for the death of "such an illustrious and unfortunate woman." Frightened by this heinous crime, the women remind themselves of how dangerous their situation is by repeating the proverb: "Hearing, seeing, and remaining silent; one who sees, hears and keeps quiet, harms no one and enjoys life to its fullest" (V, xxxii, 130).[70]

Another example of Carvajal's blatant disrespect for women narrated by Gutiérrez de Santa Clara occurs in the village of San Miguel. Upon arriving there, the commander in chief decides to take six *regidores* (councilmen) captive and hold them accountable for the town's support of the viceroy. The wives of these men immediately come to plead for their lives: "With tears in their eyes, the women went to the room of Francisco de Carvajal and knelt before him, beseeching him with loud cries and moans that he, for the love of God and of Our Lady, have pity on them and on their children, and let their husbands go. . ." (III, i, 75). Carvajal delights in tormenting these pathetic women but only kills the husband of one. The other men are exiled, divested of their property, and forced to pay a fine. Even the unfortunate widow is required to contribute money.

A similar situation is created when a plot to kill Carvajal is uncovered, and the conspirators are condemned to die. This time, however, the person who intervenes is not a relative of the jailed men but a woman of ill repute. When María Ledesma tries to have Alonso Camargo's sentence commuted by marrying him, Carvajal contributes a measure of levity to this grave scene by relating a folktale about another woman who attempted to do the same thing. Virtue, according to Gutiérrez de Santa Clara, is a woman's greatest asset and without it she is considered to be too low even by a criminal's standards. In the story told by Carvajal, the poor convict was so upset at the thought of having to wed an undesirable woman that he gladly chose execution over such a union: "On with it, gentlemen; I do not want to marry such a dirty woman. It makes me sick to look at her; I prefer one single death rather than so many [deaths] every day" (III,vlii, 191). Actually, Carvajal had no intention of freeing his prisoner, and after casting aspersions on María Ledesma's character, he has Camargo beheaded.[71]

Gutiérrez de Santa Clara also provides a profile of Doña Catalina de Leyton (Catarina Leitão), the wife of the "Devil of the Andes," as Carvajal was called. Describing her as "an honorable widow," Gutiérrez de Santa Clara recounts that she was married to Carvajal by the Viceroy of New Spain, Antonio de Mendoza (I, xxix, 222). Although references to her are scattered and sketchy, Catalina is portrayed as a dutiful and supportive wife even though she is the spouse of the *Quinquenarios'* archvillain. In contrast to the wives of ordinary soldiers, however, she appears in more formal settings where she is presented as a gracious aristocrat and the feminine ideal (IV, xxviii, 347).

The Inca in his *Historia general del Perú* is not as compassionate in his characterization of Catalina de Leyton as Gutiérrez de Santa Clara and continues his criticism of Peninsular women. According to him, she was probably more concerned with decorum in her own home than she was about the future of Peru, and he indicates this by recording Carvajal's displeasure with her when she criticizes his cohorts after a banquet. Finding his men sleeping off a night of drinking in the dining room, Catalina remarks: "Alack for Peru, look at the state of those who're running it." On hearing this, Carvajal responds to her outspokenness: "Quiet, you old besom; let them sleep a couple of hours and any of them'll be fit to govern half the world."[72] The Inca no doubt considered this remark to be justified, as she had exceeded her role as a wife and loyal companion.

Gutiérrez de Santa Clara and the Inca are among the few early historical writers who portray Spanish women creatively. Unlike the Inca, however, the Mexican historian does not dwell on their negative characteristics but clearly indicates that they do not belong in a war zone. Gutiérrez de Santa Clara's presentation of Peru's female residents caught up in Gonzalo Pizarro's rebellion affirms that cruelty to women continued after the conquest of the Indians and that Spanish women were sometimes forced to suffer the consequences of subsequent political instability and chaos in that region. While wives and lovers of combatants responded to these hardships courageously, their efforts to aid their men were generally ineffectual and often ended in tragedy.

As long as unconquered lands remained within the Spaniards' reach, their military forces pressed onward, and as a result of their advancement, continuous incursions were made into Chile. From the middle of the sixteenth century to the early part of the 1700's, three notable historico-literary works, Ercilla's *La Araucana,* Oña's *Arauco domado,* and Núñez de Pineda y Bascuñán's *Cautiverio feliz,* were written. All of them contain descriptions of both native American and Spanish women residing in Arauco. War again serves as the backdrop for the female characters, and their portrayal within the historical circumstances is both realistic and imaginative. Indian women rather than those from the Peninsula continue to capture the attention of these colonial authors just as they had done with earlier explorers, conquerors, and religious men. The tradition of idealizing the *indias*, established by the previous writers, is followed by the poets Ercilla and Oña; however, they carry this view to the extreme when they completely invent Araucanian female characters. The young soldier, Núñez de Pineda y Bascuñán, on the other hand, demonstrates the reversal of this trend by offering a more realistic assessment of the area's Indian women and their way of life.

The Spanish soldier, Alonso de Ercilla, presents the first description of women involved in the Chilean conquest in *La Araucana [The Arau-caniad]*, and he uses the image of the female warrior both to chide women for abandoning their traditional role and to praise exceptional members of their sex for their valor in the face of danger. Heroic females, drawn from the poet's imagination and shaped by the actual circumstances of war, are commonly portrayed in his epic poem, and they become the focus of several of its most famous episodes.

As early as his prologue, Ercilla indicates that the females of Arauco's militaristic state accompanied their husbands on the battlefield: "sometimes fighting like men, with great courage [they] yield themselves unto death."[73] While he acknowledges their strength and courage on this occasion, his presentation of them in physical combat is not a favorable one. Women are not by nature suited to war, according to him, although they are capable of overcoming the disadvantages of their sex and performing acts of extreme cruelty and barbarism. In *Canto X*, Ercilla describes how bands of "soft ladies, skilled with spindles" ambushed battle-worn Spanish troops with "virile ardor." They have renounced their femininity and rejected their role as wives and mothers to be professional fighters:

> As they coursed, their breasts went flapping,
> But they paid no heed to stomachs
> Occupied eight months by infants.
> Those most pregnant ran the fastest (X, 143–44)

Although Ercilla's portrayal of women as savages is generally limited to his collective presentation of them, his portrait of chief Caupolicán's wife, Fresia, reflects characteristics similar to those of these ferocious women. The poet narrates her encounter with her husband after his capture by the Spaniards, and his deliberate reversal of the traditional roles of the man and the woman reveals his strict definition of masculine and feminine. By being taken prisoner by the enemy, Caupolicán has brought disgrace upon himself and his family. This is a fate worse than death for a warrior, and Fresia publicly denounces his failure as a leader and a man:

> Broke not forth the dame in weeping,
> Nor exposed a female faintness,
> Rather, red with indignation,
> His papoose she thrust before him,
> Screeching: "Robust foreign fingers,
> Which thus bound your placid right hand,
> Would more clemently bestead you,
> If they pierced your craven bosom!
>
>   . . . . .
> "Take your son, our knot of union,
> Whereby licit love enchained me
> To your soul. All shock of sorrow
> From these fecund breasts is shriveled.
> Rear him, as your rippling sinews
> Have assumed a sexless languor.
> I reject the name of mother
> To the scion of degradation!" (XXXIII, 465–66)

Besides Fresia, four other Indian women are portrayed by Ercilla in *La Araucana*, and his characterization of them differs sharply from his view of Araucanian tribeswomen as a whole. Although they are depicted as the wives and daughters of Indian chieftains, their portrayal reflects aspects of the chivalric novel, Renaissance love sonnets, and other epic poems. These female characters, like others found in colonial literature, display both fortitude and valor during wartime; however, these attributes are now considered as moral rather than physical. Ercilla's four Araucanian women also possess a distinctly European refinement that is manifest in their appearance, customs, attitudes, and behavior.[74] The poet compares the virtue and beauty of these native American women to such historical and legendary women as Judith, Camila, Penelope, and Lucrecia, and he relates the story of the heroic yet controversial monarch, Elisa Dido. He, like Roman writers during the empire's final period of decline, looked to antiquity to provide staunch models of morality for a society lacking proper standards and values. This divergence from the mainstream of his historical account reveals how quickly he comes to the defense of women and his concept of the ideal woman.[75]

When a soldier who had read Vergil's *Aeneid* questions the reputation of the Carthaginian queen, Ercilla presents his view of the virtuous widow who commits suicide rather than break her vows to her dead husband:

> Such her character and wisdom
> Was, that she was held a goddess.
> In her day there breathed no maiden
> Who could parallel her beauty.
>
>   . . . . .
> She was comely, chaste, and wealthy,
> Shrewd, sagacious, prudent, constant. (XXXIII, 455)

Elisa Dido's character traits have particular significance to Ercilla because they represent several of the most highly prized values of his time. Her sense of honor typifies that of the age of chivalry, and her concept of love and fidelity is embodied in the canons of courtly love and is expressed in Garcilaso's poetry.[76] Many of her attributes are repeated in Ercilla's female creations, since they are also portrayed as monogamous Caucasian beauties whose moral and ethical conduct is unquestionable.[77]

Apart from using Classical models such as Dido in the creation of four of his Indian women, Ercilla appears to have been influenced by the ladies in Ariosto's *Orlando furioso* as well. The similarities between the Italian poet's female figures and those of Ercilla occur primarily in the personal relationships they have with male characters in their respective poems. The episode of Guacolda and Lautaro, for example, resembles that of Doralice and Mandricardo, and circumstances involving Isabella and Zerbino are echoed in the stories of Tegualda and Crepino and Glaura and Cariolán.[78] Although Ercilla draws the characteristics of his Araucanian women and their relationships from several sources, he skillfully and artistically combines these literary elements to provide exceptional portraits of Guacolda, Tegualda, Lauca, and Glaura. Each female character demonstrates the ideal behavior of a maiden or matron in the very real circumstances resulting from war. Ercilla himself appears in several of the episodes in which these women are described in order to lend credence to his account.

An intimate view of a warrior's life is revealed as Guacolda and her husband, Lautaro, share their love as well as their fears the night before a battle. Awakened by a dream which portends Lautaro's death and tormented by the thought of losing him, Guacolda envisions what life will be like after he is gone: "When cold earth receives your body, / Mine shall lie in death above you" (XIII, 195). Ercilla's description of their final moments together is concise and discreet. It presents Guacolda as a devoted, loving wife who relies upon her husband for strength but conveys as well her despair at their parting and the anxiety over her impending loss. Selfishly, she delays his departure for combat.

For the widow Tegualda, the anxious waiting is over. Numbed by the shock of her husband's death, she searches relentlessly for his body in order to give it a proper burial. Wandering about the battlefield, she comes upon Ercilla who is guarding the Spanish encampment and appeals to him to permit her to complete this sad and final task:

> What wouldst thou acquire of glory,
> When just Heaven's heralds published
> That thy blade betrayed a woman,
> Miserable and helpless widow?
> . . . . .
> Let my soul retrieve its body;
> Then, proceed with furious rigor,
> For my suffering has impaled me
> So that life, not death, affrights me. (XX, 286)

Tegualda's experience confirms Guacolda's fear that life would not be worth living after her husband's death and that the void created by his absence would not only be physical but spiritual as well. This same sense of loss is also expressed by the wounded Indian widow, Lauca, who finds her way into the Spanish camp later in the poem (XXXII, 443).

Ercilla's portrait of Tegualda is the most extensive of any of the women in *La Araucana*, and he includes a flashback of her life when she was single. The unfortunate daughter of the chieftain Brancol (XX, 287) confides in the poet and relates how the love of one man naturally transformed her from an arrogant, indifferent girl into a sensitive young woman (XX, 291). In a manner resembling Medieval tradition, Tegualda met her mate at a tournament for young athletes, and since he was the winner of the games, she decided to marry him.[79]

While Tegualda's recounting of these poignant memories gives substance to her character, it serves as well to intensify the pain and horror of the scene in which she encounters her husband's remains:

> Miserable Tegualda, seeing
> First the shrivelled face misshapen,
> Hied with horrified hysterics,
> Hurled herself upon the carcass,
> And supine, she clasped him closer,
> Bathed in a flood of tears in foison,
> Kissed his mouth and kissed his gashes,
> Striving to resuscitate him.

> "Woe is me!" she sobbed, "What can I
> Do amidst such dule and mishap?
> Why should I not glut forever
> Love's injustice at this juncture?
> Pusillanimous are lovers
> Gulping not this bitter goblet!
> What is this? Where tends injustice?
> Death! Is even *that* denied me?" (XXI, 296)

The vulnerability of women to be taken as spoils in wartime, as well as other moral questions involving them, is drawn into *La Araucana* through Glaura's testimony to Ercilla. After finding this lovely girl in

a thicket and before recording her suspenseful narration, he pauses
briefly to present an idealized description of her beauty:

> 'Twas a girl, well-formed and buxom,
> With entrancing eyes, joy's forehead,
> Ruddy mouth and nose perfected,
> Pearly teeth enchased in corals,
> Billowy and high of bosom,
> Lovely hands, round arms, and tapering,
> With a natural sprightly bearing
> That accentuated beauty. (XXVIII, 387)

In addition to being European in appearance, Glaura responds to lust,
incest, and rape according to the principles of Christian morality and
values her chastity above all else.[80] Regaining her composure in Ercilla's
custody, she begins the story of continuous unhappiness and pursuit
and expresses resentment of both her high station and attractiveness.
Even in her own home, Glaura's virtue had been repeatedly threatened
by Fresolano, a relative and close family friend. Appalled by his behavior, she finally expresses her indignation at his attempts to seduce
her:

> ..."Oh scoundrel,
> Ingrate and incestuous traitor,
> Friendship's curse, and law's corruptor,
> Breaker of the bond of kinship!'' (XXVIII, 389)

Later, after Spanish soldiers entered her house and killed Fresolano and
her father, she is accosted by two pillaging black men during her escape:

> "Covetously they divested
> Me of all that I was wearing.
> Woeful, I esteemed as nothing
> Loss of life and garments looted,
> But my chastity so precious
> Was about to be deflowered,
> And my cries and plaints were many,
> Moving plants and trees to mercy. (XXVIII, 391)

Ercilla's portrayal of Glaura changes somewhat when Spanish soldiers again close in around her, and she considers deserting Cariolán, the valiant young Araucanian who rescues her from the two black assailants and who loves her very deeply. Escaping captivity when he is seized, she views her own behavior as that of an "inadvertent, weak-spined woman" and one who is "timid, cowardly, inconstant" (XXVIII, 392). When Glaura's instinct for self-preservation is overcome by her concern for Cariolán's welfare, she begins searching for him. Deploring her cowardice, which Ercilla associates with being female, and wishing to be reunited with her companion under any circumstances, she arrives at the Spanish camp where Ercilla finds her. Here she learns that Cariolán had been taken into the poet's service because of his exceptional bravery. As a gesture of friendship and esteem, the notable Spaniard releases him, and the couple returns to the wilderness as man and wife.

Continuous warfare in Arauco also meant tremendous hardship for the Spanish women who occupied the region's first settlements. Barbarous hordes of Indians did not spare these defenseless newcomers, and the full extent of their cruelty is recorded in Ercilla's shocking description of a battle's piteous aftermath. In *Canto VI*, he expresses outrage at the enemy's attack on women and emphasizes the gravity of this violence by noting its toll on motherhood and the family unit:

> And for women frail and mournful,
> Due respect and care they kept not;
> But still more austere, they pierced them
> With their swords, and spurned entreaties;
> They considered not the pregnant,
> But drove blows into their bellies,
> And through wounds there were projected
> Little unborn limbs so tender. (VI, 95)

Ercilla's only detailed description of a Spanish woman is that of Doña Mencía de Nidos, who came to Chile in 1549 and died in Santiago in 1603. She was married to Cristóbal Ruiz de la Ribera, who was a conqueror of Chile and one of its first settlers.[81] The poet describes her as a "noble dame, discreet, courageous" (VII, 102–4) and depicts her during an Indian raid on Concepción when she is roused from her sickbed. Arming herself, she harangues fleeing neighbors in order to shame them into resisting.[82] Here it is a woman who voices better than anyone else some of the old Spanish chivalric virtues:

"Where is now your pristine courage,
That you shrink from those who threaten?
Where is now that great ambition
That would crown you as immortal?
Where are now your pride and bravery,
Priceless heritage bequeathed you?
Whither flee ye, so bewildered,
When no enemy pursues us? (VII, 103)

Death for her, she professes, would be better than infamy, and she pledges to be the first to give her life for the protection of the settlement and the honor of the Spanish people. Unfortunately, the disorganized and timorous residents of Concepción do not respond to Doña Mencía's call to arms, and the Spaniards are forced to seek refuge in Mapocho, a considerable distance away.[83] The choice of an ailing woman to reprimand the Spaniards for their cowardice in this instance is a critical one and underscores the obvious weakness of some settlers in defending themselves and their property. Unlike Fresia, who also has harsh words for the men, Doña Mencía's rant was meant to inspire them to act while there was still time. She was not demanding of them something she would not do herself, and she does not place military victory above the safety of family and loved ones. Doña Mencía symbolizes a highly regarded Spanish ideal, as she embodies a defiant, invincible spirit which emerges in the absence of physical strength.

The women who appear as individuals in Ercilla's epic poem generally represent their culture's greatness in times of adversity. Although war is unquestionably the domain of men, women can successfully meet its challenges and frequently offer inspiring examples of moral excellence. Because of these highly imaginative characterizations, Ercilla's portrayal of women is an outstanding literary feature of La Araucana, and his heroines inspired other Hispanic authors to incorporate them into their works. In Spain, Lope de Vega and Ricardo de Turia wrote plays about them,[84] and in the colonies, female characters with the same names appeared in an epic poem by the Chilean Pedro de Oña.

The Araucanian women who are identified in Oña's Arauco domado [Arauco Tamed], like those of Ercilla's La Araucana, are the alleged wives of prominent chieftains who historically defended their lands against the Spaniards. Although several of his Indian women were suggested by those of Ercilla, Oña's characters stand apart from their precursory models. The reason for this may have been the Chilean poet's desire to counter Ercilla's tendency to elevate Indians to the role of hero or heroine thus making them the most important participants in the conquest. The appearance of Oña's Araucanian women rather than their behavior is often the most important element of their portrayal, and his elaborately protracted visions of them exceed the qualities of feminine physical perfection enumerated by Ercilla. Because of Oña's attention to superficial aspects of his female characters, however, they appear to be artificial and out of place in a poem about war and generally lack the substance of Ercilla's creations. While Oña frequently praises the beauty and capacity for physical love of Araucanian women, he does not find their conduct morally uplifting and even indicates that they can be treacherous and slovenly.

In *Arauco domado*, Ercilla's disgraced and distraught Fresia is transformed into a voluptuous love goddess as she bathes with her husband, Caupolicán, in a lush, secluded spot that seems far from battlelines. Oña's sensuous, slowly paced description of her beauty as her nude body is submerged in the water is unmatched by Ercilla, even in his portrait of the lovely Glaura.[85] Inspired by mythological divinities and heroines of pastoral novels, Oña, like his predecessor, overlooks her Indian features and presents her as a love object:

> Her head was undulating, sleek, and smooth;
> Her forehead, neck, and hand resembled snow;
> Her ruby mouth was small and curved with grace;
> Her breast was high; her eyes were heron eyes;
> Round was her arm; like jasper was her waist,
> A column to which Paros tribute owes;
> Her tender foot of silver on the green
> Outshone for whiteness e'en the albescent swan.[86]

Oña's story of Guacolda begins where Ercilla's ended, with the death of her husband, Lautaro. She is now happily married to her second husband, Catiray, and living behind Spanish lines. Lautaro's ghost, however, is restless and seeks revenge against this chieftain who, he believes, was responsible for his death at Mataquito. Appearing before the Indian warrior, Talgueno, the apparition asks him to mete out proper punishment for this treachery. Lautaro declares that a woman's love is "fraud and sportive jest," and he offers as proof his wife's actions after his murder:

> Thou followed'st me only whilst I was alive
> To abandon me in death, as if I were
> A shadow traced whilst shines the golden sun
> And dissipated when the clouds turn gray (XIII, 468)

In contrast to Ercilla, Oña uses a negative example to demonstrate that women are expected to remain faithful to their husbands even after death.

The image of woman as a brave warrior and duteous wife emerges in Oña's wholly new creation of Tucapel's wife, Gualeva. Here, he combines exceptional beauty and military skill in a female character who is "The living portraiture in face and dress / Of Venus and Bellona, the goddessess" (XII 424). When her husband does not return from the siege at Fort Penco, she takes up arms and searches frantically and valiantly for him. Traveling through the forest for more than a day, she finds Tucapel, who is weak and stunned from the Araucanians' defeat. While she is nursing him back to health, the couple is confronted and threatened by a lioness. As a demonstration of her "virile boldness" (VII, 250), Gualeva reaches for her sword and, aided by her wounded husband, kills the animal (XII, 428–31).

Oña's collective portrayal of Araucanian women contrasts sharply with his individual portraits of chieftains' wives and reveals a lack of esteem for Arauco's culture[87] and a determination to degrade those who oppose the expansion of the Spanish empire.[88] His perception of them as a group not only emphasizes their backwardness but discloses their baseness as well. An example of this may be found in his description of one of the Araucanians' frequent drinking bouts at which the women gathered together to dance:

> In groups are other women set alone,
> Who caper madly with the madcap sons,
> All wrapped in bacchanalian fury's fumes.
> Nude halfway down the waist, and from the knees,
> Like mares that hover by the tribulum
> With fillies skittish, whirling dizzily,
> That skirmish through the heaps of unthreshed wheat
> And shred the chubby spears to beaded grains.

They are adorned with tinsel plaits and bangs,
With stones that dazzle every eye that sees.
With bluish beads like drops of pearly dew,
And shuffle with a thousand mincing twists.
'Tis there the wingèd god can penetrate
And pierce incautious youth with longing's dart,
Because if Bacchus and if Ceres keep
Close company, perforce lurks Venus nigh. (II, 72–73)

Although both Oña and Ercilla cite barbarism as a principal characteristic of Araucanian women as a whole, it is clear that they view Indian women as individuals from different perspectives. This divergence in their portraiture is due not only to their moral evaluation of them but to the attention devoted to feminine beauty as well. Oña's view of a woman as a goddess whose loveliness embodies perfection itself is unusual for a colonial epic poem, but this vision of womanhood appears throughout the lyric poetry written in early Spanish America. Peninsular and Creole women, however, are usually the subject of these verses, and idealized descriptions of *indias* are notably absent.

The third important work containing descriptions of Araucanian women is Francisco Núñez de Pineda y Bascuñán's *Cautiverio feliz [Happy Captivity]*, which provides a more realistic view of them than the poems of Ercilla and Oña.[89] As the son of the Spanish army's commander in chief, Don Alvaro Núñez de Pineda, Francisco had been born and raised near Arauco and possessed considerable knowledge of the Araucanian language and culture. In 1629, the twenty-year-old youth was captured by the Indians while he was serving in the military and spent six and a half months living among them.[90] He, like Father Las Casas, uses the mistreatment of native wives and daughters as an example of Spanish injustice toward Chile's indigenous population which, the young soldier believes, has led to the prolongation of conflict in the region.[91]

According to Núñez de Pineda y Bascuñán's presentation of Arauco's women, they were subservient to its men in every way. Not only did they perform household duties such as cooking, sewing, and cleaning, but they were required to work in the fields, and during trips they had to walk behind their husbands who were on horseback. The women-folk were also expected to entertain guests, and the head of the household often offered his daughter to visitors as a gesture of friendship and hospitality. Polygamy was practiced by the Araucanians, but the coveting of another's wife was considered a serious affront. Although the women were subordinate, they were generally well treated and respected by members of their own society. Such courtesies were not extended, however, by some Spaniards. Núñez de Pineda y Bascuñán learns of several cases in which Indians, who had befriended Spanish soldiers, later saw their wives and daughters abused by them. Colpoche, for example, recounts to him how his wife was raped while the couple was residing at a Spanish fort (pp. 78–80), and Ancan-amón relates how his wives were kidnapped and permanently taken to Paicaví (pp. 114–18). Even Spanish women abused the *indias*, according to the old chieftain Tureupillán, and he asks Francisco if his elders had told him about this cruelty:

Didn't they inform you that the ladies were so cruel and greedy that they customarily had our wives and daughters working day and night for their purposes and profits? Didn't they tell you that there were some so ferocious that they were not content to maim their servants, cutting off their noses and ears and burning their private parts but that unfortunately they condemned them to a filthy death in prison, and that there they were buried? (pp. 181–82)

Núñez de Pineda y Bascuñán's willingness to help women as well as his continual demonstration of respect for them reflect vestiges of the chivalric code. This conduct was often puzzling to his Indian captors, as it seemed uncharacteristic of the Spaniards that they knew (pp. 121–23). His positive approach toward women, however, appears to have been tempered by his strict Jesuit schooling, for he considers his morality to be threatened by what he regards as the provocative behavior of young girls.[92] The first time the captive is alone with an Indian girl in a remote place occurs when his protector, Maulicán, is hiding him from the other chieftains who demand his death. Maulicán's daughter, who brings him food during his seclusion, is attracted to Francisco, and he admits to himself that the feeling is mutual. However, on the pretense that she will divulge his location, he sends her away: "I just could not bring myself to thank her as she deserved and smooth things over. More important to me was the risk these visits entailed to my well-being, at once of body and soul" (p. 130).[93] Later he becomes the girl's protector when she is captured by the Spaniards. Remaining within the Spanish fold, she decides to become a Christian but dies of a fever shortly after her baptism (p. 132).

The young soldier's reluctance to socialize with women probably accounts for the lack of female characters who emerge as individuals in the *Cautiverio feliz*. Although he appears to be physically attracted to Indian girls, he is extremely cognizant of their alleged relationship to sin, and he finds himself repelled by their forwardness. He is, however, noticeably more comfortable with older or married women. He teaches them to pray (p. 177) and even uses his elementary knowledge of medicine on them (pp. 180–87). After he crosses the frontier and is back in Spanish territory, he sends them gifts in return for their kindness (p. 229).

Cautiverio feliz documents the fact that cruelty to Indian women continued on a wide scale into the seventeenth century but that writers such as Núñez de Pineda y Bascuñán still stood ready to help the downtrodden American natives and to come to the defense of women. While he criticizes the Spaniards in general for their dishonorable conduct, his account contains a rare description of the inhumanity of Spanish women toward members of their own sex because they were Indian servants. The young soldier's avoidance of women on a personal level, however, may be traced directly to his parochial education and constitutes a clear example of how negative attitudes toward women reached the secular population from religious sources. After continually dodging Indian women, he does finally confess to having a romantic attachment to Maulicán's daughter. Because of the sensitivity with which he conveys this episode, it later inspired a Peruvian playwright, a contemporary of Núñez de Pineda y Bascuñán, to dramatize it in one of his works.[94]

Early Spanish American history was written from the point of view of man and his experiences, and it is not surprising, therefore, to find that in the chronicles and epic poetry considered in this chapter writers tended to treat women only as they were involved in masculine endeavors or with male participants. Many of the women included by them were the wives, mistresses, sisters, daughters, mothers-in-law, or aunts of renowned men in the New World and were mentioned by them out of courtesy and deference to this relationship or to provide an added dimension to the characterization of prominent male figures in their accounts.

The most dominant image of women in historical writings is the one derived from the Spanish romances of chivalry. Because of their valiant efforts to endure the hardships of a hostile American environment, women in the New World were often portrayed as heroines who exceeded the traditional limitations imposed on their sex. Although beauty and virtue were still cited as important feminine characteristics, especially by poets, female characters frequently appear engaging in physical combat either against the enemy, as portrayed by Carvajal, Ercilla, and the Inca, or as in the case of the works of Motolinía and Oña, against the forces of evil. Other women, while not engaged in combat, are seen as assertive, powerful, independent, and self-sufficient individuals in both their actions and their manner of thinking and so represent many of the qualities usually possessed by a skilled warrior. In recognition and praise of these outstanding women, writers often described them as manly or masculine, and this was the greatest compliment an author of the time could pay them.

Although literary elements may be found in the portrayal of Peninsular women in the works of Las Casas, Gutiérrez de Santa Clara, Ercilla, and the Inca, native Americans are generally more imaginatively conceived, especially during the first century of Spanish occupation, because of the aura of mystery surrounding them. Some Indian women like Las Casas' Queen Anacaona, several of Motolinía's female converts, and the native wives of Spanish soldiers in the Inca's episode about Alvarado merely possessed idealized features while others were endowed with imaginative characteristics taken from specific literary sources as in the case of works by Bernal Díaz and Ercilla. Extended contact with indigenous populations, however, eventually altered the writers' perception of the New World's Indian women, and their descriptions become more realistic as illustrated by Núñez de Pineda y Bascuñán's portrayal of them in his *Cautiverio feliz.*

As a reflection of chivalric canons, women were generally viewed with admiration and respect in early colonial works and were defended by gallant authors imbued with an adventuresome spirit. However, in some cases the Indians were depicted as treating women more humanely than the Spaniards. These men, and even some women, who abused or mistreated members of the feminine gender were condemned for their conduct by Las Casas, Gutiérrez de Santa Clara, and Núñez de Pineda y Bascuñán, and their stories of violence against women were designed to bring dishonor to the perpetrators. Partly because of Las Casas' presentation of women as victims in his *Brevísima relación de la destrucción de las Indias,* his humanitarian ideas left a lasting imprint upon history and influenced Spain's politics both internally and externally. Since men felt compelled to be protective of women, criticism of them is rare. However, their occasional display of greed, promiscuity, bloodthirstiness, and drunkenness did not go unnoticed by the Inca, Gutiérrez de Santa Clara, Ercilla, Oña, and Núñez de Pineda y Bascuñán, and images of women as evil inspired by works of patristic literature or Rojas' *La Celestina* appeared.

The portrayal of women as extremely strong and courageous was consistent with the age of discovery and conquest. Confrontation of the unknown led to the proliferation of fantasy, and the continual threat of warfare maintained a clear definition of sex roles within society and reinforced the Spaniards' concept of patriarchy. The man was the head of the household and the sole protector of his family. Women who were exceptional under these circumstances and emerged from the place accorded them traditionally were awarded characteristics similar to those of a man because he was considered to be superior and worthy of a fearless female counterpart. Historical evidence attests to the fact that some women were, indeed, able to break with tradition and expand their societal functions. Isabel de Bobadilla and her two daughters and Beatriz de la Cueva helped to settle and govern Central America and Cuba. María de Estrada fought with Cortés in Mexico, and María Calderón and Mencía de Nidos participated in military conflicts in South America. Beatriz Coya aided in the establishment of peace between the Spaniards and Peru's Indians, and María de Toledo transferred the tradition of the performing arts to Hispaniola. The most dramatic example of this documentation, however, which may be directly attributed to her literary portrayal, is that of Doña Marina, whose importance to the Spanish in the conquest of New Spain is vividly established in Bernal Díaz' *Historia verdadera*.

For other women, however, life in America increased their dependence upon men because of the unfamiliar surroundings in which they found themselves or the constant threat of enemy attacks. Women could prove to be a liability under such circumstances but usually acted as a stabilizing force in the permanent settlement of newly acquired territories. Both historians and poets stress the importance of love, marriage, motherhood, and the family. A wife's duty was to support her husband in all his activities no matter what the cost to her, to nurse him back to health in periods of sickness or injury, and always to be faithful to him even after death.

Although the portrayal of women in historical writings had a number of social and cultural implications, it also had a literary potential that was quickly recognized by dramatists in Spain. The presentation of morally and physically strong female characters in early colonial literature was a major contribution to the development of the *mujer varonil* theme of the Spanish Golden Age theater. Such females as Carvajal's Amazon women and Ercilla's Guacolda, Fresia, Tegualda, and Doña Mencía, who had appeared only as secondary personages in Spanish American writings, were chosen to become central figures in the dramas of Lope, Tirso, and Turia. This imitation of New World characters in works written in the home country is a tribute to their artistic creation and represents an important instance in which colonial literature affected that of the Peninsula.

Notes

1. Luis Weckmann, "The Middle Ages in the Conquest of America," *Speculum* 26 (1951), pp. 131–32.

2. Although the transfer of works of fiction to the New World was prohibited by royal decree in order to protect the Indians, existing ship manifests and orders from colonial book dealers prove that quantities of these books entered Spanish America from Spain. Irving A. Leonard, *Romances of Chivalry in the Spanish Indies* (Berkeley, Calif.: University of California Press, 1933), pp. 3–15. See also José Torre Revello, *El libro, la imprenta y el periodismo en América durante la dominación española* (Buenos Aires: Talleres, Casa Jacobo Peuse, 1940), pp. 37–67, 94–107.

3. According to Otis H. Green, *Amadís de Gaula* is the most typical work illustrating a knight's duty to the ladies. Otis H. Green, *Spain and the Western Tradition*, 4 vols. (Madison, Wisc.: University of Wisconsin Press, 1963), I, 14.

4. In societies in which the warrior is honored as the ideal man, Maurice Valency notes that "women become proper objects of love in proportion as they approximate masculinity." His example of the Classical model of ideal womanhood, who is both beautiful and armed, is Athena. Maurice Valency, *In Praise of Love: An Introduction to the Love-Poetry of the Renaissance* (New York: Octagon Books, 1975), p. 12.

5. Irving A. Leonard, *Books of the Brave* (New York: Gordian Press, 1964). In chapters 4 and 5, Leonard cites numerous historical works which trace the appearance of the Amazons throughout Mexico and South America.

6. Leonard, *Books of the Brave*, pp. 36–37. Columbus' findings were re-iterated by Pedro Mártir de Anglería in his *Décadas* and were also mentioned in Las Casas' *Historia de las Indias*. Bartolomé de Las Casas, *Historia de las Indias*, 3 vols. (México, D.F.: Fondo de Cultura Económica, 1951), I, 304.

7. Garci-Rodríguez de Montalvo, *Las sergas de Esplandián*, vol. 40 of

Biblioteca de Autores Españoles (Madrid: Ediciones Atlas, 1950), p. 539. Irving Leonard conjectures that Montalvo may have been inspired by Columbus' report regarding the women on Matinino. The saga of Queen Calafia and her Amazon kingdom is continued in the chivalric novel *Lisuarte de Grecia*, which was published in 1514. Leonard, *Books of the Brave*, pp. 40–41.

8. Leonard, *Books of the Brave*, p. 46. Ralph L. Roys, *The Indian Background of Colonial Yucatan* (Washington, D.C.: Carnegie Institution of Washington, 1943), p. 13.

9. Gonzalo Fernández de Oviedo, *Historia general y natural de las Indias*, vols. 117–21 of *Biblioteca de Autores Españoles* (Madrid: Ediciones Atlas, 1959), II, 2; V, 392; V, 394. Lope de Vega was inspired by Fernández de Oviedo's account of the Amazons and wrote the Golden Age *comedia, Las mujeres sin hombres*.

10. Bernal Díaz mentions a place where the Spaniards took refuge after a storm which they called ''Punta de las Mujeres'' because they found large idols there resembling women. Roys, *The Indian Background of Colonial Yucatan*, p. 13. Bernal Díaz del Castillo, *Historia verdadera de la conquista de la Nueva España* (México, D.F.: Editorial Porrúa, 1970), p. 49.

11. Leonard, *Books of the Brave*, p. 46.

12. Hernán Cortés, *Cartas de relación* (México, D.F.: Editorial Porrúa, 1970), pp. 183–84. Leonard, *Books of the Brave*, pp. 48–49.

13. The notoriety resulting from the alleged Amazon kingdom's discovery during Orellana's expedition permanently affixed the name of this tribe of women warriors to the river and basin area and obscured the name of the prominent Spanish explorer. Orellana had originally joined Gonzalo Pizarro's expedition in search of El Dorado and the Land of Cinnamon. His encounter with the warring women was dramatized by Tirso de Molina in his trilogy *Las amazonas en las Indias*.

14. Fray Gaspar de Carvajal, *Relación del nuevo descubrimiento del famoso río Grande de las Amazonas* (México, D.F.: Fondo de Cultura Económica, 1955), pp. 97–98. Other references to this work appear in the text. The English translation has been taken from Friar Gaspar de Carvajal's *The Discovery of the Amazons*, trans. H. C. Heaton (New York: American Geographical Society, 1934), p. 214. This episode is retold by Fernández de Oviedo in his *Historia*.

15. El Inca Garcilaso de la Vega, *Obras completas*, vols. 132–35 of *Biblioteca de Autores Españoles* (Madrid: Ediciones Atlas, 1960), I, 404–5; I, 442–43. John Varner comments on the only reaction a true gentleman and worthy knight could have under these circumstances: ''Somewhere in the annals of chivalry, knight errants must have encountered Amazonian women who were equally clever, but the code of the cavalier seems to have left him no more protection than that of courtesy; Amadis of Gaul would not lay hands on a woman though she stood a good chance of blotting out his life.'' John Grier Varner and Jeanette

Johnson Varner, trans. and eds., *The Florida of the Inca*, by the Inca Garcilaso de la Vega (Austin, Tex.: University of Texas Press, 1951), p. 455.

16. The *mujer varonil* [manly woman] became a popular theme in Spanish Golden Age theater. Lundelius traces its development from figures of Classical mythology such as Athena (Minerva), Artemis (Diana), and the Amazons to dramatic works produced in sixteenth- and seventeenth-century Spain and notes the importance the discovery of America had in reinforcing this image of womanhood. M. Ruth Lundelius, "The *Mujer Varonil* in the Theater of the *Siglo de Oro*," (Dissertation, University of Pennsylvania, 1969), pp. 26–196.

Women who resided in the New World and who were portrayed by Golden Age dramatists are discussed at the end of chapter 4, "Women in Drama."

17. Julie Greer Johnson, "Bernal Díaz and the Women of the Conquest," *Hispanófila* 82 (1984).

Page numbers appearing in the text of this section refer to the 1970 Spanish edition of Bernal Díaz del Castillo's work. The English translations of his history have been taken from Bernal Díaz's *The Discovery and Conquest of Mexico*, trans. A. P. Maudslay, ed. Genaro García (New York: Farrar, Straus and Cudahy, 1956), pp. 62, 135, 64, 176, 43, 243. Hernán Cortés scarcely mentions women at all in his official communiques to the King of Spain, and the Anonymous Conqueror treats them very superficially. The latter's chapters on women's dress and marriage are informative, however. El Conquistador anónimo, *Relación de algunas cosas de la Nueva España y de la gran ciudad de Temestitan México, hecha por un gentilhombre del señor Fernando Cortés* (México, D.F.: José Porrúa e Hijos, 1961), pp. 48, 68.

18. Cortés refers to Doña Marina in his second letter to the King of Spain as "the Indian woman" and mentions her by name in the fifth. Cortés, *Cartas de relación*, pp. 44, 242.

19. Women were often considered by the Indians to be a form of property and were given by them as gifts and taken as tribute. The Spaniards as well thought of these women as one of the spoils of war, and disagreements arose among Cortés's soldiers over which of their number would receive the prettiest girls. The Spanish troops also auctioned and branded their Indian women (CXXXV, 279–80).

20. According to Church doctrine, an Indian woman must become a Christian before having sexual intercourse with a Spaniard. Ann M. Pescatello, *Power and Pawn: The Female in Iberian Families, Societies, and Cultures* (Westport, Conn.: Greenwood Press, 1976), p. 135.

21. This description of Marina contrasts sharply with that of Cortés and his men on two occasions when they are insulted by the Indians who call them *mujeres* (CXXVI, 249; CXLI, 300).

22. Manuel Alvar López, *Americanismos en la "Historia" de Bernal Díaz del Castillo* (Madrid: Imprenta Márquez, 1970), p. 78. Although Bernal Díaz's

view of Marina, like that of many Spaniards, is positive, the name Malinche will later signify "traitor" among members of the indigenous population and supporters of Mexican nationalism.

23. Garci-Rodríguez de Montalvo, *Amadís de Gaula*, 4 vols., ed. Edwin B. Place (Madrid: S. Aguirre Torre, 1969). The influence of *Amadís de Gaula* upon Bernal Díaz' history in general is well known. Stephen Gilman, "Bernal Díaz del Castillo and *Amadís de Gaula*," in *Studia Philologica, Homenaje a Dámaso Alonso*, 2 vols. (Madrid: Editorial Gredos, 1961), II, 99–114. Gilman does not, however, discuss the role of Doña Marina but mentions in the final note to his study the *Storia letteraria delle scoperte geografiche* by Leonardo Olschki in which a comparison is made between her and selected characters of Medieval literature. Although Olschki presents many interesting ideas on the subject, including an analogy between Doña Marina and Bramimonde of the *Chanson de Roland*, he does not relate the development of her role to specific works of Spanish literature. Leonard Olschki, *Storia letteraria delle scoperte geografiche* (Florence: Leo S. Olschki, 1937), pp. 64–72.

24. Díaz del Castillo, *Historia verdadera*, XXXVII, 61. Montalvo, *Amadís*, I, i, 22–24. The abandonment of the hero at birth is not uncommon in folklore. See Stith Thompson, *Motif-Index of Folk-Literature* (Bloomington, Ind.: Indiana University Press, 1955), I, 118.

25. Díaz del Castillo, *Historia verdadera*; XXXVII, 62. Montalvo, *Amadís*, I, x, 85.

26. Gilman, "Bernal Díaz," pp. 103–4.

27. The literary figure of the Celestina influenced to some extent the portrayal of immoral, evil women in colonial literature. Celestinesque types were often associated with witches and witchcraft of the New World's Indian and black cultures. See discussions of Juan Rodríguez Freile's *El carnero* and Fernán González de Eslava's *Coloquio VII* in chapters 3 and 4.

28. Fernando de Rojas, *La Celestina*, ed. Bruno Mario Damiani (Madrid: Cátedra, 1976), pp. 119–20.

29. Díaz del Castillo's reference to the relationship of Xicotenga's daughter with Pedro de Alvarado, one of Cortés' most trusted officers and the future conqueror of Guatemala, presents some important genealogical information which spans several generations of the Alvarado family (LXXVII, 133–34). The author receives a noble Indian woman from Moctezuma's court in a brief episode designed to show Bernal Díaz' importance among Cortés' men and the Aztec chieftain's admiration for him (XCVII, 189).

30. The first Spanish woman to reach the New World accompanied Columbus on his third voyage (1497–1498). Charles R. Boxer, *Women in Iberian Expansion Overseas, 1415–1815* (New York: Oxford University Press, 1975), p. 35.

31. The *noche triste* (Sad Night) occurred on June 30, 1520, when Cortés

and his army were forced to make a disastrous retreat from Tenochtitlán to Tacuba.

Díaz del Castillo also mentions a shipwrecked Jamaican woman who served unsuccessfully as a messenger for the Grijalva expedition (VIII, 17).

32. Cortés's marriage to Catalina Xuarez was the subject of conjecture. In his *Historia de las Indias*, Las Casas cites Gómara's opinion that the future conqueror was at first unwilling to wed. Faced with the disapproval of Diego Velázquez, Cortés decided to solemnize the union although Catalina was a poor girl of humble origin. Later he reportedly said that "he was as happy with her as if she were the daughter of a duchess." Las Casas, *Historia de las Indias*, II, 530.

33. Salvador de Madariaga, *Hernán Cortés, Conqueror of Mexico* (Chicago: Henry Regnery Company, 1955), pp. 416–17; 457.

34. The Indians called her "tececiguata" (XXXVI, 59) which means "great lady." Alvar López, *Americanismos*, pp. 95–96.

35. Although women were often presented in a positive light because they, like the Virgin Mary, are creators of life, Eve's role in the fall of man was not forgotten by early religious writers. The story of Adam and Eve and their expulsion from the Garden of Eden was an initial theme dramatized by the first friars in New Spain, and a description of its presentation offers clear evidence of the transfer of the clergy's misogynistic tendencies to the colonies. Motolinía, *Memoriales e Historia de los indios de la Nueva España*, vol. 240 of *Biblioteca de Autores Españoles* (Madrid: Ediciones Atlas, 1970), pp. 239–40. For a discussion of this play, see chapter 4, "Women in Drama."

36. Vern L. Bullough, *The Subordinate Sex, A History of Attitudes toward Women* (Urbana, Ill.: University of Illinois Press, 1973), pp. 100–101.

37. References noted in the text have been taken from the 1951 edition of Las Casas' work previously cited.

38. Las Casas also alludes to Anacaona's tragic story in his *Brevísima relación de la destrucción de las Indias* (Paris and Buenos Aires: Sociedad de Ediciones Louis-Michaud, 1957), pp. 32–33.

39. Fernández de Oviedo describes the *areitos* as a combination of music, dance, and drama and mentions the one presented by Anacaona in honor of the Spanish official, Nicolás de Ovando. Fernández de Oviedo, *Historia general*, I, 114.

40. When the Spaniards come to retrieve their tribute, the matriarch is in the center of the excitement. Las Casas' description of her on this occasion is endearing as well as humorous as he divulges her natural curiosity, generosity, and contentment. After bestowing many luxurious gifts upon Don Bartholomew, she goes to see the Spaniards' boats loaded for their return to Santo Domingo and even boards one of the vessels herself. Just as she is about to set foot on deck, however, the launch in which she is riding capsizes, hurling the queen

into the water. An incident is averted when she sees how much amusement her spill brings to Don Bartholomew, and she happily completes her inspection of the boat (I, 447–48).

41. Manuel Giménez Fernández suggests that Las Casas may have accompanied the troops on this occasion because of the vividness of his description. Manuel Giménez Fernández, "Fray Bartolomé de Las Casas: A Biographical Sketch," in *Bartolomé de Las Casas in History*, eds. Juan Friede and Benjamin Keen (DeKalb, Ill.: Northern Illinois University Press, 1971), p. 70.

42. Anacaona's generosity was not just a pretense, since she offered her daughter, Higueymota, in marriage to a Spaniard (II, 143). This gesture indicates that women as well observed the custom of giving women to outsiders as a means of formalizing alliances.

43. According to law, emigrants from Spain must be accompanied by their wives unless royal dispensation was granted to them. Pescatello, *Power and Pawn*, p. 132.

44. Perestrelo served Prince Henry the Navigator and aided in the colonization of the islands of Porto Santo and Madeira in 1425. Because of his distinguished service to Portugal, he was awarded the captaincy of Porto Santo. Samuel Eliot Morison, *Admiral of the Ocean Sea* (Boston: Little, Brown and Company, 1942), p. 38.

45. Very little is known about Felipa Moñiz. Morison conjectures that she was probably married to Columbus in 1479, since the birth of their only child took place the following year. By the time Columbus left Portugal in 1485, she was no longer living. Morison, *Admiral of the Ocean Sea*, pp 38–39.

46. Las Casas also mentions Diego Velázquez' marriage to María de Cuéllar, who had come over from Spain with María de Toledo. The governor of Cuba was married on a Sunday and became a widower within a week. Recording this in his history, the Dominican observes: "It was as if God wanted that lady for Himself, because they say that she was very virtuous, and He wanted to take precautions with her untimely death because perhaps time and prosperity would change her" (II, 523). His comment emphasizes the importance of virtue in women and points out as well that they are easily tempted and prone to sinful activities.

47. Díaz del Castillo mentions this tragic event in his *Historia verdadera*. Díaz del Castillo, CCXIV, 612. María later married the conqueror and governor of Nicaragua, Rodrigo de Contreras, and became the mother of the Contreras brothers, who led a rebellion against the Crown. El Inca, *Obras completas,* IV, 27–28.

48. El Inca, *Obras completas*, I, 268. The English translation has been taken from the Varners' edition of the Inca's *Florida* cited previously. The Inca Garcilaso de la Vega, *The Florida of the Inca*, p. 47.

49. Notations included in the chapter proper have been taken from the 1957 edition of this previously mentioned work.

50. This book was quickly translated into English and circulated widely in Protestant countries. It was first entitled *The Tears of the Indians* to enhance its propagandistic purpose.

Pedrarias was governor of Panama at the time that these atrocities were committed.

51. An *encomienda* or grant of Indians was awarded to a soldier in return for his loyal service to the Crown. According to the provisions of the New Laws, new *encomiendas* were prohibited, and present ones were to be dissolved on the death of the original holder and could not be passed on to his descendants. Many of the men who possessed *encomiendas* had served Spain well by conquering and colonizing this new land and felt passionately and sincerely that what they received was just reward for their hard work and suffering. Because of the enactment of the New Laws, rebellions broke out in Central America and Peru.

52. Moctezuma uses this Nahuatl word to describe Díaz del Castillo's lack of material possessions. Díaz del Castillo, *Historia verdadera*, XCVII, 189.

53. Motolinía, *Memoriales e Historia*, p. 253. Page numbers cited in the text have been taken from this 1970 edition. For the English translation, see *Motolinía's History of the Indians of New Spain*, trans. and ed. Elizabeth Andros Foster (Westport, Conn.: Greenwood Press, 1973), pp. 131–32.

Motolinía mentions several similar episodes in which women successfully defended their honor against evil men and the devil himself. One of the young women threatened by rape defends herself "in a manly way" (pp. 321–22).

54. The first Spanish woman to arrive in Peru accompanied this 1535 expedition. According to Agustín de Zarate's account, which the Inca quotes, she, her husband, and two daughters were frozen to death crossing the mountains from Quito. El Inca, *Obras completas*, III, 82–83. The woman's name is not given by the Inca; however, O'Sullivan-Beare suggests that she was Doña Francisca de Valterra, the wife of Pedro de Guzmán, who was mentioned by Bernal Díaz as having perished in Peru in this manner. Nancy O'Sullivan-Beare, *Las mujeres de los conquistadores* (Madrid: Compañía Bibliográfica Española, 1956), p. 137. Díaz del Castillo, *Historia verdadera*, p. 567.

55. Julie Greer Johnson, "A Caricature of Spanish Women in the New World by the Inca Garcilaso de la Vega," *Latin American Literary Review* 9, no. 18 (1981), 47–51.

56. El Inca, *Obras completas*, III, 81. References noted in the text have been taken from this Spanish edition. For the English translations in this section, see El Inca Garcilaso de la Vega, *Royal Commentaries of the Incas and General History of Peru*, trans. Harold V. Livermore (Austin, Tex.: University of Texas Press, 1966), II, i, 733–34; II, vi. 1230.

57. Boxer, *Women in Iberian Expansion Overseas*, pp. 35–39.

58. Pescatello, *Power and Pawn*, p. 139.

59. After the death of his first wife, Doña Francisca de la Cueva, Alvarado married his sister-in-law, Doña Beatriz. She became the governor of Guatemala when he was killed in Mexico during a skirmish. She died in an earthquake when water was released from a volcanic lake and flooded the palace grounds. William Lytle Schurz, *This New World* (New York: E. P. Dutton and Co., 1964), p. 291.

60. Pupo-Walker has studied the autobiographical structure of the Inca's *Comentarios reales* and notes that the author's purpose for selecting such a design was to praise the cultural ideals that he embodied as a proud *mestizo*. Enrique Pupo-Walker, "Sobre la configuración narrativa de los *Comentarios reales*," *Revista Hispánica Moderna* 39 (1976-1977), p. 124.

61. The Inca names Martín de Bustincia as the late husband of the princess in this anecdote; however, according to Aurelio Miró Quesada, Martín was one of the children of Beatriz and Pedro. Aurelio Miró Quesada, *El Inca Garcilaso y otros estudios garcilasistas* (Madrid: Ediciones Cultural Hispánica, 1971), p. 309. Doña Beatriz was one of the most powerful women in Peru during the middle of the sixteenth century because of her property and influence. Elinor C. Burkett, "Indian Women and White Society: The Case of Sixteenth-Century Peru," in *Latin American Women: Historical Perspectives*, ed. Asunción Lavrin (Westport, Conn.: Greenwood Press, 1978), p. 106. In this article, the author recounts how noble Inca women were able to maintain positions of prominence in Spanish society through intermarriage while this was denied to native males.

62. Few of the many relatives of Huayna Capac remained by the time the Inca Garcilaso was born. Most were cruelly murdered by Atahuallpa to remove any threat they might pose to his claim as Inca, heir to the entire kingdom. In addition to Beatriz Coya, the Inca's mother, the niece of Huayna Capac, survived this holocaust as well.

63. The decision of all outside parties to endorse this union seems extremely hasty when considering the seriousness of the matter and much too obvious an attempt to disregard social differences. Selfishness seems to be the chief motive in this instance, as the family of the bride probably saw this as a way to continue to keep favor under the new regime and the Spaniards viewed it as a means of maintaining control of previously held wealth and property.

64. José Durand cites the word *ichach* as an indication of the princess's reticence and finds her response to be typically Indian. He also attributes the tendency of the Inca to omit certain sensitive details of his account to his Indian heritage. José Durand, "Los silencios del Inca Garcilaso," *Mundo Nuevo* 5 (1966), pp. 71, 70.

65. Lewis Hanke, ed., *History of Latin American Civilization*, 2d ed. (Boston: Little, Brown and Company, 1973), I, 141.

66. While the defiant acts of the princess are unequaled, the Inca does tell a story about a very determined woman who was formerly a concubine of Tupac

Inca Yupanqui. According to popular belief and perhaps in light of chivalric tradition, the Inca Huayna Capac had the reputation of never denying a request made by a woman. His generosity was tested, however, when he sought to punish a town that had openly rebelled against him. The village was saved when this prominent *mamacuna* [matron] and other female residents protested the Inca's decision to destroy it and begged for his mercy (II, 341–42).

67. Pedro Gutiérrez de Santa Clara, *Quinquenarios*, vols. 165–67 of *Biblioteca de Autores Españoles* (Madrid: Ediciones Atlas, 1963). Other references to this edition have been included in the text. Gonzalo Pizarro's rebellion against Spanish domination from 1544 to 1548 resulted primarily from the passage of the New Laws in 1542, which called for the abolition of the *encomienda* system in the colonies.

68. Gutiérrez de Santa Clara probably went to Peru in 1544, if he went at all. Although he claims to have served under Captain Pablo Meneses on the loyalist side and later joined the *pizarristas* as Captain Lorenzo de Aldana's secretary (I, 142), his name does not appear on any existing list of soldiers on either side of the conflict. Marcel Bataillon suggests that his absence from the wars may have contributed significantly to the creative interpretation of these historical events. Marcel Bataillon, "Gutiérrez de Santa Clara, escritor mexicano," *Nueva Revista de Filología Hispánica* 15, nos. 3–4 (1961), pp. 408–9, 418.

69. El Inca, *Obras completas*, III, 398. For the English translation, see El Inca, *Royal Commentaries*, II, v, 1214.

70. Gonzalo Correas, *Vocabulario de refranes y frases proverbiales y otras fórmulas comunes de lengua castellana en que van todos los impresos antes y otra gran copia* (Madrid: Tip. de la "Rev. de archivos, bibliotecas y museos," 1924), VI, 15.

71. Diego Fernández, El Palentino, refers to this incident as well in his account of the civil wars. However, the name of the woman is not María Ledesma but María de Toledo. Diego Fernández, *Historia del Perú*, vols. 164–65 of *Biblioteca de Autores Españoles* (Madrid: Ediciones Atlas, 1963), I, 114.

In his *War of Chupas*, Cieza de León mentions a case in which a condemned man is married the night before his execution. Antonio Picado, who was Francisco Pizarro's secretary, was captured and tortured by Diego de Almagro and his men in order to find out where the conqueror had hidden his treasure. His wedding to Ana Suárez takes place only hours before his beheading. Pedro Cieza de León, *The War of Chupas*, trans. Sir Clements R. Markham (London: Chiswick Press, 1917), pp. 140–44.

72. El Inca, *Obras completas*, III, 398. For the English translation, see El Inca, *Royal Commentaries*, II, v, 1213.

73. Alonso de Ercilla, *La Araucana* (México, D.F.: Editorial Porrúa, 1977), p. 12. Other references to this work appear in the chapter proper. Passages in

58   Women in Colonial Spanish American Literature

English have been taken from Alonso de Ercilla's *The Araucaniad*, trans. Charles Maxwell Lancaster and Paul Thomas Manchester (Nashville, Tenn.: Vanderbilt University Press, 1945), p. 28; X, 109; XXXIII, 299–300; XXXIII, 293; XIII, 139; XX, 192; XXI, 197–98; XXVIII, 250–53; VI, 80; VII, 85–86.

74. Julio Caillet-Bois, *Análisis de La Araucana* (Buenos Aires: Centro Editor de América Latina, 1967), p. 24. According to Caillet-Bois, Ercilla's interpretation of the Araucanians adds to the artistic value of his poem and does not diminish its historical importance. Although José Toribio Medina contends that Ercilla's Indian women were based upon historical personages, more recent critics believe that his characterizations were inspired by other literary figures, especially those of Ariosto's *Orlando furioso*. Lerner, for example, associates both episodes and characters of *La Araucana* with this work. José Toribio Medina, "Las mujeres de *La Araucana*," *Hispania* 11 (1928), pp. 1–12. Lía Schwartz Lerner, "Tradición literaria y heroínas indias en *La Araucana*," *Revista Iberoamericana* 38, no. 81 (1972), pp. 615–25.

75. María Rosa Lida de Malkiel, "Dido y su defensa en la literatura española," *Revista de Filología Hispánica* 4 (1942), p. 379. After defending several women in his poem, women come to his assistance when he is condemned to die for fighting with another Spaniard (XXXVI, 496). O'Sullivan-Beare, *Las mujeres de los conquistadores,* pp. 235-36.

76. Lerner, "Tradición literaria," pp. 618–19.

77. Frank Pierce, "Some Themes and Their Sources in the Heroic Poem of the Golden Age," *Hispanic Review* 14, no. 2 (1946), p. 98.

78. Maxime Chevalier, *L'Arioste en Espagne* (Bordeaux: Imprimeries Delmas, 1966), p. 152.

79. Lerner, "Tradición literaria," pp. 620–21.

80. Charles Aubrun, "Poesía épica y novela: El episodio de Glaura en *La Araucana* de Ercilla," *Revista Iberoamericana* 21, nos. 41–42 (1956), p. 268.

81. Tomás Thayer Ojeda, *Formación de la sociedad chilena y censo de la población de Chile en los años de 1540 a 1565* (Santiago, Chile: Prensas de la Universidad de Chile, 1943), III, 164–65.

Another Spanish woman who is mentioned by Ercilla with particular fondness, although she did not come to the New World, is Doña María de Bazán (XVIII, 269). After the Chilean campaigns, the poet returned to Spain and married her in 1570. José Toribio Medina, *Vida de Ercilla* (México, D.F.: Fondo de Cultura Económica, 1948), p. 109.

82. According to Francisco A. Encina, the defiance of Juana Jiménez, one of Valdivia's mistresses, inspired Ercilla to invent this episode about Doña Mencía. Francisco A. Encina, *Historia de Chile* (Santiago, Chile: Editorial Nascimento, 1940), I, 333–34.

83. An Araucanian, who lived in the valley near Concepción, came upon a Christianized Indian who had fled the city. Instead of killing the convert, he

rebuked him for his cowardice: "Thou must be a very woman, / Since from slash of steel thou shrinkest" (VII, 105).

84. Lope de Vega wrote a play entitled *La Araucana* in which Indian women appear, and Ricardo de Turia portrayed Doña Mencía de Nidos as a *mujer varonil* in his *comedia, La belígera española*. See chapter 4.

85. Dinamarca compares Oña's Fresia to Garcilaso's Camila and the episode in which Fresia and Caupolicán appear to that of Guacolda and Lautaro in *La Araucana*. Salvador Dinamarca, *Estudio del "Arauco domado" de Pedro de Oña* (New York: Hispanic Institute in the United States, 1952), pp. 105, 147–48.

86. Pedro de Oña, *Arauco domado* (Santiago, Chile: Imprenta Universitaria, 1917), V, 172–73. Other references to this edition are noted in the text. The English translations in this section have been taken from Pedro de Oña's *Arauco Tamed*, trans. Charles Maxwell Lancaster and Paul Thomas Manchester (Albuquerque, N.M.: University of New Mexico Press, 1948), V, 84; XIII, 196; XII, 178; VII, 111; II, 45.

87. Although Oña does not share Ercilla's admiration for Arauco's culture, he is sympathetic to the Indians' suffering at the hands of some greedy, lawless Spaniards. His description of the women forced to work in Chile's mines and fields is heart-rending (III, 102–3).

88. The women of Quito are also portrayed as immoral because they participate in a rebellion against the Spanish government (XV, 537–38).

89. Francisco Núñez de Pineda y Bascuñán, *El cautiverio feliz*, ed. Angel C. González, Segunda Edición (Abreviada) (Santiago, Chile: Empresa Editora Zig-Zag, 1967). Notations appearing in the text have been taken from this edition.

90. José Anadón, *Pineda y Bascuñán, defensor del araucano* (Santiago, Chile: Editorial Universitaria Seminario de Filología Hispánica, 1977), pp. 34–35.

91. Raquel Chang-Rodríguez, "El propósito del *Cautiverio feliz* y la crítica," *Cuadernos Hispanoamericanos* 297 (1975), pp. 662–63.

92. Anadón, *Pineda y Bascuñán*, p. 31. Although many churchmen associated women with evil, the founder of the Jesuits, Ignatius Loyola, is reported to have uncovered similarities between women and Satan. Mary Daly, *The Church and the Second Sex* (New York: Harper and Row, 1975), p. 101.

93. This English translation has been taken from Francisco Núñez de Pineda y Bascuñán's *The Happy Captive*, trans. William C. Atkinson (London: The Folio Society, 1977), p. 77.

94. Guillermo Lohmann Villena, *El arte dramático en Lima durante el virreinato* (Madrid: Estades, Artes Gráficas, 1945), pp. 214–15. Unfortunately, the dramatist's name and the title of the play are unknown.

CHAPTER 2

EXPRESSIONS OF LOVE AND PRAISE

In an age when historical events generally dominated the thoughts and lives of colonial writers, few literary works were written specifically in appreciation and honor of womanhood. However, a small number of poets, inspired by the feminine ideal, by the fame of prominent Spanish or American women, or by the affection they had for close lady friends, composed lyric verse of an amatory or encomiastic nature. Their poetry occasionally contains biographical information about these women and references to their accomplishments in civic matters, religion, or the arts. Feminine social traits such as manners, appearance, and dress during the colonial period are also alluded to in these poetic descriptions of women. Although many of the poems honoring women were written in deference to the wives of monarchs and government officials, others reflect the intimate emotions of the poet and thus reveal some aspect of his personal life.

The attitude of colonial poets toward women and their portrayal of them in their works closely parallel European concepts and models. Renaissance views of love, which combine chivalric tradition with neo-platonism, may be found throughout the early lyric poetry written in the New World. Given this perspective, the poet's position toward his feminine subject is like that of an ideal knight who, instead of engaging in battle, proves his strength of character by serving his lady no matter what the consequences may be.[1] He is a courtly lover who elevates his beloved to a place of superiority over him and worships her from afar.[2]

She, in turn, ennobles him in a spiritual sense because her beauty is a source of divine virtue and the embodiment of human perfection. While this approach toward women remains relatively constant throughout the colonial period, it often becomes more realistic and sensual during the seventeenth and eighteenth centuries than it was in the sixteenth as the distance between the poet and his lady diminishes.[3]

Both love poetry and laudatory verse, much of which is elegiac in tone, share a glorified image of womanhood. This view is characterized by a description of the lady's flawlessness in encomiastic terms[4] and a comparison of aspects of her loveliness to splendorous phenomena found in nature and the heavens. The poet may suggest this idealized vision of femininity through several references to the lady's grandeur or outline it specifically through his enumeration of her physical attributes. A woman's youth and beauty, for example, are often likened to a flower, especially the rose, and her radiance or prominence is frequently conveyed by the mention of celestial light. The meticulous delineation of a lady's attractiveness is generally provided by poetic portraiture which focuses on her facial features. Special emphasis is given to her eyes, which are thought to reflect a woman's divinity,[5] and they are often compared to stars, planets, or suns. During the latter part of the colonial period, however, some portraits of women were expanded to include a description of their entire body.

The literary precedents set by European poets regarding the relationship between the writer and his female subject and the poetic vision of a woman became conventionalized in colonial lyric poetry and were followed in the characterization of both imaginary and real women. American elements are usually limited to the identification of the lady being acclaimed or mourned and the mention of a particular place, but even these references are frequently omitted. For this reason, the portrayal of leading Spanish American women in the Church, state, intellectual community, and the poet's own circle of friends almost always resembles that of Petrarch's Laura,[6] Garcilaso de la Vega's Isabel Freyre,[7] or Quevedo's Lisi.[8]

One of the first writers of amatory verse in Spain's American colonies was the sixteenth-century Mexican poet, Francisco de Terrazas, referred to by Cervantes in *La Galatea* as the "new Apollo."[9] Several sonnets and an *Epístola amatoria [Love Letter]* written in tercets are all that remain of his lyric poetry,[10] and these compositions reflect an Italianate influence which may have been transmitted to him by Gutierre de Cetina.[11]

Terrazas' exaltation of feminine beauty and charm is best demonstrated by a superb sonnet from the early collection of poetry entitled *Flores de varia poesía [Flowers of Varied Poetry]*.[12] The descriptive language and technique that he employs clearly mirror the Renaissance concept of womanhood and are typical of that used by many colonial poets who succeeded him:

> Give up the golden hair
> which binds my soul
> and thus return to pure snow
> the blended whiteness of those roses.
>
> Give up the pearls and the precious coral
> which so lavishly adorn your mouth,
> and to heaven, by whom you are envied,
> return the suns which you have stolen.
>
> The grace and discretion that have been
> bestowed on you by the Celestial Master
> Return them to angelic nature.
>
> And all this thus restored
> You will see that what is left is all yours;
> To be harsh, cruel, ungrateful and obstinate. (p.13)

In the sonnet's quatrains Terrazas concentrates upon the lady's physical beauty, the source of her attractiveness, but confines his description to her head as an indication of the chaste intentions of his overtures. Each of her facial features is compared to the element in nature that most precisely duplicates its color or intensity and whose rarity suggests the degree of her extraordinary loveliness. The poet then dedicates his tercets to a description of the lady's behavior. His mention of her grace and discretion, which he considers of divine origin, hints at his deification of her. However, in the poem's final line, when all of his beloved's outward physical beauty has been reclaimed by nature, he finds that she is in her inner essence: "harsh, cruel, ungrateful and obstinate." This reaction, which was no doubt prompted by the woman's disdain for him, is common in the disappointed courtly lover. He is customarily portrayed as complaining about his beloved when he realizes that she is unattainable and that his love for her is hopeless.

A similar rejection is also the theme of Terrazas' "Soneto a una dama que despabiló una vela con los dedos" (p. 14) ["Sonnet To A Lady Who Snuffed Out a Candle With Her Fingers"]. In this poem he alleges that a woman can control her emotions as quickly and easily as snuffing out a candle and laments that she can be totally indifferent to his petitions of love. As a suitor, however, he must suffer miserably because of her callousness. In spite of her scorn and his pain, he will continue to endure his burning desire until he is finally consumed by its fire.

Praise of a specific Spanish American woman, rather than an imaginary one, is found in the works of the Spaniard Bernardo de Balbuena, and his description of her sheds light not only upon her personal life but upon that of the poet as well. In the introduction to *La grandeza mexicana [Mexican Grandeur]*, he provides a portrait of Doña Isabel de Tobar y Guzmán, the lady to whom his lengthy poetic description of Mexico City is dedicated. He describes Doña Isabel as "a lady so rare in her make-up, of such remarkable intelligence, of such degrees of honesty, and of such excellence of beauty, that any one of these virtues could easily place her among the most famous women in the world."[13] She was the daughter of Pedro de Tobar, one of the principal colonizers of New Galicia,[14] and the granddaughter of the governor of Cuba on her mother's side. At the time Balbuena writes his dedicatory preface, she is already a widow and the mother of an only son, who has become a member of the Jesuit Order.[15] Although the tribute that the poet pays to Doña Isabel on this occasion is glowing, it is, in reality, a traditional encomium accorded women of her stature.

Until this century, little was known about the relationship between Balbuena and Doña Isabel represented by this succinct, formal statement. However, according to Balbuena's biographers, John Van Horne and José Rojas Garcidueñas, the poet made a trip to San Miguel de Culiacán in New Galicia to visit Doña Isabel before going to Mexico City. When he left her, he promised to write and tell her what the viceregal capital was like. She herself would be going there soon to enter the convent of San Lorenzo, an alternative often chosen by widows who did not wish to remarry but to remain faithful to their late husbands. Balbuena kept his word, and *La grandeza mexicana*, published in 1604, is the letter in poetic form that he addressed to her.[16]

Aware that Balbuena and Doña Isabel grew up together in New Galicia, Rojas Garcidueñas began to search the poet's pastoral novel, *Siglo de Oro en las selvas de Erífile [Golden Age in the Forests of*

Eryphyle], for evidence that might link the couple romantically. While the amatory sentiments contained in this youthful novel are similar to those found in Montemayor's *Diana* and Gil Polo's *Diana enamorada*, Rojas Garcidueñas is able to identify specific descriptions and events which, he believes, are autobiographical. The most convincing proof of his theory is found in the eighth eclogue when the shepherd Rosanio praises his beloved in a courtly manner and reveals the name of Doña Isabel in the sonnet's acrostic. Rojas Garcidueñas also states that more direct references to her were probably made in the original manuscript; however, these were presumably dropped when it was revised by Balbuena before being published.[17]

Balbuena may have employed the love theme in other writings, but, unfortunately, they were destroyed some years later when Dutch pirates raided San Juan during his tenure as Bishop of Puerto Rico. The title of one of the lost pieces, "La alteza de Laura" ["The Sublimity of Laura"], seems to indicate some degree of Petrarchan influence.[18]

Many poems honoring women both in life and in death are contained in one of the first anthologies of Spanish American poetry, *Ramillete de varias flores recogidas y cultivadas en los primeros abriles de sus años [Bouquet of Various Flowers Gathered and Cultivated During the Early Years of the Poet's Life]*. This collection, published in the Spanish city of Alcalá de Henares in 1675, is comprised of the works of its compiler, Jacinto de Evia, and those of Padre Antonio de Bastidas and Hernando Domínguez Camargo.[19] The rose is the symbol chosen by the *Ramillete's* contributors as a motif of their poetry, and it often appears in their descriptions of women. It is considered to be the ideal expression of a woman's most prized qualities and a symbolic representation of the life cycle. Both Evia and Bastidas use the rose in their verses, and they base their use of the image on Camargo's translation of Vergil's poem to that flower.[20]

The Ecuadorian poet, Jacinto de Evia, explores the beauty and nature of women and the effects and consequences of love in several poems of the *Ramillete*. His female subjects, like those of Terrazas, are visionary; however, he identifies them with pastoral names. For him, the rose is the perfect replica of a woman because it can be both lovely and dangerous. In his "A una rosa" (pp. 317–18) ["To a Rose"], he compares his beloved's comely features to the flower's delicate structure and her refusal to listen to his expressions of love to its thorns.

Evia's poems "Anfrisa por malograda y mal empleada es llorada" (pp. 305–6) ["Anfrisa Because She Is Spoiled and Misused, She Is Pitied"], "Quéjase Fabio de su poca suerte en los desdenes de su Anfrisa" (pp. 311–12) ["Fabio Complains About His Lack of Luck Upon Being Slighted by Anfrisa"], and "A un corazón de cristal que presentó" (pp. 301–2) ["To a Heart of Glass That Showed"] again voice the lover's reaction to his beloved's disdain. In each of these works, the imagery used to describe the lady's contradictory nature varies. All of the poet's metaphors, however, express an appreciation for the woman's beauty or her potential for love along with a painful awareness of her insensitivity toward him. Anfrisa is a "beautiful diamond" (p. 306) in the first *romance* (ballad), and Fabio mentions "her snowy breasts" (p. 311) in the second. Amarilis, who is described in the last poem, is indifferent to her lover's pleas because she has a "crystal heart" (p. 301).

To ease his suffering and to vent his frustration, a poet in love sometimes addresses outside forces concerning his predicament. In his *glosa* (gloss) "Cupido, que rindes las almas" (pp. 303–4) ["Cupid, You Who Conquer Souls"], Evia implores the love god to tell Belisa how much he adores her, and in "Anfrisa por malograda," he questions Heaven about having created such a perplexing woman who has the characteristics of both an angel and a monster. In spite of this apparent incongruity, however, he constantly describes women as being divine. They are regarded as celestial beings (p. 301) and even classified as goddesses who are worshiped faithfully by their lovers (p. 312).

Apart from presenting the effects of love upon men, Evia also indicates that women may be hurt by it as well. In "A las lágrimas de una dama" (pp. 299–300) ["To a Lady's Tears"] and "A las lágrimas que lloraba una dama" (pp. 313–14) ["To the Tears that a Lady Shed"], the poet describes two women who are sad because they believe that they have lost the opportunity to enjoy love. Using the conventional imagery of feminine portraiture, he relates how their crying changes their lovely appearance. Amarilis is weeping because she is jealous of her husband, and the flood of tears "withers the flowers that her face displays" (p. 299). Likewise, when Belisa bemoans the absence of her lover, her weeping drowns her splendor, and her eyes expire like bright stars in the sea (pp. 313–14).[21]

In another of his poems, "Descubre un amante algo más la llama que albergaba su pecho" (pp. 307–9) ["A Lover Discovers Something Else, the Flame that He Harbors in His Heart"], Evia uses the common metaphor of a moth being drawn to a light to describe how compelling the force of love is and how fatal its attraction may be.[22] Here the lover gladly surrenders to this overwhelming power and is undaunted by the perils it poses: ". . .if I have to give up my life, / it is bliss to surrender it to your flame" (p. 307). The lady possesses his soul, and his death, therefore, will be a pleasurable one.

A number of elegiac poems to prominent women of the seventeenth century were contributed to the *Ramillete* by Padre Antonio de Bastidas, who was also an Ecuadorian and Evia's teacher. The image of woman as a flower is used in several of these works not only to denote the past beauty of the deceased but also to underscore the brevity of her life. In his *glosa* to Doña Francisca de Santa Clara y de la Cueva (pp. 99–100), for example, Bastidas combines both floral and light imagery when he characterizes her passing as a transformation from a flower to a shining star (p. 100). By doing this, he recognizes her loveliness and fragility and at the same time emphasizes her lasting contribution to Quito's religious life, the founding of the city's Santa Clara Convent. The Church offered many women the opportunity to be active outside the home, and they were responsible for much of the altruism of the period.

Bastidas also wrote a poetic lament on the death of Doña Tomasa Vera (p. 123), the wife of the governor of Popayán, where he taught for ten years as a member of the Jesuit Order.[23] An attractive young wife is always an asset to a man in public office, and she probably accompanied her husband in some of his administrative duties to have gained this recognition. Bastidas was particularly grieved by the untimeliness of her death and conventionally compares her existence to that of a rose. A portion of the last line, "On living, she is born and dies like a rose" (p. 123), is repeated as the sonnet's acrostic.[24]

Queens as well as kings were mourned in the colonies, and Father Bastidas wrote several poems in commemoration of the death of Philip IV's wife, Isabel, in 1644 (pp. 82–92). Although the dead queen is the subject of these short compositions, little is actually said about her as an individual or about the importance of her accomplishments.[25] More attention is given to the general outpouring of grief in Quito and to the poetic reflection of that emotion in nature. Bastidas' references to Isabel in his poetry are traditional and dwell on her former radiance. Metaphors of brightness, especially those related to the sun, convey her past warmth, charm, and love as well as her importance as the king's wife. In the

following excerpt from one of Bastidas' *romances*, which echoes the
Ubi sunt? theme, the sharp contrast between light and dark imagery is
employed in an effort to characterize the dramatic effect of her death
on a Spanish American city:

> Shepherds of these peaks
> who bestow so much honor on Quito
> where is the rosy dawn
> of the Bourbons hiding now?
>
> If you search from the height
> of the first light of dawn,
> where has the sun transposed
> the florid beams of Isabel?
>
> I only witness, shepherds,
> in place of her splendor,
> the silence of the night,
> the confusion of the shadows. (p. 83)[26]

The late queen as well as five of her predecessors also named Isabel
were praised by the Mexican poet Juan Ortiz de Torres.[27] His com-
position written in 1645 differs from that of Father Bastidas in that he
gives some attention to the specific details concerning several of the
deceased monarchs. This monologue, entitled "Alabanza de las insignes
Isabeles de España" ["In Praise of the Illustrious Isabels of Spain"],
is appropriately presented by a woman.[28] The theme of her speech is
introduced by a direct question which she, herself, answers in subsequent stanzas, and it reflects what Méndez Plancarte refers to as "a
light intellectual feminism"[29]: "Are only men to take credit for everything? . . . / Indeed, there were women who contributed to the sciences
and the arts. . . ." As these lines indicate, the poet realized that the
accomplishments of women were often slighted, but his attempt to
rectify this oversight is not altogether successful. His description of
Isabel the Catholic, for example, is informative because it is based upon
historical fact. As he mentions in his poem, she expelled the Jews from
Spain, established the Inquisition in Castile, and "because of her faith
and unparalleled zeal / a New World was discovered unintentionally."
In addition to these signal achievements, Ortiz de Torres alleges that
she had a eucharistic vessel made from the first gold that Columbus

brought back from the Indies to commemorate his voyage and discovery. Although the poet openly acknowledges Isabel's participation in the unification of Spain and the expansion of the empire, he attributes this to her spiritual strength rather than her intelligence or political foresight.

Just as memorials were written by Father Bastidas and Ortiz de Torres on the death of Spanish queens, so the poet Diego de Ribera described Mexico's observances of Philip IV's demise in 1665. His "Funerales pompas de D. Felipe IV y plausible aclamación de D. Carlos II"[30] ["Funeral Ceremony of H. M., Philip IV and Plausible Acclamation of H. M., Charles II"] contains a description of the viceroy's wife as she fulfilled her official responsibilities by accepting condolences on the royal family's behalf. Doña Leonor de Carreto was married to Don Antonio Sebastián de Toledo, the Marquis of Mancera, who governed New Spain from 1664 to 1673. Known for her patronage of the arts, she invited Juana Inés de Asbaje to become one of her ladies-in-waiting before the young girl decided to enter a convent and so launched the career of the most renowned literary figure of the Spanish American colonies.[31] According to Ribera, the vicereine was a striking woman who illuminated the gathering of mourners by her presence, and he likens her loveliness to that of mythology's most beautiful goddesses, Venus[32] and Minerva. The poet's reference to her as "the Marchioness Pallas" reflects the continuance of the image of the female warrior to characterize exceptional women and was probably chosen by the poet to denote that she performed her husband's duties on certain occasions.

In depicting Doña Leonor's ladies-in-waiting, Ribera uses the customary language of love poetry in recognition of their pulchritude; however, a more outstanding aspect of his presentation is the attention accorded the appropriateness of their attire. His itemized account of the proper mourning dress of the time is one of the few realistic descriptions of women's clothing in lyric poetry, and it shows to some extent how these ladies conformed to the masculine image of the feminine ideal:

> Over their hoop underskirts
> of thick flannel
> skirts were seen trailing,
> a custom of the times.
>
> Their coiffure was so modest,
> and so artfully done,

that there was not even
one hair out of place.

Their black taffeta headdresses
fitted snuggly on their heads.
They fell like youthful hair
to reach the floor.

This time their mantles
were not folded in corners
since they were as delicate
as their thoughts.

From Ribera's account the clothing worn by these ladies was decorative rather than functional, and its elaborateness attests to the court's reputation as a center of fashion in Spanish America. Garments were tastefully chosen to fit the occasion, and emphasis was placed upon creating a flowing effect from the head and a delicateness about the waist. Farthingales, which were in vogue at the time, often improved a woman's proportions by accentuating her narrow midsection while adding fullness to her hips. Although the appearance of these aristocratic ladies was elegant and so permitted them to extend their influence at court, they were no doubt uncomfortable and physically restricted in their activities by these costumes.[33]

A more sensitive and sincere elegy to a woman than those written to the wives of heads of state or government officials is Luis de Sandoval y Zapata's[34] sonnet, "A una cómica difunta" ["To a Dead Actress"].[35] She is one of the few actual women who is not a member of the social elite to be extolled in lyric poetry, and this tribute confirms the fact that women were allowed to work in colonial theaters and became accomplished thespians. Describing the deceased actress as graceful, elegant, and lovely, this seventeenth-century Mexican poet praises her as a versatile and convincing performer:

and—loving, cold, disdainful—thou didst feign
so well that even Death was unresolved
if thou didst simulate him as one dead
or didst submit to him as one alive. (II, 103)

Apart from expressing personal admiration for a popular entertainer, Sandoval y Zapata pays homage to the feminine ideal. In his "Belleza a un balcón del ocaso'' [''Beauty on a Western Balcony''], the radiant, elusive woman is still pursued by the lowly, suffering lover, but conventional imagery is artfully fragmented in order to create an unusual poetic illusion:

> On the Occident she shed her light
> who kindled in the Orient of her beauty;
> him to detain who hastened to his doom
> the heaven of the West sought out the Sun.
>
> I, in the Occident guitaring light,
> in a love-distracted dying burned;
> (the consummation of my little day
> was Moon, because my life was up betimes).
>
> Thou gainest from the Occident on the Sun;
> fatal wounds he fugitive inflicts,
> thou motionless inflictest wounds of healing.
>
> In the Orient still he fans his pyres;
> and thou, from out the West, a livelier Sun,
> still fannest lives to life-consuming love. (II, 104)[36]

The lovely shepherdess or country girl, praised in Evia's poems, is also the principal subject of Juan del Valle y Caviedes' love poetry written in Peru during the late 1600's. Amorous verse, while not as well known as his feminine satire, comprises a substantial part of his literary production. Sixteen *romances amorosos* [love ballads], as well as a number of other pieces from the poet's *Poesías varias y jocosas [Varied and Jocose Poems]*, present his ideas about love and his vision of the ideal woman.[37] The poems are generally similar in their compliance with courtly convention, since most consist of the lover's complaints at his beloved's failure to return his affection.

A concise statement of Caviedes' feelings toward love is his poem ''Da el autor catorce definiciones al amor'' (pp. 94–95) [''The Author Defines Love in Fourteen Different Ways''] where he concludes that it is an ''enigma'' and a ''labyrinth.'' This typically baroque conception of the emotion is evident throughout his amatory verse, but he continues to bring new perspectives to this definition. In ''A dos amigas que se educaban en un monasterio'' (pp. 73–77) [''To Two Friends Who Were

Being Educated in a Monastery''], he appropriately chooses cloistered women as the objects of his affection because they were generally noted for their refinement and purity. The Church provided the only formalized training for young girls in its convents, and their innocence was assured by the protective atmosphere within these religious communities. Caviedes describes love as a "jail" or an "inferno" in this poem and reveals the sacrifice a lover has to make to court his lady properly. He must not only relinquish his freedom, according to the poet, but surrender his soul to his beloved as well. In other poetic works, Caviedes classifies love as a sickness or a wound and alludes to the suffering and pain to be endured by one who is enamored. However, with regard to this discomfort, he admits in his sixth and seventh "Romances amorosos": "the wounds are sweet" (p. 65) and "I am dying to die" (p.66). No matter what the consequences of courtship are, the rational side of the poet philosophically disavows any responsibility for his infatuation (p. 47).

The women described in Caviedes' love poems are all beautiful, but this quality is generally implied rather than stated. Names such as Amarinda (p. 73), Filis (p. 63), Lisi (p. 61), and Lucinda (p. 68), commonly associated with bucolic scenes, evoke visions of natural, wholesome beauty. Caviedes emphasizes a woman's eyes, however, because he, like other lyric poets before him, was captivated by their sparkle and movement. His poems "A los ojos de una dama" ["To the Eyes of a Lady"], "A los ojos de otra dama" ["To the Eyes of Another Lady"],[38] "Romance amoroso VI" (pp. 65–66) ["Love Ballad VI"], and his *coplas* [couplets] "De Menga los ojos" (pp. 78–79) ["Menga's Eyes"], all reveal the damaging and even fatal effects of a woman's glances. In the first poem the function of the lady's eyes and their capacity for harm are paradoxical:

> I strain my eyes looking at them,
> Argus of your two bright stars,
> and when I take a good look at them,
> I go blind,

and in other verses of these poems, Belisa's eyes are condemnatory court judges,[39] and Catalina's are poised arrows (p. 65). The latter metaphor in particular denotes the kinship between the image of the

female warrior and the beloved, as the use of military conceits establishes Athena as the prototype of the ideal woman.[40] The ability of a
woman's eyes to represent celestial beauty and divine goodness, however, is not forgotten by Caviedes. Those of an unidentified woman are
"two bright stars," and those of Belisa, like the eyes of Terraza's
unnamed lady, are "divine suns." Belisa's gaze also produces a "sweet
tyranny" which finally leads the poet to entreat her: ". . . since God
bestowed beautiful eyes on you, / go ahead and use them, Belisa."[41]

Caviedes' examination of a woman's inner nature is far more lengthy
and specific than his treatment of her physical aspects. Various feminine
charmers are described as "tyrants" (p. 77), "murderesses" (p. 62),
and "pirates" (p. 75), and they are generally evasive, indifferent, cold,
cruel, ungrateful, and, under certain circumstances, deadly. While these
epithets and attributes should serve as a deterrent to the lover, their
effect is antithetical as the poet admits in his "Romance amoroso XIV"
["Love Ballad XIV"]:

> In your ungratefulness and elusiveness
> you blend the necessary adornments,
> for I find you more beautiful
> the more ungrateful you are.
> For, to be beautiful and elusive
> in pretty women always appears natural
> so it can be said that these things
> were both born from the same womb. (p. 70)

Several of Caviedes' descriptions of women, like Balbuena's portrait
of Doña Isabel de Tobar, reflect love or admiration for a real person
and so shed some light on the poet's life. In his *romance* "En la muerte
de mi esposa" ["On the Death of My Wife"], the bereaved poet expresses his disbelief and sense of isolation at his wife's passing. Although little is said about her, her importance to him is conveyed by
the poetic exclamations: "My sun! My sun has died!" (p. 78).[42]

Another poetic work by Caviedes reveals not only his own fame as
a poet but that of the colonial period's greatest literary figure, Sor Juana
Inés de la Cruz. By the last quarter of the seventeenth century, Caviedes
was already an author of some renown in Peru, and word of his talent
had reached as far north as the viceroyalty of New Spain. In Mexico,
Sor Juana wrote him expressing her high regard for his poetry and

asking for a copy of his work. Although her letter to Caviedes has been lost, his rhymed reply to her has been preserved and is reprinted in Vargas Ugarte's collection of the poet's *Obras*. When Caviedes received Sor Juana's letter, he was no doubt very flattered by the request from such an illustrious poetess, and he wanted to pay her only the highest possible compliments in return. While the language he chose to describe her is conventional, he did not employ the imagery usually associated with the literature of women worshipers but used that related to the female warrior. He, like Diego de Ribera in his description of Leonor de Carreto, reserved this symbolism for a truly remarkable woman and one who assumes the role of a man. Because women lacked the opportunity to develop their intellectual ability, scholarly and literary pursuits were commonly associated with men. Sor Juana's accomplishments, therefore, were considered exceptional for her sex, and her mental agility and poetic talent were regarded as manly:

> You have men confused,
> because you overcome their arrogance,
> Amazon of discretion,
> with skillful and sharp weapons.
> And since anyone can make
> a coat in verse out of his cape,
> make in honor of creativity,
> a pair of trousers out of your skirt.
> Like the Nun Ensign did[43]
> in order to add splendor to her arms,
> for letters, there is
> in you a nun captain. (p.35)

On April 17, 1695, Sor Juana died, and she was greatly mourned by her admirers throughout the Spanish empire. Carlos Sigüenza y Góngora delivered the eulogy at his dear friend's funeral, and other notable individuals offered eloquent tributes to Mexico's Muse on that sad occasion.[44] Although these first testimonials have been lost, many others, written shortly after her death, have been preserved and were published along with some of Sor Juana's works in *Fama, y obras pósthumas del fénix de México [Fame and Posthumous works of the Phoenix of Mexico]*. This collection of elegiac poetry and prose was gathered by Dr. Juan Ignacio de Castorena y Ursúa, who was the prebend and chaplain of Mexico City's cathedral. It includes laments by such prominent persons as the Count of Galve, who was the viceroy of New Spain at the time of Sor Juana's death, Don Jerónimo Monforte y Vera, a Spanish dramatist residing in Peru, and Dr. Jacinto Muñoz de Castilblanque, the Archbishop-elect of Manila.[45]

The poetic vision of Sor Juana expressed in these memorials is similar to those of other great women of the time. Light imagery commonly associated with queens and vicereines is consistently used in the description of the famous Hieronymite nun as well. In a sonnet by the Mexican poet, Don Diego Martínez, the light representing the poetess changes sources but remains constantly shining:

> Sunset, then, endure your fading light,
> for if the sun does not die as a sunset
> the stars do not attain their brightness. (p. 282)

Sor Juana is often referred to by her poetic name, Julia,[46] or by an appropriate designation of mythological origin. Don Joseph Miguel de Torres, the secretary of Mexico's Royal University, like Caviedes, evokes the image of the female warrior in his poetic tribute to her. By addressing her as Minerva, he pays homage to her feminine beauty and her masculine intellect (p. 284).

In addition to the traditional poetic aspects of Sor Juana's portrayal, many of her admirers who eulogized her affectionately mentioned specific elements of her life and works. Her ability to read at age three (pp. 5, 8, 28), her desire to dress like a man in order to attend the university (p. 11),[47] and the sale of her library and scientific instruments to help the poor (pp. 57, 61) are among the fond memories they recall throughout more than fifty entries.[48] Dr. Juan de Aviles' poetic encomium to Sor Juana incorporates the theme and imagery from her sonnet, "En que da moral censura a una rosa, y en ella a sus semejantes" ["In Which She Morally Censures a Rose, and Likewise Things Similar to It"] and a simple statement of one of her intellectual goals from her *Respuesta a Sor Filotea de la Cruz [Reply to Sister Philotea of the Cross]*:

> Well, if this Rose that Fame bemoans
> in forty-five years has lived centuries,
> now she does not have to know more,
> now she is ignorant of nothing (p. 292).[49]

Of course, Sor Juana and her contributions to colonial culture would have been remembered without these poetic encomiums written for her; however, their existence indicates that she attained considerable fame throughout the Spanish empire during her lifetime. She had dedicated much of her poetry to officials of both church and state as well as friends and acquaintances, and at her death they responded with admiration and affection for her in the form of expression that she loved. Many of the poems based upon particular events in her life contributed to the compilation of her first biography by Padre Diego Calleja.[50]

Expressions of love and praise continued to be written in the colonies during the eighteenth century; however, the conception of the woman is often more realistic than it had been previously, and her description may contain sensual or erotic allusions. An example of this relative frankness toward womanhood is found in the amorous verses of the Ecuadorian Jesuit, Father Juan Bautista Aguirre, who spent nearly twenty years in Italy after leaving Spanish America. In the brief prelude to his love poems, contained in his *Versos castellanos, obras juveniles, misceláneas [Castilian Verses, Youthful and Miscellaneous Works]*,[51] he states that he wrote these compositions for "entertainment" and "exercise," and he provides his reader with two alternatives for their interpretation: "if you can, attribute them to the divine, and if not, judge them to be compliments from Don Quixote to Dulcinea."[52] Although many members of the religious community composed love poetry, Padre Aguirre may have felt that such a statement was a necessary precaution because of the sensuous nature of several of his descriptions.[53]

In his "A una dama imaginaria" (pp. 501–2) ["To an Imaginary Lady"] and "A unos ojos hermosos" (pp. 505–6) ["To a Pair of Beautiful Eyes"], Aguirre treats familiar themes found in love poetry; however, in these particular pieces he humanizes the feminine ideal. His ornate portrait of a woman in the former poem reveals that her beauty is still the source of her attractiveness but that her loveliness is not limited to her face alone. After carefully citing each one of her facial features, he continues his description of her with a reference to her feminine form but veils it in spirituality:

> Beauty and pleasure are
> in your figure and in your face
> your whole body is breath
> and all of your breath is soul. (pp. 501–2)

Aguirre's view of women is based upon the pleasure of beholding them rather than their representation of lofty ideals, and as a result he sees them as a very real obstacle to man's spiritual well-being. Describing a woman's eyes, he condemns them as a worldly source of evil: "And although you look like angels / you do not deserve such a name / for they are the guardians of mankind / and you are the ruin of men" (pp. 505–6).[54] In a fragment of one of his *romances* (p. 501), the poet places the responsibility for man's thoughts and actions directly upon the woman because of her irresistable physical attractiveness. Although Aguirre's manner of expression is courtly, his complaints about women do not reflect the customary ambivalence of a spurned lover but the diverse attitudes of the Church toward women represented by the Virgin Mary and Eve. The poet considers ladies to be alluring yet basically sinful, and this tendency was probably accentuated by his celibacy.

Definite traces of sensuality and even eroticism are evident in a number of odes written by the Mexican poet, Fray Manuel Navarrete. These pieces, however, represent only a portion of his amatory verse contained in his *Entretenimientos poéticos [Poetic Entertainment]*, which was published posthumously in 1823.[55] His poems generally present love as a "refined game" between shepherds and shepherdesses and reflect the influence of the Spanish poet, Meléndez Valdés.[56] In a traditional vein, his epigram "Del amor" ["Concerning Love"] synthesizes his view of romance, which is typical of that of the courtly lover:

> It is said about love,
> that it is a prison and a sickness: I say,
> my friend Fabio, that I want,
> neither health, nor freedom. (II, 182)

Country girls abound in his poetry, and he admits in his "Influjos de amor" (I, 281) ["The Influences of Love"] that he would quickly give up life in Mexico's magnificent capital to enjoy the company of a rustic beauty. Conventional imagery usually prevails in these works as in his sonnet "De la hermosura" (I, 294). ["Concerning Beauty"], when he warns Lisi that her loveliness, like that of the rose, will soon disappear.

While allegedly remaining an observer of the feminine sex, Navarrete refers to women of flesh and blood and carnal love in numerous poems.[57] In his "Retrato de Celia" (I, 164–69) ["Portrait of Celia"], a complete view of the lady is suggested as he, like fellow churchman Aguirre, merges physical and spiritual imagery:

> I shall paint your breasts
> temple in which hearts
> offer their libations
> of love on the sacred altar (I, 167).

Other literary devices are also used by the poet in order to conceal his licentiousness. In his ode "A Clorila con unas frutitas de pasta" (I, 123–24) ["To Clorila with Pastry Fruit"], he captures the sensuality of a lady eating and experiences her touch vicariously:

> Such delicate kisses!
> Such soft bites
> In truth, I feel
> the sweetest envy (I, 124),

and he veils reality with dream imagery in his ode "El triunfo del amor" (I, 115–17) ["Love's Triumph"]. The scene, in which Anarda appears at her lover's bedside and atones for having made him jealous, is not only sensual but erotic.

The tendency to introduce elements of realism into the physical description of women and to express candidly the relationship between the lover and the beloved, an approach only suggested by such seventeenth-century poets as Sandoval y Zapata in his sonnet "Riesgo grande de un galán en metáfora de mariposa," becomes apparent during the eighteenth century but is by no means a dominant feature of late colonial poetry. Taste and discretion were demonstrated by both Padre Aguirre and Fray Navarrete in their portraits of women, and they are careful to place realistic details within a spiritual or dreamlike context to detach themselves personally from their amatory verse. Although these changes intensify the courtly portrayal of women, the general view of womanhood in colonial lyric poetry is only slightly altered. Beauty remains woman's most prized attribute, and a respectable distance between her and the poet is still cautiously maintained.

The colonial lyric poetry examined in this chapter generally reveals the direct transfer rather than the adaptation of the Renaissance concept of ideal womanhood to New World literature. From the time of Terrazas to that of Navarrete, the few poems written in praise of women usually reflect the superiority of the female subject over her lover or the poet and the importance of beauty in her description. Conventionalized nature imagery delineates the specific aspects or the extent of her pulchritude, and it is used in the portraits of historical and fictional women alike. The rose, for example, is used by Evia to describe the perfection and delicateness of his beloved's silhouette and by Bastidas to characterize the former loveliness and youth of the deceased Doña Tomasa Vera. Light imagery as well is used in a similar fashion. Sandoval y Zapata's conception of the feminine ideal appears to merge harmoniously with the sunset as the woman fades out of view, and Doña Leonor's ladies-in-waiting are pictured by Ribera as "suns" in a somber setting. Although imaginary women are more frequently portrayed in idyllic scenes than actual women, pastoral names and episodes occasionally disguised the poet's true feelings about women or concealed their identity. Balbuena divulges the name of Doña Isabel de Tobar in a sonnet taken from his *Siglo de Oro en las selvas de Erífile*, and Navarrete's shepherdesses may have represented several of his lady friends.

The highly idealized image of the woman in courtly love poetry was embraced by lyric poets in the colonies, since it resembled a feminine type that was somewhat of a rarity in Spanish America. During the conquest years, white females were scarce, and with the settlement and growth of urbanization, upper-class women were often inaccessible to the majority of men because of the traditional social restrictions placed upon them. Some men as well were isolated from women in observance of stringent monastic rules, and their celibacy influenced them to perceive women in idealized terms. Enforced continence, however, is known to have engendered misogyny in some cases. The glorification of aristocratic white women is due in part to their lack of availability, but it is also indicative of their embodiment of racial purity. Unlike the Spanish men who had engaged in sexual relationships indiscriminately, Spanish women had been sheltered from interracial contact, and their bloodlines had remained unbroken, a quality greatly admired by the Spaniards. The refined lady, therefore, provided the perfect partner for the poet in his amorous or erotic fantasies and a worthy subject for his exaltation, and she, not the female warrior, represented society's advancement after the conquest.

Although women drawn from the poet's imagination rather than his experience appear more frequently as subjects of poems of love and praise, the names and descriptions of a small group of Spanish America's female residents have been preserved in colonial lyric poetry. These women, however, are often described in the same metaphorical language because they displayed the standards of femininity that were so highly prized by the poets. They were the most likely segment of the female population to have been brought up on Spanish educational treatises such as Fray Martín de Córdoba's *Jardín de nobles doncellas,* Fray Luis de León's *La perfecta casada,* and Luis Vives' *Instrucción de la mujer cristiana,* and out of a desire to be pleasing to men and subsequently loved by them, they willingly imitated this image. They were rewarded for their efforts with social approval, and they often assured a life of luxury for themselves.

In the lyric poems dedicated to historical Spanish and Creole women, the particular facets of a woman's beauty, as well as the complaints about her nature found in encomiums to unidentifiable females, are often replaced by limited personal information. Their portrayal depicts either some aspect of their public life in the viceroyalties or their private life with the poet. Both the court and the Church are presented in this genre as offering women the opportunity to channel their energies outside of the home, and cultural activities are reported to have occupied the leisure of some. Ribera's description of Doña Leonor de Carreto and her ladies-in-waiting and Bastida's tribute to Doña Tomasa Vera underscore the ceremonial importance of women and show how their proper appearance and appropriate conduct reflected favorably upon the status and prestige of their husbands. Among her stately duties, the vicereine was often charged with maintaining an atmosphere of refinement at court and invited scholars and artists such as Sor Juana to demonstrate their talents before the viceroyalty's most notable individuals. Women were not only the entrepreneurs and creators of the arts but participated in their interpretation as well as Sandoval y Zapata's sonnet to a popular actress attests. After leaving Doña Leonor's retinue, Sor Juana looked to the Church to provide the proper environment for study and pursued a literary career from the convent. In Quito, Doña Francisca de Santa Clara y de la Cueva actively promoted the Catholic monastic life among Ecuadorian women, and in Mexico, Balbuena's lady friend, Doña Isabel de Tobar, also sought fulfillment through conventual duties after she became a widow.

While the accomplishments of these women are generally not as demonstrative as the display of heroism by women in wartime, the poets occasionally used warrior imagery to indicate that these women were just as exceptional in their respective spheres of interest as fearless frontier women and that their success was considered by them to be uncommon for their sex. Sor Juana is portrayed as an intellectual Amazon in a letter written by Caviedes and as the armed goddess, Minerva, in Torres' sonnet. Military conceits also appear in descriptions of unidentified women, and their usage establishes a close tie between the two positive views of women, that of the female warrior and that of the ideal woman.

Poetry expressing praise and love of women adds a new perspective to the portrayal of women in colonial literature in that it presents them not as glorified participants in military campaigns but as contributors to the civic, religious, and cultural life of the colonies after the conquest years. This view of them, however, is limited and lacking in imagination and obscures to a large extent the individual identities of these colonial women. The image of the woman on a pedestal was difficult for poets to maintain because of its standardization and unreality, and as a result, satirists of the period found the destruction of such a consistently perfect vision to be both quick and easy.

Notes

1. Maurice Valency, *In Praise of Love: An Introduction to the Love-Poetry of the Renaissance* (New York: Octagon Books, 1975), p. 83. A lover may have to suffer intensely and even die for his lady's sake, but his duty, in this case, is often considered to be a delight. Otis H. Green, *Spain and the Western Tradition*, 4 vols. (Madison, Wisc.: University of Wisconsin Press, 1963), I, 75.

2. A lover's expression of adoration for his lady may often resemble prayers to the Virgin. This religious tone is not derived from the Cult of Mary, but some hymns and supplications to the Reverend Mother may reflect the rhetoric of love poetry. C. S. Lewis, *The Allegory of Love* (Oxford: Oxford University Press, 1967), pp. 21, 8.

3. Green, *Spain,* I, 73–82, ix.

4. Valency, *In Praise of Love,* p. 26.

5. Ibid., p. 33.

6. Denis de Rougemont, *Love in the Western World* (New York: Pantheon, 1956), pp. 180–84.

7. Hayward Keniston, *Garcilaso de la Vega: A Critical Study of his Life and Works* (New York: Hispanic Society of America, 1922), pp. 192–203.

8. Otis H. Green, *Courtly Love in Quevedo* (Boulder, Colo.: University of Colorado Press, 1952), pp. 29–38.

9. This reference is from "Canto de Calíope" in *La Galatea*'s eighth book. Joaquín García Icazbalceta, *Francisco Terrazas y otros poetas del siglo XVI* (Madrid: Ediciones José Porrúa Turanzas, 1962), p. 7. Other references to Terrazas' poetry have been taken from this edition and cited in the text of the chapter.

10. Francisco de Terrazas, *Poesías,* ed. Antonio Castro Leal (México, D.F.: Librería de Porrúa Hnos. y Cía., 1941), pp. 3–16.

11. Marcelino Menéndez y Pelayo, *Obras completas* (Madrid: Imprenta Fortanet, 1911), II, 39. Gutierre de Cetina came to New Spain in 1546 and was killed in Puebla in 1554. His death may have resulted from a love triangle, as he was mortally wounded in front of Doña Leonor de Osma's house by Hernando de Nava, whose father had arrived in New Spain with Pánfilo de Narváez' army. Carlos González Peña, *Historia de la literatura mexicana* (México, D.F.: Editorial Porrúa, 1975), pp. 49–50.

12. This collection, discovered in Spain during the seventeenth century, was probably compiled while Juan de la Cueva was in Mexico, as many of the verses in it are his. Terrazas, *Poesías*, p. xxiv. Menéndez y Pelayo, *Obras completas*, II, 38–39.

13. Bernardo de Balbuena, *La grandeza mexicana* (México, D.F.: Editorial Porrúa, 1971), p. 55.

14. John Van Horne, *Bernardo de Balbuena: biografía y crítica* (Guadalajara, Méx.: Imprenta Font, 1940), pp. 54, 119.

15. Balbuena, *La grandeza mexicana,* pp. 55–56.

16. Van Horne, *Bernardo de Balbuena*, pp. 119–20. José Rojas Garcidueñas, *Bernardo de Balbuena: la vida y la obra* (México, D.F.: Imprenta Universitaria, 1958), pp. 17–19.

17. Bernardo de Balbuena, *Siglo de Oro en las selvas de Erífile* (Madrid: Ibarra, Impresor de Cámara de S. M., 1821), pp. 166–67. Rojas Garcidueñas, *Bernardo de Balbuena*, pp. 54–72. In his search for references to Doña Isabel in Balbuena's work, Rojas Garcidueñas has also found two allusions to her in his epic poem, *El Bernardo*.

18. Rojas Garcidueñas, *Bernardo de Balbuena*, pp. 45, 190.

19. Aurelio Espinosa Pólit, ed., *Los dos primeros poetas coloniales ecuatorianos* (Puebla, Méx.: Editorial J. M. Cajica, Jr., 1960), pp. 25, 27–29. Although this book deals mainly with Antonio de Bastidas and Juan Bautista Aguirre, some works of Jacinto de Evia are also reprinted in this edition. Selections of poetry by both Evia and Bastidas have been translated from this volume, and references to it appear in the text.

20. Isaac J. Barrera, *Literatura ecuatoriana* (Quito: Editorial Ecuatoriana, 1939), pp. 36–39.

21. In his "A la profesión de doña Sebastiana de San Buenaventura" (pp. 269–72) ["To the Profession of Doña Sebastiana of Saint Bonaventure"], Evia

describes the joy of a woman's spiritual love as an earthly experience. Traditional imagery delineates her purity and beauty. Entering a convent was the only suitable alternative for a woman in the colonies who did not choose to marry.

22. This conventional metaphor is also used by Juan del Valle y Caviedes in his "Romance amoroso XV" ["Love Ballad XV"] and by Luis Sandoval y Zapata in his sonnet, "Un galán en metáfora de mariposa" ["Grievous Peril of a Gallant in Moth Metaphor"]. Juan del Valle y Caviedes, *Obras*, ed. Rubén Vargas Ugarte (Lima: Talleres Gráficos de la Tipografía Peruana, 1947), pp. 71–72. Alfonso Méndez Plancarte, *Poetas novohispanos, segundo siglo (1621–1721)*, primera parte, 3 vols. (México, D.F.: Ediciones de la Universidad Nacional Autónoma, 1943), II, 105.

23. Espinosa Pólit, *Los dos primeros poetas*, p. 23.

24. The use of floral imagery continues into the eighteenth century as well and is the principal motif of Lucas Fernández del Rincón's "Llanto de Flora, desatado en rosas sepulcrales" ["The Cry of Flora, Loose in Funeral Roses"]. The piece was written to commemorate the death of Doña María Luisa Gabriela de Saboya, who was the wife of Philip V and Queen of Spain from 1710–1714. Méndez Plancarte, ed., *Poetas novohispanos, segundo siglo, (1621–1721)*, parte segunda, 3 vols. (México, D.F.: Ediciones de la Universidad Nacional Autónoma, 1945), III, 190–93.

25. This is also true of his sonnet to Doña Hipólita de Córdova y Cardona, the wife of Luis Henríquez de Guzmán (p. 119). In this poem, her lineage and the fact that her husband was viceroy of both New Spain and Peru are presented as her most outstanding characteristics.

26. In addition to these poems, Bastidas also describes an unidentified woman at her husband's tomb. This sonnet, "A una mujer que mira atenta el túmulo de su esposo" (p. 121) ["To a Woman Who Looks Attentively at the Grave of Her Husband"] is confined to her outpouring of grief at this loss.

27. Ortiz de Torres, like Padre Bastidas, wrote several elegies; however, this lament is the only one honoring women. Frank Dauster, *Breve historia de la poesía mexicana* (México, D.F.: Ediciones de Andrea, 1956), p. 40. In his sonnet honoring Isabel de Borbón, Ortiz de Torres resorts to traditional courtly imagery:

> There were two pearls of unbounded fortune,
> Isabel, who glorifies Spain,
> and her virtue, which makes her a saint. (p. 53)

28. Méndez Plancarte, *Poetas novohispanos*, II, 51–53.

29. Ibid., II, xli.

30. Ibid., II, 143–49.

31. Sor Juana and Doña Leonor enjoyed an unusually close friendship, and the poetess later dedicated several poems to her. Alfonso Méndez Plancarte and Alberto G. Salceda, eds., *Obras completas de Sor Juana Inés de la Cruz*, 4 vols. (México, D.F.: Imprenta Nuevo Mundo, 1955), I, 299–301. Sor Juana's portraits of the vicereine are discussed in chapter 5; however, it should be noted here that the talented nun does not depart from the traditional language of courtly love in these descriptions.

32. Méndez Plancarte notes that Ribera has borrowed the descriptive phrase "The German Venus" from Góngora's sonnet "Clavar victoríoso." It is used by Ribera in this case to denote Doña Leonor's fair complexion. Méndez Plancarte, *Poetas novohispanos*, II, 149.

33. Ribera's description of the ladies' celebration of Charles II's ascension to the throne is incomplete in Méndez Plancarte's *Poetas novohispanos*; however, he does include a sonnet in which the poet depicts the vicereine and her female entourage in conventional terms as they stand on the palace balconies (II, 147).

34. Carlos Sigüenza y Góngora refers to Sandoval y Zapata as the "Mexican Homer" in his *Triunfo parthénico [Parthian Triumph],* which contains the prize-winning poetry written to honor the Virgin in 1682 and 1683. Carlos Sigüenza y Góngora, *Triunfo parthénico* (México, D.F.: Ediciones Xochitl, 1945), p. 173. Irving A. Leonard, *Don Carlos Sigüenza y Góngora: A Savant of the Seventeenth Century* (Berkeley, Calif.: University of California Press, 1929), p. 23.

In one of his sonnets to the Virgin of Guadalupe, Mexico's patron saint, Sandoval y Zapata poetically describes how the roses fell from Juan Diego's mantle to reveal her colorful portrait. Méndez Plancarte, *Poetas novohispanos*, II, 120.

35. Méndez Plancarte, *Poetas novohispanos*, II, 103. References to Sandoval y Zapata's poetry appearing in the text correspond to this collection. For the English translations of his work, see Samuel Beckett, trans., *Anthology of Mexican Poetry*, ed. Octavio Paz (Bloomington, Ind.: Indiana University Press, 1958), pp. 73–76.

36. An element of eroticism is noted by Alfonso Reyes in another of Sandoval y Zapata's sonnets, "Riesgo grande de un galán en metáfora de mariposa": "In the fire of thy seeking be consumed. / Joyfully amid its flames flagrate. . ." (II, 105). Alfonso Reyes, *Obras completas*, 19 vols. (México, D.F.: Fondo de Cultura Económica, 1960), XII, 362.

37. Much of Juan del Valle y Caviedes' love poetry appears in Rubén Vargas Ugarte's collection of his *Obras*. References appearing in the text have been taken from this edition unless otherwise indicated. Reedy lists thirty-five examples of his amorous verse in the appendix of his study on Caviedes. Daniel R. Reedy, *The Poetic Art of Juan del Valle Caviedes* (Chapel Hill, N.C.: University of North Carolina Press, 1964), pp. 150–51.

38. Daniel R. Reedy, "Poesías inéditas de Juan del Valle Caviedes," *Revista Iberoamericana* 29, no. 55 (1963), pp. 161–62.

39. Reedy, "Poesías inéditas," p. 162.

40. Valency, *In Praise of Love*, p. 12.

41. Reedy, "Poesías inéditas," p. 162.

42. According to Glen L. Kolb, Caviedes' "A una dama que lo era del interés" ["To A Woman Who Was of Interest"] reflects a past romantic relationship of his. The cause of the lady's rejection, in this case, is believed to have been the poet's poverty. Glen L. Kolb, *Juan del Valle y Caviedes: A Study of the Life, Times and Poetry of a Spanish Colonial Satirist* (New London, Conn.: Stonington Publishing Company, 1959), p. 31.

43. Catalina de Erauso, the nun ensign, was a Spanish novice who came to the New World during the early seventeenth century and fought the Indians in Peru and Chile as a soldier in the army. James Fitzmaurice-Kelly, *The Nun Ensign* (London: T. Fisher Unwin, 1908, pp. xvi, xix. This volume also contains Juan Pérez de Montalbán's Golden Age *comedia* featuring Catalina de Erauso as *la mujer varonil* (the manly woman). The play, *La monja alférez*, is discussed in chapter 4.

44. Irving A. Leonard, *Baroque Times in Old Mexico* (Ann Arbor, Mich.: University of Michigan Press, 1966), pp. 189, 191. Anita Arroyo, *Razón y pasión de Sor Juana* (México, D. F.: Gráfica Panamericana, 1952), p. 151.

45. Sor Juana Inés de la Cruz, *Fama, y obras pósthumas del fénix de México* (Madrid: La Imprenta de Antonio Gonçález de Reyes, 1714), pp. xi-xxxi, 65, 46, 68. Other references to this edition have been included in the text. Sor Juana had written a poem praising the viceroy after the Spanish fleet's victory over the French in the Caribbean. She also mentions him in verses dedicated to his wife. Méndez Plancarte, *Obras completas de Sor Juana*, I, 331, 119–20.

46. Menéndez y Pelayo, *Obras completas*, II, 82.

47. Unlike Catalina de Erauso, however, Sor Juana did not wish to be a man but only to enjoy some of the freedoms generally accorded men.

48. This number includes tributes by six women: María Jacinta de Abogader y Mendoza, Francisca de Echavarri, Catalina de Alfaro Fernández de Córdova, Marcelina de San Martín, Inés de Vargas, and one unidentified *señora* (pp. 52–60). While all of these ladies were learned women and poetesses like Sor Juana, one might think that a different perspective from that of the men would be presented in their encomiums to her. Unfortunately, they too depended upon standardized metaphors to describe her.

49. Méndez Plancarte, *Obras completas de Sor Juana*, I, 278; IV, 444.

50. Calleja's brief biography is contained in *Fama, y obras pósthumas del fénix de México*, pp. xi-xxxi.

51. Emilio Carilla, *Un olvidado poeta colonial* (Buenos Aires: Imprenta de la Universidad, 1943), p. 15.

52. Espinosa Pólit, *Los dos primeros poetas*, p. 501. Selections of Aguirre's poetry have been translated from this edition, and references to it appear in the text.

53. Both Juan María Gutiérrez and Gonzalo Zaldumbide mention this characteristic of Aguirre's poetry. Their criticism is included in *Los dos primeros poetas coloniales ecuatorianos*, pp. 332–34, 397–401.

54. Father Aguirre, like Caviedes in his "Romance amoroso VI," also describes the lady's eyes using military conceits.

55. Manuel Navarrete, *Entretenimientos poéticos*, 2 vols., (México, D.F.: Imprenta de Valdés, 1823). References to Navarrete's verse have been taken from this first edition of his works and included in the text.

56. Francisco Monterde, ed., *Poesías profanas* (México, D.F.: Ediciones de la Universidad Nacional Autónoma, 1939), pp. xii, x.

57. In spite of the distance the poet creates between him and his subject, Manuel Toussaint contends that his erotic odes were a reflection of his experience and offers proof of his relationships with Josefa Camargo de Celia, Ana Coria, Rosalía Guevara, and Dolores Viteli. Manuel Toussaint, "Nuevos aspectos en la biografía de Fray Manuel Navarrete," *Revista de Literatura Mexicana* 1, no. 2 (1940), pp. 226–34.

Navarrete wrote *La divina providencia [Divine Providence]* as an act of penance for his realistic love poems. He also destroyed some of them to prevent their publication.

CHAPTER 3

FEMININE SATIRE

Although colonial writers, like those of the Peninsula, generally presented a favorable image of women in their literary works,[1] criticism of womanhood is a prominent theme when they engage in satirical writing. While the character, physical attributes, and customs of women have always been the frequent targets of satirists, America's quickly paced, highly changeable life-style, its wide-scale racial intermingling, and its primitive conditions gave the New World's satirical writers the opportunity to stir up past controversy and to formulate new complaints about the feminine gender. Satire also proved to be a socially acceptable way of expressing hostility toward women, admonishing them for not following masculine codes of appearance and dress, and reacting against the overidealization of femininity brought on by the excesses of courtly love.[2] Following the feminine models of Fernando de Rojas, Francisco Quevedo, and various picaresque novelists, colonial satirists viewed women in the colonies as ugly and immoral and made every effort to expose them in order to warn men of their faults.

The relaxed moral climate, the atmosphere of superstition, and the existence of so-called demonic cults in the Indies provided ideal conditions for the literary transfer of Rojas' Celestina whose many trades included pandering and sorcery.[3] The appearance of Celestinesque figures in early Spanish American literature tended to be concentrated in the one-hundred-year period following the publication of Rojas' masterpiece; however, the interest his work generated in prostitutes, go-betweens, and old hags as literary characters continued throughout the colonial period. Quevedo's misogynic work, *Los sueños*, offered a variety of scathing portraits for colonial satirists to follow as well. In addition to deriding prostitutes, he was especially critical of wives and chaperons and frequently condemned them for their deceptive nature.[4] The vehemence of his attacks may also account for the force with which satirists in the colonies ridiculed females.

Early satirical writers in the New World also often followed the structure and critical tone of picaresque novels such as *Lazarillo de Tormes*, Quevedo's *El buscón*, and Mateo Alemán's *Guzmán de Alfarache*, and this affected the manner in which they portrayed their female characters. Since women do not appear as protagonists in colonial picaresque works, their development as secondary characters is limited by the episodic plots characteristic of the genre. Within this framework, many brief personal views of women are presented with attention quickly drawn to a single fault or offense of each character.[5] These negative rather than positive examples of behavior are designed to instruct the reader on how to live a prudent life.

Using Spain's satirical tradition as a guide, Mateo Rosas de Oquendo, Juan Rodríguez Freile, Juan del Valle y Caviedes, Alonso Carrió de la Vandera, and Esteban Terralla y Landa portray a wide variety of Spanish America's female residents immersed in the routine of daily living. These women live in urban centers as well as remote areas of the viceroyalties, and they represent every segment of the colonial population. Although the tone of these presentations ranges from lightly humorous to blatantly misogynistic, their purpose is a single one, which is to prove that women are a detrimental force to men and society. In addition to conveying men's negative impressions and judgments about the opposite sex, works of colonial satire shed some light on the economic, social, and racial problems facing women in the colonies after the conquest.

Both Peruvian and Mexican women are the victims of the colonial period's first known satirist, the Spanish writer Mateo Rosas de Oquendo. He purports to have considerable knowledge of feminine faults and follies, especially those of married women, because of his many amorous encounters involving them.[6] Criticism is directed at the female population in general as well as at specific historical figures in his satirical works, and he is intent upon deriding women who establish their own identities and function independently of men. Although he is aware of a number of their imperfections, he is particularly concerned about their lack of morality.

In his "Sátira a cosas que pasan en el Perú año de 1598" ["Satire of Things that Happen in Peru in 1598"], Rosas de Oquendo reviews his lengthy stay in Lima in a picaresque vein and uses female characters to exemplify the city's moral degeneration. After describing them as "ugly women who appear beautiful / in view of their money," "virgins who give birth," and "lambs by day and hawks by night" (pp. 9, 6), he proceeds to elaborate on this antithetical image of womanhood, and his narration of several specific episodes focuses on how and why women delude men. As a deterrent to their deceptiveness, Rosas de Oquendo proposes that the men become more attuned to the needs of their wives, and he offers particular points of advice as to how this should be accomplished.

For example, during the absence of the breadwinner, the wife must continue to maintain her family, and she cannot always count on selling *tamales* or the popular Peruvian beverage, *chicha,* to meet household expenses. Finding herself in a financial predicament, she sometimes resorts to bartering her attentions for required goods and services from neighborhood merchants. When her husband returns home, he assumes that all is well because his wife appears happy and his home looks prosperous (pp. 16–17). In this brief account, Rosas de Oquendo portrays the woman as deliberately deceitful and evil and contrasts her to the man who is considered to be merely foolish and simply in need of the author's guidance. Although this illustration is obviously oversimplified and distorted by him, it does shed some light on a woman's place in colonial society and divulges the cause of much of her questionable behavior. Women, like the wife in this anecdote, were economically dependent upon men, as they rarely had any income other than that provided by their husbands. Because they were continually asking for things, satirists often portrayed them as greedy, materialistic individuals. When a woman was single or when she could not obtain these items from her husband, she might decide to go outside the home in her search, and since she was usually unskilled, her only alternative was to sell herself. In order to save your honor and your marriage, the poet recommends to husbands, you should be attentive to your wives and not mistreat them, watch what you say about them in public, and above all give them gifts (pp. 30–31).

Various images of streetwalkers are employed by Rosas de Oquendo to emphasize the ostensibly degrading and scandalous effects of several favorite pastimes upon the residents of colonial Lima. Women, therefore, who chose to spend their leisure engaged in such diversions were not only unladylike but immoral as well. Card playing, according to him, is like dealing with one of the many bawds who roamed the downtown area:

> This game is a go-between
> and there are major losses.
> The first is respect,
> lost in the first hand
> and then honor is at stake
> if you start losing money. (p. 28)[7]

Dancing was also another popular form of entertainment, and his description of several dances of the period focuses upon the suggestive movements of the female participants:

> The music begins
> and the maidens dance,
> for there isn't a prostitute in Geneva
> who attains such motion.
> Not even a swirling gypsy
> gyrates as much as
> the girl with no morals
> who doesn't know any better;
> according to their movements,
> their postures, and the looks on their faces,
> it appears that they have
> a windmill in their hips. (p. 29)[8]

While Rosas de Oquendo criticized Lima's female population in general terms in his ''Sátira a las cosas que pasan en el Perú año de 1598,'' he specifically ridicules one woman, the wife of viceroy García Hurtado de Mendoza, in ''La victoria naval Peruntina'' [''The Peruntine Naval Victory'']. Having had close contact with her as a member of the viceregal staff, he feels qualified to comment on the negative aspects of her personality and presents her in an extremely unfavorable light. Rosas de Oquendo probably characterizes her as a nuisance at court because he considers her to be an obstruction to the patriarchal system.

Depicting Doña Teresa de Castro y de la Cueva when she receives the news of her brother's defeat of the English pirate, Sir Richard Hawkins, he describes her as self-centered and eccentric. The vicereine took great pride in her noble lineage, prestigious position, and religious devotion to the Catholic Church, and Rosas de Oquendo mocks her for this. In enumerating her many distinctions such as being descended from the Cañete and Lemos families and being mentioned in Oña's dedication of his *Arauco domado,*[9] he jeeringly adds several titles of his own invention like "illustrious *mamacona* of Galicia" (p. 77). The Quechua word *mamacona* was the name given to elderly matrons who were in charge of the Inca's Virgins of the Sun. However, in Argentina, where Rosas de Oquendo had lived before coming to Peru, it meant old and fat.[10] Another detail of her unattractive appearance is conveyed by the neologism *anchicara* (p. 79), which refers to the vicereine's broad face. He also calls her Preste Juana de Lemos in order to underscore her sanctimoniousness.[11]

Rosas de Oquendo is less critical of Mexican women than he is of Peruvians.[12] In his "Romance que envió un amigo a otro de Guadiana a México" ["A Poem That One Friend Sent to Another From Guadiana to Mexico City"], he depicts a young man who journeys to a small town and misses the excitement of the capital. In order to emphasize just how dull the countryside is, and perhaps to shatter the image of the beautiful country lass of pastoral literature, he chooses to describe a local spinster. A single woman was generally considered to be a misfit in colonial society because women who did not marry at an early age or join a convent had no place of their own.[13]

Although the reasons for Rosas de Oquendo's continual choice of women as his targets are unclear, there is some evidence to indicate that they are more personal than cultural. In his short poem entitled simply "Romance" ["Ballad"], he complains:

> It is the women who follow me,
> for women I lost my country
> and for women I am losing now,
> Mexico, your beautiful ladies.[14]

Because of his constant attraction to the ladies and its influence upon his life, it is possible that he lashes out against women in order to react to his dependence on them. Pleasure of any description, however, from sexual gratification to frivolous amusement appears to elicit feelings of guilt in the poet, which cause him to regard enjoyable experiences as immoral. His literary treatment of women, nonetheless, is probably the least scathing of any colonial satirist, and he often expresses the belief that men must occasionally share the blame for women's impropriety.

After Rosas de Oquendo had warned men about women in Peru and in New Spain, Juan Rodríguez Freile, a native of Bogotá, began gathering information about New Granada's female residents for the same satirical purpose. However, rather than drawing upon his own personal experience to prove that women are detrimental to society, Rodríguez Freile uncovers a historical pattern in which they caused scandal and even crime among the region's first Spanish families. Although his attitude toward women in *El carnero [The Conquest of New Granada]* was influenced by the Bible, patristic literature, and European history, his portrayal of them was guided by *La Celestina*.[15] His direct criticism of prominent aristocratic ladies is interspersed throughout his twenty-one-chapter account, but his underlying view of womanhood is summarized in a line that he borrows from a speech by Rojas' character, Sempronio: "Women are called limbs of Satan, the fountainhead of sin, and the destroyers of paradise" (p. 296).[16] Eve, he alleges, was the instigator of calamity in the world, and Spanish women brought this stigma with them to New Granada.[17] While ugly women are clearly a nuisance, according to Rodríguez Freile, beautiful women pose the real threat to society (p. 243). Beauty, described by him as a "silent deception" (p. 148), is misused by them, and he recalls its condemnation by the Spanish moralist, Fray Antonio de Guevara, and the Roman satirist, Juvenal, as a cause of madness and immorality. The latter's *Sixth Satire*, an attack on wives for overstepping the bounds of propriety, is often cited by satirists as proof of women's turpitude and links them with the collapse of the Roman empire.[18]

Rodríguez Freile's series of historical incidents in which women's actions have brought pain and hardship to both friends and family are succinctly written to emphasize their didactic purpose, and the various descriptions of female characters and their circumstances in each of them are generally quite similar. Married ladies of prominent social standing who are young, beautiful, and wealthy are principal figures in these episodes. The wife usually initiates the action by being unfaithful to her husband, and she then tries to rid herself of him. He, out of jealousy and disgrace, seeks revenge. A crime is committed in which other people are involved, and injuries, death, and property damage result.[19] The story is then concluded when poetic justice finally prevails. Following this basic pattern, Rodríguez Freile exposes the adulterous relationships among New Granada's elite on no less than five separate occasions.

In the first of these examples, Doña Inés de Hinojosa lived with her husband, Don Pedro de Avila, in Carora, now part of Venezuela. Attracted by a newly arrived music and dance instructor, Jorge Voto, she falls in love, and the two lovers plot to kill her husband. After their marriage, they move to Tunja where Inés becomes romantically involved with Don Pedro Bravo de Rivera, the commissioner of Chivatá, and he and a couple of friends murder Voto. All are ultimately punished, however, and Doña Inés is hanged (pp. 147–57). The name of a certain aristocratic adultress is undisclosed in another of Rodríguez Freile's episodes when he narrates her involvement with Bogotá's public prosecutor, a Licenciado Orozco. Comparing her to Eve, he enumerates the catastrophic consequences of her affair, which include civil disturbances and the jailing of Inspector Monzón under false pretenses. In the end, the lady is allegedly poisoned by her own husband (pp. 204–34, 241).

In 1584, Gaspar de Peralta discovered by chance that his wife had been unfaithful to him. While attending a party in Bogotá, he heard another guest tell an amusing story about breaking the bed while visiting a lady friend. He thought nothing about the anecdote at the time; however, several days later, when his wife asked him to contact the carpenter to repair the bed, he realized the truth. After telling his wife that he was leaving on a business trip, he returns home unexpectedly. Finding the two lovers together, he kills them both (pp. 243–47). Another incident involving Doña Luisa de Tafur, the wife of Francisco Vela, and her paramour, Don Diego de Fuenmayor, occurred during Don Francisco de Sandi's presidency of the *Audiencia Real* or Royal High Court of Justice. When her husband finds out about this, he wounds her, and her brother avenges this assault by killing his brother-in-law. In order to avoid the ensuing scandal, Luisa becomes a nun and enters the convent of La Concepción (pp. 300–305).

The most highly developed of these five episodes concerns one of the initial cases to come before New Granada's first bishop and chief inquisitor and was that of a black woman, Juana García, who was accused of being a witch. The charges were brought against her by the husband of a young and beautiful aristocrat who had engaged her services some years before. Rodríguez Freile uses the practice of witchcraft by African slaves in the area as an opportunity to introduce a Celestin-esque figure into his account and appears to reconstruct this historical episode loosely upon the framework of Act X of Rojas' *Tragicomedia*.[20]

The testimony presented in the case revealed that while the husband was away on business in Spain, the wife became pregnant. On hearing news of the Spanish flotilla's arrival in Cartagena, the expectant mother, fearing that her returning spouse would learn of her condition, went to a local midwife, Juana García, for an abortion. The black woman, uncertain that the husband was indeed on his way to Bogotá, did not perform the surgery immediately but decided to postpone it until the next day. The following night, the wife, who was then in great pain, pleaded with Juana to alleviate her misery. At the wife's insistence, she conjured up the husband's image in a washbasin in order to learn his whereabouts. Peering into the water, the two women could see a scene taking place on the island of Hispaniola in which her husband and his mistress were with a tailor who was making a dress for the lady. After one of the sleeves was cut out, Juana García magically retrieved it and gave it to her young client for safekeeping. Assured that his appearance in the capital was not imminent, the midwife re-marked: ''Now. . .you can see what a hurry your husband is in to get back to you. You needn't worry about being with child. You have time for another one for that matter'' (p. 135).[21] Business kept the young merchant away from his home for some time, and when he finally returned, the child, no longer an infant, was being raised by his wife as an orphan. Although the couple seemed happy at first, the wife began to hint that she had some knowledge of the affair that he had during his extended leave. When she produced the sleeve as proof of the illicit relationship and related the story of how she got it, her disclosure ultimately resulted in Juana's banishment from the territory (pp. 132–39).[22]

In both *El carnero* and *La Celestina* young women are in physical pain over the guilt of having lost their honor and must depend upon old *curanderas* (medicine women) for a quick remedy. The two prac-titioners of the occult arts not only readily acquiesce to their clients' promiscuity and immediately console them but encourage the contin-uance of their hedonistic life-style as well. As these respective works come to a close, both Juana García and the Celestina are required to pay for their questionable activities. The newly freed slave stands apart from her literary precursor, however, in that her race rather than her occupation is an indication of her low social station. Her magic as well is ostensibly from Africa and not from Europe, although Rodríguez Freile describes her incantation like that of a Medieval sorcerer. Both of these elements, the participation of members of the lower class and the involvement of witchcraft, are used by the author to discredit midwifery, a common vocation for women in the colonies.[23]

Rodríguez Freile is one of the few colonial satirists to portray women living outside Peru or Mexico and to concentrate especially on exposing the faults of Spanish women. His tendency to characterize aristocratic ladies as fallen infers that women have a basic moral weakness and are not always the victims of social prejudice or economic reversals. His standardization of their portrayal also implies that members of the opposite sex are generally all alike. Although he, like Rosas de Oquendo, criticizes women for their adulterous relationships, he is not concerned with the extenuating circumstances that caused them to be unfaithful or with their ingenuity at deceiving their husbands. He simply portrays women as ruthless, vengeful, and violent, and he emphasizes the cost of their uncontrollable passions to families, communities, and the empire.

The satirical attack on women begun by Rosas de Oquendo and Rodríguez Freile in the first half of the colonial period was continued with vigor by the Spaniard Juan del Valle y Caviedes during the latter part of the seventeenth century. He, like Quevedo, wrote both courtly love poetry and feminine satire, and his scathing portraits of women, like those of the Spanish master, have become his more notable vision of femininity. He is the era's most skillful satirist, and while women were not his prime target, ridicule of them was one of his favorite literary themes. In his *Poesías varias y jocosas [Varied and Jocose Poems]*, Caviedes uses several of the same literary devices such as pastoral names and portraiture that he employed in his love poetry; however, the view of womanhood he presents is exactly opposite from the one he outlines in his amorous verse, considered in the preceding chapter. His female subjects are no longer wholesome country girls but often prostitutes, and he identifies them as ugly women, go-betweens, "ladies," *mestizas* (women of mixed Spanish and Indian blood), or old crones. Their unsightly appearance and disgusting behavior, rather than their beauty and grace, are accentuated, and many of these women instead of being virtuous are immoral. Just as the poet focused his attention on a woman's eyes in his love poetry as a reflection of her divinity, so he describes her sex organs in his satire as an indication of her baser instincts. Although Caviedes criticizes the *limeñas* for their ignorance and gullibility in such poems as his "A una dama que se sacó una muela por dar a entender que las tenía" ["To a Woman Who Pulled Out One of Her Teeth to Prove that She Had Them"] and "A un mozo pobre que casó con una mujer vieja, fea y rica" ["To a Poor Youth Who Married an Old Woman Who Was Ugly and Rich"], his severest censure is reserved for women of easy virtue.[24]

Six detailed and most unflattering portraits of women are to be found among Caviedes' satirical poems. The best example of his defiance of courtly expression and a piece in which he parodies the lofty image of the female warrior as well is "Pintura de una fea buscona en metáfora de guerra" ["The Portrait of an Ugly Camp Follower in War Metaphor"]. Caviedes unorthodoxly begins his portrait with her feet, and then, in lumbering *pie quebrado*,[25] he crudely compares parts of her body to instruments of war and her sexual activities to recruiting procedures:

> From a variety of soldiers
> you will have every kind,
> but you will always make infantrymen (infants)
>   out of cavalrymen (riders).
> You will have in your company
> people that you pick up and draft,
> for everyone fits into the many
>   maneuvers that you have.
> Artillery you will have
> simply to be loaded,
> for everyone knows what a good
>   piece you are.
>
>   . . . . .
>
> Bombs you have in your breasts
> because they burst with milk,
> for nipples, you have little
>   fuses.
>
>   . . . . .
>
> Your face, without cosmetics,
> is a leather shield with a hideous mask
> and your rust-colored hair
>   is arranged like two escutcheons on your head. (pp. 169–70)

Although Caviedes obscenely alludes to female genitalia in several of his portraits,[26] they become the focal point of "A una dama que rodó del cerro de San Cristóbal" ["To a Woman Who Rolled Down the Hill of Saint Christopher"]. In this poem, he presents a pornographic and scatological description of Juana as she takes an awkward spill:

> As she fell she exposed
> what is known as the cucumber's bitter part,
> which is where the melon smells
> and women stink the most.
> Openly she revealed
> the causes of a storm,
> where it pours and
> often thunders.
>
> . . . . .
>
> Paradise from which Adam's
> successors are set free,
> where all of us
> inherit original sin.
> The sun shone on her
> where they say it never shines,
> although Juana's parts
> are never lonely.[27]

The frequent appearance of prostitutes as the subjects of Caviedes' verse and his detailed description of various aspects of their trade indicate that prostitution had been permitted to thrive in Lima since Rosas de Oquendo's documentation of it in the late sixteenth century. Organization characterized the profession, and it provided a means of survival for many unemployed, single women. Since their lack of training greatly limited their opportunities, harlotry offered substantial and immediate financial rewards. In an atmosphere in which men were striking it rich, it was hard for women to choose to work their way up in a legitimate business especially when society traditionally frowned on their working outside the home in any capacity. Racially mixed women, who were generally members of the lower social strata, most frequently found themselves in these circumstances, and the absence of a protective environment for them made their enlistment into the profession easy.[28] Caviedes criticizes these public women for their commercialization of sex rather than for their loose morals and usually avoids using derogatory names for them by simply calling them "ladies."[29]

In his poem "Remedios para ser lo que quisieres" ["Recommendations On How To Be What You Want"], Caviedes imitates the manuals on genteel women's behavior and gives these "ladies" of Lima advice on how to be successful whores.[30] The art of soliciting is basic to the trade, and the poet recommends exaggerated dress, gait, and diction to catch the eye of a prospective client and to clinch a suitable deal. An absolute necessity for an enterprising streetwalker is a capable go-between or "aunt" as she is often called, and as a veteran of the profession, she counsels and protects young aspirants. In his poem "A una vieja que habiendo sido dama paró en ser alcahueta" (pp. 109–10) ["To an Old Woman Who Having Been a Prostitute Became a Go-Between"], Caviedes stresses the indignities of advancing age that old bawds must endure, and in "A una vieja del Cuzco, grande alcahueta y revendedora de dos hijas, mestizas como ella" (pp. 166–67) ["To an Old Woman From Cuzco, a Great Go-Between and Seller of Her Daughters, Who Are Half-Breeds Like She Is"], he outlines a greedy mother's instructions to her own daughters.

The women who lived and worked in the streets of Peru's cities and towns are not threatened by the poet with dishonor or perdition but are presented with the very real yet ironic consequences of promiscuity. A common problem among women involved in prostitution was venereal disease, and Caviedes takes note of the intense suffering of its victims as well as one method of treatment. Hospitalization was frequently required for those afflicted, and he describes the discomfort of Belisa, who was a patient in Lima's La Caridad (Charity Hospital):

> Love takes its payment in pains
> what was lent in tickles,
> for you pay with tears
> what you acquired in laughter.[31]

In alluding to a remedy for this common malady, Caviedes uses a mythological play on words: "For all that Venus caused / can be done away with by Mercury," and he even mentions that this therapeutic element is found in the Andean town of Huancavelica.[32] When the sickness was too advanced, however, as in Belisa's case, visible deterioration took place:

> Her body is a skeleton
> from so many examinations

due to so much probing
in her intestines and entrails.[33]

In "A la bella Arnarda" ["To Beautiful Arnarda"], grim humor characterizes a more graphic description of the effects of syphilis. Here, Caviedes refers to one of the female reproductive organs as a bell:

They say that the clapper
is inevitably falling out
or cracking from the blows
because of so much stroking.[34]

Caviedes' reason for composing feminine satire appears to have been his desire for a challenging literary exercise because he systematically undermines the idealized vision of womanhood depicted in chivalric novels and the poetry of courtly love. He was well acquainted with the technical intricacies of these positive images in literature and had frequently utilized them to describe exceptionally beautiful or able women in his amorous or encomiastic verse. His satiric poetry, however, is indicative of his dexterity and creativity as a poet, and his candor and explicitness give some insight into the seriousness and extent of two urban problems that plagued the capital, prostitution and disease. Although the *limeñas* continue to be satirized during the eighteenth century by Carrió and Terralla y Landa, the ingenuity with which Caviedes caricatures them is unmatched during the colonial period.

Perhaps the best satirical overview of women in the Spanish American colonies is contained in a journal written by the Asturian Alonso Carrió de la Vandera when he was commissioned by King Charles III to inspect the colonial postal system in 1771.[35] *El lazarillo de ciegos caminantes [El lazarillo: A Guide for Inexperienced Travelers Between Buenos Aires and Lima]* is not only a report of his inspection tour but an instructive guide book for wayfarers as well. Just as the young *pícaro* (rascal) Lazarillo de Tormes led his blind master, so Carrió intended to direct untutored and unwary individuals traveling South America's commercial routes.[36] One of the pitfalls he warns against in his travelogue is precisely that of contact with the opposite sex. At each stop along the way, he writes a description of a woman who he feels is representative of the area and one who casts a shadow over previously lauded female types.

Much of *El lazarillo de ciegos caminantes* is brisk repartee between

Inspector Carrió and his seemingly naive native American guide, Con-colorcorvo, and the latter introduces the theme of feminine satire.[37] In the journal's "Prologue," Concolorcorvo recounts his sordid past in the former Incan capital in a manner reminiscent of the picaresque novel, and here he has occasion to reflect ruefully upon the moral conduct of his mother and several other female relatives.[38] His statement "I am an Indian pure and proud, except for the malpractices of my mother, for which I do not stand security" shatters not only the pure and unsullied image of the matriarchal figure but also dispels the aura surrounding the native American women immortalized in the early chronicles and epic poetry. The Church as well comes under the Indian guide's attack for its role in the protection and education of young girls: "Two cousins of mine are preserving their virginity, to their sorrow, in a convent in Cuzco, where the King our lord supports them." After obliterating society's most hallowed female figure and assailing one of the few organizations that looked after the welfare of women, Concolorcorvo and the Inspector continue their mockery of New World female residents, and their complaints about them are as diverse as the women themselves.

The most unusual women of the entire trip, who represent a unique breed of American females, are encountered by the two men as they leave Buenos Aires and cross the Argentine pampa. They are the rugged helpmates of the region's cow-punchers or *gauderios*, known today as gauchos, and the description of them in *El lazarillo* is the first to appear in colonial literature. By the eighteenth century, frontier women were rarely extolled, and the masculine traits assigned to them were deni-grative. Imitating Francisco Quevedo's creation of "pobras" (poor women) from "pobres" (poor men or poor people), Carrió refers to these crude, rustic women as "machas" (virile women). This laconic caricature, he feels, aptly depicts their lack of femininity in both ap-pearance and demeanor (p. 252).

Carrió's contemptuous view of America's miscegenation and the part Indian women played in it is suggested by the cutting imagery he uses in describing the location of Jujuy in the northern part of the Viceroyalty of Río de la Plata: "The city is surrounded by a voluminous river, formed by the convergence of two large streams, of which one is of crystalline water, the other muddy, resulting in a mixture like that of a Spaniard and an Indian woman" (p. 243). Racial intermingling, ac-cording to him, had not served to bring the two cultures together or to

create a new race of Spanish Americans but only tainted the pure bloodlines of emigrants from Spain.[39]

Female characters from diverse social backgrounds are used by Carrió
to indicate the various excesses and moral problems of the unusual
boom town of Potosí, and their descriptions whittle away at the image
of women in courtly love poetry. This settlement in Alto Perú was the
site of the largest and richest silver lode in the New World. Here, as
in Lima, prostitution thrived, and it was eagerly supported by the legions
of prospectors and miners in the area. Considering it a menace to society,
Carrió is especially intent upon exposing female reprobates who, after
leading a life of sin, wish to rejoin polite social circles. He is no less
harsh, however, with the apathetic men who no longer perceive virginity
as a woman's most important feature and wind up married to these
women (p. 181).

Besides affording his readers a glimpse of the seamy side of Potosian
life, Carrió employs the critical appraisal of a woman's wardrobe to
focus attention on the town's unseemly opulence because he, like many
other Spaniards traveling in the New World, is shocked to see profuse
wealth casually displayed by ordinary colonists, and he frowns upon
this practice as extravagant and ostentatious. The choice of a woman
to illustrate his disdain is particularly appropriate because some women
carried the importance of their appearance to extremes, and materialism
rather than spirituality became their most outstanding trait: "The principal luxury of this city, as is the case in all other large cities in the
kingdom, is composed of magnificent clothing; there is a common lady
here who has more dresses adorned with gold and silver than the Princess
of Asturias" (p. 281).

The tendency of some women to lie blatantly about their age is also
mocked by Carrió on passing through the remote yet salubrious village
of Compabata. In order to ridicule such prevarication, he has Concolorcorvo cite an extreme case in which a lady resident claimed to be
137 years old but was reported by a fellow citizen to be at least 145
(pp. 322–23). Although his choice of an elderly woman as a literary
subject may have been determined by her direct opposition to the young
ladies of courtly literature, it is also used to illustrate that women in
the New World generally lived longer than men.[40]

From the amount of attention Inspector Carrió devotes to women in
his description of Lima, it would appear that he considers them an
outstanding feature of the viceregal city, the final destination and cul-

minating point of his long journey.[41] While he follows the satiric tradition of Rosas de Oquendo and Caviedes, he presents yet another view of these controversial females. His assessment of them touches several socioeconomic levels and meticulously depicts the manners, wearing apparel, customs, and physical characteristics of the women of the metropolis. Courtly conventions again come under attack in his descriptions of the *limeñas*, and he also compares them with those of New Spain's capital in order to determine which city better represents the low point of femininity.

Because women generally behave well in public, and especially on ceremonial occasions, Carrió seeks to catch them at unguarded moments, when he thinks they are more likely to reveal the disagreeable disposition that underlies their façade of refinement. He further points out their failure to perform the simple domestic tasks required of their sex with efficiency and ease. The aristocratic ladies of Mexico and Peru, for example, have completely different ways of dealing with their servants, and according to him, the women of both regions are deserving of censure. In a sarcastic tone, and under the guise of praising them, the Inspector insinuates that the *mexicanas* are simple, and the Indian guide deliberately elaborates on this innuendo to divulge the blatant and noisy aggressiveness of the ladies of Lima:

"They [the Mexican women] make better use of a few servants. They speak to them very little and very slowly, and in gatherings: *Loquantur arcana per digitos*; they are the most clever pantomimists in the world, but I have noticed that their gestures do not follow any general rule, because I have observed that some servants who returned to service in a house confessed that they still did not understand the signs of their mistress because they varied from those used before."

"I am amazed," I said to the Inspector, "at the ability and skill of the Mexican ladies who succeed in expressing themselves and being understood by means of gestures. . . . I understand that this word corresponds to those movements of the hand and face with which newborn babies and deaf mutes express themselves, which is understood by those who deal with them; it is a pity that the ladies of Lima do not introduce this language into their houses in order to relieve themselves of so much shouting."(pp.452–53)

Although much of the feminine attire worn in the colonies was influenced by European fashions, the ladies of Lima, emulating Moorish women, wrapped themselves in lengthy garments and wore a heavy facial veil. Because they were cloaked from head to foot, these women became known as *tapadas*, and this popular style of dress was later considered a symbol of colonial Peru.[42] Designed to protect a woman from men's gazes in public, this form of concealment was turned to the advantage of the *limeñas*, who appeared alluring and even provocative, according to Carrió, by selecting delicate and costly footwear and raising their petticoats to reveal their legs.[43] The Inspector also makes fun of the flirtatious manner in which they draped their headdresses to reveal only one eye, and he contends that the tendency of women to cover a considerable part of their faces with veils or with handkerchieves, as the Mexican women did, was really functional and disguised the effect of their lack of dental hygiene. In contrast to the beloved's coral-colored lips and her pearl-like teeth, he describes their gaping mouths and toothless gums like inkwells, an image he borrows from Quevedo,[44] and notes the ugliness and cacophonous speech of women wearing dentures.[45]

Although Carrió de la Vandera's ridicule of women echoes many of the previous complaints of colonial satirists, his presentation of such a wide variety of female subjects from all parts of Spanish America implies that women were the cause of controversy everywhere. Like Rosas de Oquendo, the Inspector finds women living in the provinces to be more morally upstanding than those residing in urban areas but less exciting and often backward. Racial prejudice frequently figures prominently in *El lazarillo*'s descriptions of women, and the author seriously questions the role of Indian women in the conquest. This resentment of members of other races, only suggested by Caviedes in his assignment of "mestizas" to a certain group of females, indicates that deep divisions still existed in the New World's population long after miscegenation had begun, and it continues to be a factor in the work of the colonial period's last major satirist.

Lima por dentro y fuera [Lima Inside and Out], written by the Andalusian traveler Esteban Terralla y Landa, contains a more detailed description of Lima's female population during the eighteenth century than that of Carrió. He too wished to warn visitors about the city's women, but his criticism of them is far lengthier and harsher than that of his compatriot. Assuming the role of both narrator and guide, the satirist conducts an unsuspecting friend through the capital counseling him on its most obvious dangers.[46] This imaginary excursion bears a certain similarity to Quevedo's *sueño*, "El mundo por de dentro," and shares with it some satiric comments concerning women.[47]

Like the Spanish master before him, Terralla y Landa attributes man's misjudgment of women to their deliberately deceptive nature, and he focuses his attack on the *tapadas*. He vehemently warns his friend against pursuing these cloaked women and divulges what he considers to be the most shocking and wretched example of womanhood:

> Never flatter   a cloaked woman
> for she may be a negress   or a horrible skeleton.[48]

p. 67

His sardonic assessment of the female anatomy is also reminiscent of Quevedo and parodies feminine portraiture.[49] According to him, the *limeñas* powdered and padded themselves to accentuate certain appealing features while masking a myriad of defects:

> You will see many whitened faces,   false teeth and wigs,
> brows of spirit gum   and soot from a kettle,
> cotton calves,   and breasts of the same,
> crammed shoes   and stuffed cheeks,
> padding below the waist,   on the back and neck,
> and on the hips a bustle   made of linen and wicker. (pp. 48–49)

Throughout *Lima por dentro y fuera*, Terralla y Landa portrays women who victimize men, and his descriptions of them provide further evidence of a woman's economic dependence upon a man because of her lack of skills. Prostitutes in the viceregal capital command much of the poet's attention throughout his lengthy diatribe, and he describes them in their usual haunts from the alleys to the highways and from the inns to the theaters. After arranging a casual encounter or engineering an intricate trap, they dupe many clients, and the ensuing events provide the inspiration for several of the most amusing experiences of his alleged sojourn in Lima. Terralla y Landa's treatment of these streetwalkers is at first glance quite polite, but the narration of their deception and thievery evokes harsh criticism. The very nature of the subject matter affords the author an opportunity to employ off-color allusions and blatant vulgarity which at times add sarcastic humor to his account. His attack on Lima's network of public women is, like that of Caviedes, directed toward the commercialization of sex.

After describing the city's elegant bordellos along with their shapely, well-dressed occupants, Terralla y Landa imagines his companion as a participant in several amorous adventures with Lima's enterprising young women, and the result is a deliberately planned spoof of the canons of courtly love. Courting is still presented as a game in which the lover is forced to suffer while the beloved remains inaccessible, but the circumstances surrounding their attachment are now entirely different. Women are often portrayed making overtures to men either personally or through go-betweens, and they follow up these initiatives with eager pursuit. The attraction between the two parties is no longer spiritual but carnal and materialistic, and the effects of the relationship are degrading rather than ennobling. Because the duty of Lima's prostitutes is to extort as much money and as many gifts from their customers as they can, while granting few sexual favors in return, the poet warns his friend of the consequences by illustrating what can happen to him:

> At midnight you'll see how   a woman in brocade,
> lamé, and velvet,   calls through an opening in the door,
> who after taking off   her dress and accessories,
> orders out the window   for four things with a half [dollar];
> she asks for a half a loaf of bread,   a half a block of cheese,
> a half a bunch of bananas,   and the rest goes for fermented cane
>   liquor.
> You'll see how full she is   if not with dinner, with gas,
> finding herself tuned   louder than a stringed instrument. (p.13)

On another occasion, Terralla y Landa vividly relates a series of events in which his friend is not only denied access to his female companion but is called before a judge because of her. At the invitation of a gentleman on the street, Terralla y Landa's comrade allegedly joins one of his lady friends for lunch. Despite the disgusting local cuisine and the deplorable table manners of the guests, he becomes entranced by the young woman's beauty and decides to return this hospitality by inviting her to dinner. The following evening the poet's companion finds that he is not only obligated to entertain his new acquaintance and perhaps several of her friends but an entire entourage which Terralla y Landa likens to the "army of Croesus." Each guest, claiming to be a relative, orders something different as the night of feasting begins, and the innkeeper, who sees the opportunity for his own personal gain, prepares a plethora of unappetizing dishes. While the dinner is in progress, all the guests praise him, but as the evening concludes, they chatter about his rudeness and the fact that he is a foreigner. The next day, Terralla y Landa's companion goes to his lady friend's house expecting to find her ill from overeating, but to his surprise, she is in excellent health and surrounded by people. Her demands for amusement and expensive gifts continue as does the clamor of her cohorts. Nevertheless, believing he is in love, the poet's friend tries to fulfill her every wish. Later, when he requests more attention from her, she makes a formal complaint against him for being such a nuisance. After hearing the case, the magistrate and members of his staff are taken in by the young woman and are sympathetic to her because she avows that she is married and that he has improperly pursued her (pp. 26–31).[50]

In addition to prostitutes, Terralla y Landa describes other women who are supposedly engaged in legitimate trades. They too, however, are portrayed as greedy and thieving. Although Lima may have been a haven for female criminals, the poet's frequent presentation of women living outside the law may be attributable to their economic woes. Either women could not live on the wages earned in these vocations, or females were paid less for their labor than males and forced to steal to survive. On the street named Peligro (Danger), Terralla y Landa identifies a couple of Indian fisherwomen, who are picking pockets, and sarcastically comments that "Sometimes they catch more than the day's haul they brought in" (p. 8). Another woman who allegedly does his friend's laundry is equally dishonest, and the poet uses a pun to denote her fraudulence. Changing the Spanish word for "washwoman" *(lavandera)* to *la bandera* meaning "the flag" or in this case "the Jolly Roger," he likens her tendency to rob to that of a pirate (p. 38).[51]

Terralla y Landa's lengthy *Lima por dentro y fuera* contains a much more extensive presentation of women living in the viceregal capital than the previous satirical writings by Rosas de Oquendo, Caviedes, or Carrió, and it is particularly informative with regard to the growth and organization of prostitution in the City of Kings. He is the last major satirist to deride the ladies of Lima, and his account provides a view of them during the final years of Spanish domination. Although he wrote at a time in which enlightened ideas circulated in the colonies and influenced slightly the portrayal of women in newspapers and journals,[52] Terralla y Landa offers little constructive criticism of women and no solutions to the problems in which they found themselves. Education was proposed by some men who were well acquainted with the dilemmas faced by women, but neither Terralla y Landa nor any of his predecessors viewed this as a means of changing the behavior of women whom they considered to be social misfits.

In summary, the ridicule of women may be found consistently in the works of the colonial period's most outstanding satirists, although it varies considerably in its focus and intensity, and it generally follows that of Quevedo, Rojas, and the picaresque novelists. Females, however, are usually portrayed as secondary characters in this critical genre, and when criticism of them is placed in perspective, it represents only one facet of a society whose status quo is under wide-ranging attack for its ignorance, ugliness, artificiality, and hypocrisy. Women from various cultural, geographical, occupational, and racial backgrounds of early Spanish America are derided by satirical writers, and their scathing commentary denigrates traditionally idealized feminine types such as the matriarchal figure, the aristocratic spouse of a Spanish official, the Indian maiden, the cloistered woman, the female warrior, and the country girl. While ill will toward the feminine gender may stem from personal experience or may be the result of acculturation, their expressions of disapproval in colonial literature often indicate men's prejudices and preoccupations in the New World and outline the adversity encountered by the women there as well. Daily life provides the setting for the female characters devised by the satirists, and they are pictured as being inordinately subjected to poverty, sickness, loneliness, and perversion.

Women in Spanish America's cities, especially the viceregal capitals, were more frequently portrayed in satirical works than rural women. Of the many imperfections of these city residents, their sexual excesses were most noted and were often presented in a crude and vulgar manner. On the light side, a hint of scandal and promiscuity often added a comic element to colonial feminine satire, but from a serious standpoint, it frequently prefaced the exposure of urban social ills such as prostitution and venereal disease. The prostitute emerges as the predominant female character not only because of her conspicuous presence in society but because she is a universally reprehensible figure and draws the complaints of diversely dissatisfied males. While women living in the countryside from the outskirts of Mexico City to the Argentine pampa generally escaped these problems, they were, on the other hand, portrayed as uninteresting or uncivilized in the works of Rosas de Oquendo, Carrió de la Vandera, and Terralla y Landa.

Existing antifeminist attitudes and prior personal animosity toward women were no doubt exacerbated by environmental conditions in the New World. Settlements rapidly grew into cities, and life in these municipalities could no longer be strictly controlled by church and state. The number of women increased dramatically after the conquest, and many who were unmarried were forced to leave home in order to support themselves. The women who lacked provisions for their financial security were usually from the lower nonwhite sectors of society. The types of work for which they were suited were quite limited and often unsavory, and their success hinged upon their aggressiveness and ingenuity. Upper-class women were also affected by urbanization in the colonies and enjoyed greater leisure than ever before. The manner in which they spent their free time, however, was a matter of controversy, as women were charged with everything from meddling in matters of state to paving the way for the moral collapse of the empire with their extramarital affairs. These women from opposite extremes of society, it was felt, endangered the continuance of normal family life and the stability of the patriarchal system.

In addition to criticizing women, satirists strike out at other minorities through their female caricatures. The treatment of Indian, black, or racially mixed women, for example, attest to the existence of racial prejudice in the colonies. These females, often identified only by their race, are portrayed in an unfavorable light by Caviedes, Carrió, and Terralla y Landa because of their color. Rodríguez Freile, on the other hand, points out a cultural distinction between blacks and whites in his creation of Juana García and alludes to the atmosphere of evil and superstition associated with New Granada's black culture. Racism, while affecting the descriptions of members of both sexes, may have surfaced more in relation to nonwhite women because they had been able to progress through the social ranks by marrying Spaniards, an option denied to males of similar racial make-up. These men had remained on the periphery of society and posed no threat to the order established by the Spanish. At the opposite end of the colonial social ladder, Peninsular women were maligned by Rosas de Oquendo, Rodríguez Freile, and Carrió. These aristocratic ladies often acted as if they were superior to native Americans, and colonial satirists mocked them for their arrogance and hypocrisy. This type of criticism appears to hint at the growing national consciousness in the viceroyalties.

The men who satirized women did so openly and freely in their works, since they feared no serious reprisals from the opposite sex. Little was done by women to dispute their distorted image or to call men into account for the discrepancies between their conduct and women's expectations of them. Many female residents of the colonies were simply not aware of their negative literary portrayal because they were unable to read or because those who could read were restricted to a form of literature more befitting a lady. Sor Juana Inés de la Cruz is the only female writer to take men to task for supporting a double standard of behavior for the sexes, and she was ultimately made to suffer for her liberal views.

The portrait of women in colonial satire offers a striking alternative to the heroic frontier woman and the courtly vision of the feminine ideal presented in the preceding chapters. Satiric literature gave men the opportunity to vent their frustrations and to express their antagonism toward women in a manner that would generally not have been condoned if enacted publicly. Although their purpose remains essentially the same as the satirists before them, their spirited commentary, based upon observations of Spanish American women during the postconquest years, provides a unique combination of the age-old complaints about the feminine gender and an intriguing profile of colonial women, especially those who were not members of a socially elite group.

Notes

1. For insights into the treatment of women in Spanish literature, see Jacob Ornstein, "La misoginía y el profeminismo en la literatura castellana," *Revista de Filología Hispánica* 3, no. 3 (1941), pp. 219–32; María del Pilar Oñate, *El feminismo en la literatura española* (Madrid: Espasa-Calpe, 1938); and Edna Niecie Sims, "El antifeminismo en la literatura española hasta 1560," (dissertation, The Catholic University of America, 1970).

2. Otis H. Green, *Spain and the Western Tradition*, 4 vols. (Madison, Wisc.: University of Wisconsin Press, 1963), I, 103, 113. Complaints about women were voiced in both early historical writings and lyric poetry produced in the colonies; however, the works considered in this chapter were written specifically to deride members of the opposite sex. Drama containing feminine satire is discussed in chapter 4.

3. María Rosa Lida de Malkiel, *La originalidad artística de La Celestina* (Buenos Aires: Editorial Universitaria de Buenos Aires, 1962), p. 509. She also discusses all aspects of the Celestina's character and the influence of colorful forerunners, such as the female figures in *El corbacho* and the *Libro de buen amor,* had upon her creation. See pp. 506–93.

4. José Antonio Castro, "Estructura y estilo de *Los sueños* de Quevedo," *Anuario de Filología* 1 (1962), pp. 82–83.

5. Stuart Miller, *The Picaresque Novel* (Cleveland, Ohio: The Press of Case Western University, 1967), pp. 12, 44–45.

6. Rosas de Oquendo even boasts that on several occasions they showed him their gratitude by making his offspring the beneficiary of their husbands' estates. Rubén Vargas Ugarte, *Rosas de Oquendo y otros* (Lima: Clásicos Peruanos, 1955), pp. 10–11. Page numbers appearing in the text refer to this edition of Rosas de Oquendo's works.

7. Alfonso Reyes attributes the poem "Romance a México" ["Ballad to Mexico"] to Rosas de Oquendo because the author criticizes Mexican women for their addiction to card playing. Alfonso Reyes, *Obras completas*, 19 vols. (México, D.F.: Fondo de Cultura Económica, 1957), VI, 41–43.

8. "Sátira a las cosas que pasan en el Perú año de 1598" is Rosas de Oquendo's lengthiest attack on women. He may have criticized the *limeñas* on another occasion, however. In a sonnet believed to have been written by him, the poet refers to them generally as immoral women. Reyes, *Obras completas*, VI, 35.

9. Pedro de Oña, *Arauco domado* (Santiago, Chile: Imprenta Universitaria, 1917), p. 24.

10. Francisco J. Santamaría, 3 vols. *Diccionario general de americanismos* (México, D.F.: Editorial Pedro Robredo, 1942), II, 223.

11. When Rosas de Oquendo narrates Don Beltrán de Castro y de la Cueva's arrival in Callao, he presents a portrait of him that is even less flattering than that of his sister. According to him, the hero was a weak person, insecure person who only undertook the mission out of greed. The satirist may have portrayed Don Beltrán in this way to suggest that his shortcomings were a result of having such an overbearing sibling.

12. In his "Carta de las damas de Lima a las de México" ["Letter from the Ladies of Lima to Those of Mexico"], Rosas de Oquendo pretends that the *limeñas* accepted his criticism without rancor. According to this poem, the ladies of Lima confide to the *mexicanas* that Rosas de Oquendo was never their enemy, and they call him by his alias, Juan Sánchez (p. 59).

13. A. Paz y Melia, "Cartapacio de diferentes versos a diversos asuntos compuestos ó recogidos por Mateo Rosas de Oquendo," *Bulletin Hispanique* 8 (1906), p. 170.

14. Ibid., p. 171.

15. According to Miguel Aguilera, Juan Rodríguez Freile learned how to expose scandal by reading *La Celestina*. Miguel Aguilera, ed., *El carnero* by Juan Rodríguez Freile (Bogotá: Imprenta Nacional, 1963), p. 13. References to this edition of Rodríguez Freile's work appear in the text. See also Enrique Pupo-Walker, "La reconstrucción imaginativa del pasado en *El carnero* de Rodríguez Freyle," *Nueva Revista de Filología Hispánica* 27, no. 2 (1978), pp. 348–49.

16. Fernando de Rojas, *La Celestina*, ed. Bruno Mario Damiani (Madrid: Cátedra, 1976), p. 63. For the English translation, see Lesley Byrd Simpson, trans., *The Celestina*, by Fernando de Rojas (Berkeley and Los Angeles, Calif.: University of California Press, 1955), p. 8. Gabriel Giraldo Jaramillo, "Don Juan Rodríguez Freyle y *La Celestina*," *Boletín de Historia y Antigüedades* 27, nos. 308–9 (1940), pp. 585–86.

17. This association fulfills a purpose of Rodríguez Freile's account, which was to link universal history to that of New Granada. Raquel Chang-Rodríguez, "El 'Prólogo al lector' de *El carnero*," *Thesaurus* 29 (1974), p. 74.

18. Vern L. Bullough, *The Subordinate Sex: A History of Attitudes toward Women* (Urbana, Ill.: University of Illinois Press, 1973), p. 93.

19. Silvia Benso, "Técnica narrativa de Rodríguez Freyle," *Thesaurus* 32, no. 1 (1977), pp. 109, 119.

20. Rojas, *La Celestina*, pp. 196–206. Pupo-Walker discusses at length the similarities between this particular episode from *El carnero* and various features of *La Celestina*. Pupo-Walker, "La reconstrucción," pp. 353–55. See also Julie Greer Johnson, "Three Celestinesque Figures of Colonial Spanish American Literature," *Celestinesca* 5, no. 1 (1981), pp. 43–44.

21. The English translation has been taken from Juan Rodríguez Freile's *The Conquest of New Granada*, trans. William C. Atkinson (London: Folio Society, 1961), p. 72.

22. Rodríguez Freile also includes two episodes in which the wife is innocent of charges of infidelity, but because the husband assumes she is guilty, he murders her. Francisco Martínez Bello uses his jealousy of a friar as an excuse to kill his spouse, Doña María de Olivares. Feeling neglected because of his first child's birth, he asks his wife to do away with the infant. Her refusals bring reprisals from him which conclude with her untimely death (pp. 319–23). Uxoricide also results when Don García de Vargas misinterprets the sign language of a deaf mute. Returning to his home in Tocaima, Don García meets a *sordomudo* who had just come from his house where a celebration was in preparation. When he inquired about happenings there, the man tried to tell him that the steer had just been butchered; however, by raising his hands to his head in a manner resembling horns, he unintentionally gave Don García the wrong impression. Thinking that his wife was unfaithful to him, García hastened home and killed her (pp. 265–66). Both Martínez Bello and García de Vargas,

like those guilty of other crimes, were swiftly brought to justice and duly punished.

23. Ann M. Pescatello, *Power and Pawn: The Female in Iberian Families, Societies, and Cultures* (Westport, Conn.: Greenwood Press, 1976), p. 144.

24. Rubén Vargas Ugarte, ed., *Obras de Don Juan del Valle y Caviedes* (Lima: Talleres Gráficos de la Tipografía Peruana, 1947), pp. 208, 179–81. Selections of poetry taken from this edition are noted in the text. A complete list of Caviedes' feminine satire is contained in Appendix I of Reedy's study. Daniel R. Reedy, *The Poetic Art of Juan del Valle y Caviedes* (Chapel Hill, N.C.: University of North Carolina Press, 1964), pp. 154–55.

25. *Pie quebrado*, two eight-syllable lines followed by a half line of four syllables, was used by Jorge Manrique in his tribute to his dead father, *Coplas a la muerte del Maestre don Rodrigo, su padre,* and resembles the cadence of a funeral dirge.

26. See Caviedes' poems: "Pintura de una dama en metáfora de astrología" (pp. 45–46) ["Portrait of a Woman in Astrological Metaphor"], "Pintura de una dama en seguidillas" (pp. 49–50) ["A Poetic Portrait of a Woman"], and "Una pintura en metáfora de los naipes" (pp. 50–52) ["Portrait of a Woman in Card Metaphor"].

27. Ricardo Palma, ed., *Flor de Academias, y Diente del Parnaso* (Lima: Oficina Tipográfica de El Tiempo por L. H. Jiménez, 1899), p. 451. Another poem, "Romance alevoso á las seguidillas de una dama" ["A Treacherous Ballad to a Woman's Diarrhea"] offers a similar description. Palma, pp. 414–15.

28. The first known house of prostitution in the New World was established in Puerto Rico in 1526. Pescatello, *Power and Pawn*, p. 153.

29. Glen L. Kolb, *Juan del Valle y Caviedes: A Study of the Life, Times and Poetry of a Spanish Colonial Satirist* (New London, Conn.: Stonington Publishing Company, 1959), p. 34.

30. The rules governing a woman's conduct were clearly expressed in the Spanish works of Fray Martín de Córdoba, Fray Hernando de Talavera, Luis Vives, and Fray Luis de León. Their standards influenced the education of women in the colonies, and all of these writers stress purity and honor as a woman's most valuable assets. Asunción Lavrin, "In Search of Colonial Woman in Mexico: The Seventeenth and Eighteenth Centuries," in her *Latin American Women* (Westport, Conn.: Greenwood Press, 1978), pp. 25–27.

31. Palma, *Flor de Academias*, pp. 413–14.

32. Ibid., p. 414.

33. Ibid.

34. Ibid., p. 417. Another very revealing description of the same prostitute is found in his "A una dama que cayó de la mula en que iba a Miraflores" ["To a Woman Who Fell Off the Mule on Which She Was Traveling to

Miraflores"]. Daniel R. Reedy, "Poesías inéditas de Juan del Valle Caviedes," *Revista Iberoamericana* 29, no. 55 (1963), pp. 165–68.

35. Julie Greer Johnson, "Feminine Satire in Concolorcorvo's *El lazarillo de ciegos caminantes,*" *South Atlantic Bulletin* 45, no. 1 (1980), pp. 11–20.

36. Richard A. Mazzara, "Some Picaresque Elements in Concolorcorvo's *El lazarillo de ciegos caminantes,*" *Hispania* 46, no. 2 (1963), pp. 323–27.

37. The colorful native guide, while being a historical personage, is a cleverly conceived literary device through which the Inspector channels his offensive commentary or ostensibly innocent queries that elicit his own critical responses. Marcel Bataillon, "Introducción a Concolorcorvo y a su itinerario de Buenos Aires a Lima," *Cuadernos Americanos* 19 (1960), pp. 197–216. While the use of mask-persona is a necessary deception in terms of many of the opinions that the author expresses, it hardly seems relevant in his criticism of women, as the most severe penalty he might suffer would be the scorn of some of his lady friends.

38. Alonso Carrió de la Vandera (Concolorcorvo), *El lazarillo de ciegos caminantes,* ed. Emilio Carilla (Barcelona: Editorial Labor, 1973), p. 116. References to this edition appear within the text. English translations appearing in this section have been taken from Alonso Carrió de la Vandera's *El lazarillo: A Guide for Inexperienced Travelers Between Buenos Aires and Lima,* trans. Walter D. Kline (Bloomington, Ind.: Indiana University Press, 1965), pp. 40, 137, 168, 288. Carrió also criticizes mothers for overindulging their children (p. 444), and Concolorcorvo derides mothers-to-be for having strange cravings during pregnancy (pp. 259–60).

39. As they leave the ancient city of Cuzco, Carrió and his guide again discuss the topic of racial intermingling, and the Inspector mentions the varying availability of Spanish women for men residing in the colonies (pp. 389–90). While the information presented in this passage is of historical value, its condescending manner of presentation reveals the author's arrogance and sense of superiority in describing women and their role in society and his blatant racism. Elsewhere Carrió's low opinion of blacks is divulged by Concolorcorvo's characterization of a *negra* as malodorous (p. 463). Carlos Inca, alias Concolorcorvo, also tells an anecdote about a *mulata* (a woman of mixed Spanish and African ancestry) who did not observe the limitations of her class (p. 169).

40. In a manner resembling Feijoo, he also provides information concerning the fertility or infertility of women in various areas of the New World (pp. 131, 388–89).

41. In his "Foreword" to the English translation of *El lazarillo de ciegos caminantes,* Irving A. Leonard suggests that Carrió's work may be a parody of travel literature, specifically *Relación histórica del viage a la América Meridional.* Carrió, *El lazarillo: A Guide,* p. 12. Jorge Juan and Antonio de Ulloa, who visited Lima during the eighteenth century, thought that the ladies were a

special attraction of the city and wrote a detailed description of them in their journal. Jorge Juan and Antonio de Ulloa, *Relacion Historica del Viage hecho de Orden de S. Mag. a la America Meridional para Medir Algunos Grados de Meridiano Terrestre, y venir por ellos en conocimiento de la verdadera Figura, y Magnitud de la Tierra, con otras varias Observaciones Astronomicas, y Phisicas,* Segunda Parte, 3 vols. (Madrid: Antonio Marín, 1748), III, 72–82.

42. The controversy over whether women could appear veiled in public began in the colonies during the 1580's, and this custom is the subject of jest in works of the seventeenth century. Raquel Chang-Rodríguez, "Tapadas limeñas en un cancionerillo peruano del siglo XVII," *Revista Interamericana de Bibliografía* 28, no. 1 (1978), pp. 57–62.

43. In addition to the dress of the *limeñas*, Carrió also describes that of Mexican *mestizas* (pp. 451–52). They tended to wear the cotton shirts and wraps of their Aztec ancestors.

44. Quevedo uses this image in his *sueño*, "El mundo por de dentro." Francisco de Quevedo y Villegas, *Obras completas,* 2 vols. (Madrid: Aguilar, 1958), I, 172.

45. Concolorcorvo also describes women who suffer from an iodine deficiency and who attempt to conceal the resultant goiter with a scarf (pp. 200–201).

46. Terralla y Landa wrote under the pseudonym Simón Ayanque. Ventura García Calderón, *Costumbristas y satíricos* (Paris: Desclée de Brouwer, 1938), p. 18.

47. The same structure was used by Quevedo's disciple Diego Torres Villarroel in his *Visiones y visitas* when he takes Spain's most renowned satirist on a tour of eighteenth-century Madrid.

48. Esteban Terralla y Landa, *Lima por dentro y fuera*, ed Alan Soons (Exeter, England: Exeter University Printing Unit, 1978), p. 67. All quotations have been translated from this reproduction of the work and referenced by page number only within the text.

49. Quevedo, *Obras completas*, I, 172.

50. Terralla y Landa, like Caviedes, also mentions problems confronting members of this notorious profession. One difficulty is the anguish of aging after such a short career, and another concern is that of venereal disease. For those who are suffering from this malady, the author recommends with tongue in cheek the provincial town of Piura as a good place to recover (p. 6).

51. Terralla y Landa also presents women as wives and mothers and criticizes them for their vanity and egotism (pp. 46–47). After pointing out these flaws in their character, he warns his friend against marriage (p. 48).

52. Johanna S. R. Mendelson, "The Feminine Press: The View of Women in the Colonial Journals of Spanish America, 1790–1810," in *Latin American Women: Historical Perspectives,* ed. Asunción Lavrin (Westport, Conn.: Greenwood Press, 1978), pp. 198–218.

CHAPTER 4

WOMEN IN DRAMA

The presence of women in almost every facet of colonial drama distinguishes it from other literary art forms brought to the New World from Spain. Plays usually included female characters whose roles were performed in churches by women parishioners and in theaters by actresses. Themes concerning women were frequently presented, and audiences throughout the three hundred years of Peninsular rule were composed of a significant number of females. Lady entrepreneurs contributed to the establishment of theaters in Spanish America,[1] and the era's most accomplished dramatist writing in the colonies was a Hieronymite nun from New Spain.[2]

The appearance of female characters in dramatic works performed before American spectators began shortly after the first Spanish friars' arrival on the Mexican mainland in the early sixteenth century. Their religious dramas, which were similar to the earliest Spanish *autos* (religious plays) and *églogas* (eclogues), were used primarily to teach New Spain's inhabitants about the Bible and about Christian doctrine.[3] Efforts were made to Americanize these dramatic pieces in order to assimilate Indian women into Spanish culture and to acclimate Spanish women to Spain's new territories. Native American women played a number of roles, usually in their own language, and natural settings reflected the New World environment. Women were warned about sin, instructed in the responsibilities of marriage, and cautioned about witchcraft in some of these early skits, and occasionally men were alerted to the dangers of following the advice of the feminine sex. This tendency to criticize women turned to ridicule by the end of the sixteenth century as religious programs became increasingly secularized, and dramatic works were presented outside the church.

The theater became a popular form of entertainment in the American viceroyalties during the seventeenth and eighteenth centuries, and plays were generally directed toward sophisticated Spanish and Creole audiences rather than at indigenous populations. The Americanization of Spanish drama was halted by the early 1600's, and elements of local color would not appear again for nearly a hundred years. Various types of Spanish Golden Age drama, especially the *comedia*, monopolized colonial theaters,[4] and playwrights living in the colonies endeavored to imitate such dramatizations. Women played prominent roles in them, and feminine themes were interwoven with the plot. Representatives of an idealized Spanish society such as the lady, the servant girl, and the female comic were frequent characters,[5] and the conflicts of honor and love in which they became involved customarily reflect the literary tradition of courtly love.[6] One of the period's greatest dramatist was a woman, Sor Juana Inés de la Cruz, and her theatrical works include both religious and secular representations.[7] By the eighteenth century, drama in the colonies had begun to take a significant, new direction although it was still influenced to a large extent by the Peninsular theater. American characters and themes reemerged, and the figure of the *criolla* (a woman born in the New World of Spanish ancestry) attained greater definition in drama than in other genres. Evidence of this change may be found in several plays in which Creole women are principal figures and historical events or current situations in the colonies are depicted.[8]

Over the three-hundred-year development of colonial drama, Indian, black, Spanish, and Creole women played the roles of heroines, models of femininity, comic figures, and villains. Their treatment by dramatists ranges from a highly idealistic approach to one that includes elements of realism, and the works in which they appear often echo many of the themes prominent in other genres. Because of the diversity of drama during the colonial period, it documents certain trends generally present in early Spanish American literature. One is the shifting focus away from women of native or Peninsular origin to those of Spanish ancestry born in the New World, and another is the nascent desire of colonial writers to break away from Spanish literary models and to create a totally new, American female type in their works. These changes reveal to some degree the varying requirements, attitudes, and tastes of the residents of Spain's American possessions.

One of the first female characters to appear in a dramatic work written in the New World was Fray Andrés de Olmos' Lucía.[9] She has the leading role in his *Auto del Juicio Final [Play About the Final Judgment]*, one of the earliest plays performed to provide moral guidance for young women. Lucía is an unmarried Indian girl who is living with a Spaniard, and although she had been warned repeatedly that cohabitation is a sin, she defiantly continues this arrangement until the final day of judgment when she is beyond redemption. As the play concludes, she is condemned by God for her immorality and sentenced to death.[10] The theme of this early religious drama is indicative of the Church's interest in women's welfare; however, this concern is based upon the assumption that women are easily tempted and often motivated by evil. Since they, not the men, are morally weak, according to the ecclesiastical point of view, they therefore bear the sole responsibility for their illicit relationships.[11] Lucía's exceedingly harsh, irrevocable punishment attests to the unwavering position of the Church in such matters and probably accounts for the success the *Auto del Juicio Final* had in discouraging unsanctioned unions between Indian women and Spanish soldiers. Praising the effects of this drama in an antifeminist tone, the Spanish historian, Father Juan de Torquemada, comments, "It opened the eyes of many Indians and Spaniards to turn to virtue and abandon their evil ways, and many erring women, moved by terror, became converted."[12]

Women are also featured as main characters in two early biblical plays presented in the New World, *Los pastores [The Shepherds]* and the *Auto de la caída de Adán y Eva [Play About the Fall of Adam and Eve]*.[13] Unfortunately, the original version of *Los pastores* has been lost, and the precise character of the shepherdess Gila and her role in visiting the Christ child cannot be determined.[14] However, a portion of the dramatization depicting Adam and Eve in the Garden of Eden has been preserved, and Fray Toribio de Benavente, known also as Motolinía, wrote a detailed description of its presentation. In his *Historia de los indios de la Nueva España [History of the Indians of New Spain]*, he recounts Tlaxcala's religious festivities held in 1538, when the *Auto de la caída de Adán y Eva* was performed in Nahuatl.[15]

Although the play was designed to acquaint the Indians with the explanation of man's origin according to the Bible, the argument of the work is viewed as a primary source of misogyny in the Christian Church,[16] and Motolinía clearly conveys this attitude in his preliminary observations about the enactment and his summary of its action. Offering a behind-the-scenes view of the spectacle, he mentions an incident involving the female lead when she stands too close to a pair of ocelots that are part of its authentic setting: "Once Eve carelessly collided with one of them and the well-bred beast moved aside. This was before she had sinned, for if it had been afterward, she would not have been so lucky" (p. 66). Although the Franciscan's remark was made in jest, his predisposition regarding her is evident and continues to surface in his depiction of the couple's banishment from paradise when he focuses on Eve's persistence and deceit:

Eve went back and forth three or four times between her husband and the serpent, Adam always resisting and pushing Eve away as if he were indignant. She, beseeching him and worrying him, said that it was evident how little he loved her, and that she loved him much more than he did her and, throwing herself into his arms, importuned him so that finally he went with her to the forbidden tree and she, in his presence, ate some and gave him some also. (pp. 66–67)

Eve's guilt is further emphasized in the *villancico* (church carol) sung at the conclusion of the performance which reiterates the essence of the *auto*. These are the first lines of Spanish poetry learned by native Americans,[17] and they instill an unfavorable image of womanhood in the impressionable new converts:

> Oh, why did she eat
> —that first married woman—
> Oh, why did she eat
> The forbidden fruit?
> That first married woman
> —she and her husband—
> Have brought Our Lord down
> To a humble abode
> Because they both ate
> The forbidden fruit. (p. 67)

In addition to casting suspicion on the first woman and describing her as a vehicle for the powers of evil, this brief dramatic piece also defines the female role. When Adam and Eve are cast out of the Garden, they are assigned specific duties to be accomplished in the world. The wife receives a spindle as a symbol of her domestic tasks. She is obviously subordinate to her husband and must care for him and their children. Since this arrangement was supposedly determined by God, particular credence was given to it, and its effects would be long-ranging.

The Church's antagonism toward women and its relegation of them to a position of inferiority were introduced very early in the conversion of the Indians through the *Auto de la caída de Adán y Eva*, and its translation into Nahuatl made the understanding of these concepts by natives a virtual certainty. The presentation of this play may have also served to reinforce the previously acquired attitudes of the Spaniards who either saw the play performed or who were instrumental in its staging. Regardless of the recipients of these ideas, their ramifications are enormous, and their continuance reveals how concepts emanated from a religious source to influence secular society. The criticism of women was frequently based upon criteria set by the Church, and it manifested itself not only in dramatic works such as the one discussed previously by Olmos but also as an undertone in early Spanish American chronicles and as a constant feature in satirical writings of the colonial period.

By the end of the sixteenth century, colonial dramatists introduced secular elements into their religious drama as the Spaniard Juan del Encina had done in his *églogas,* and programs presented in Spanish America's churches often included farcical sketches similar to Lope de Rueda's *pasos* written in Spain. These changes reduced the austerity of indoctrination and later served to stimulate the development of totally lay dramatizations.[18] The roles that women played in these dramatic works were generally not as serious as they had been in the early *autos*, and at times they were even comic. The purpose of their inclusion in these plays, however, was still didactic. Fernán González de Eslava, a Spanish resident of Mexico, uses female characters not only to interject levity into his spiritual and sacramental colloquies but to contribute to their solemn meaning as well. These literary figures are instrumental in his defense of the sanctity of marriage based upon the wife's obedience and respect for her husband in two of his interludes accompanying colloquies VII and XVI.

Because the characters in González de Eslava's *Coloquios [Collo-*

quies] are generally allegorical, representing in many cases abstract forces in the conflict between good and evil, only one real woman, Teresa, appears in his entire dramatic series. She is introduced, together with her husband Diego, in the prelude to the seventh colloquy, and they immediately become involved in a marital dispute over an unpopular trade regulation. During the reign of Philip II, the production of silk was forbidden in the colonies in compliance with the mercantilistic principles governing the commerce between Spain and America.[19] Although this restriction must have outraged many colonists, Eslava dramatizes an aristocratic woman's anger in this case because of what he regards as the Spanish American ladies' love of expensive finery and their obsession with their appearance. In addition to voicing these age-old complaints about women, he also takes a satirical jab at the pretentiousness of the upper class, and his portrayal of Teresa reflects the sheltered upbringing provided for girls by many prominent Spanish families.

Diego's wife has a distorted view of her own self-worth, and she, like many Spaniards and Creoles, views outsiders with scorn. As she reminds Diego, she is the direct descendant of a conqueror, and she humiliates him for his lack of social prominence by calling him a "little good-for-nothing husband" (I, 204). Vanity, envy, and selfishness prompt Teresa to chide Diego about his inability to provide her with luxury as well, and her complaints are indicative of her reliance upon him for material items:

> I don't have two dresses
> and I see a hundred thousand women
> with velvets down to the floor. (I, 205)

In order to emphasize further her lack of elegant dress and express her disdain for Indians, Teresa likens her distressing situation to that of a "mujer huipil" (I, 206), or squaw.[20] After insulting Diego's intelligence and his lineage and lamenting his failure as a provider, all of which are far removed from the Crown's enforcement of the silk ban, Teresa's arguments are exhausted. Her only recourse is to assault Diego corporally, and her violence leads to mayhem. This makes Teresa look even more ridiculous. Her barrage of blows ceases only when the hapless Diego agrees to take her to China where silk is plentiful, and the *entremés* (interlude) concludes as they board a galleon for the Orient. The vicissitudes of Teresa and Diego do not stop at the end of the interlude but extend into the main body of the *coloquio* as well. After a brief *loa* (prologue), in which González de Eslava recounts the prophet Jonah's flight from Ninevah and foreshadows his being swallowed by the whale, action resumes on shipboard where Jonah is among the passengers. When a storm comes up and envelops the ship, he is not the only one to respond emotionally. Teresa as well reviews her life, and fearing that her irresponsible behavior may have provoked this display of God's wrath, she dutifully promises to be a good wife in return for calm seas (I, 227).

Conjugal strife is again depicted in González de Eslava's other *entremés* in which the obligations of a responsible spouse are stressed.[21] In *Coloquio XVI*, however, the marriage partners are abstractions endowed with human qualities, and a female character who personifies evil is introduced.[22] When the interlude begins, Espión (Spy) is beating his wife, Ocasión (Occasion), because of her alleged infidelity.[23] Distraught by her husband's jealousy and rage, Ocasión consults an old Indian woman, known as Doña Murmuración (Lady Slander), who is accustomed to counseling women in her predicament and who attempts to resolve the problem through witchcraft:

> I went to Lady Slander
> for a solution,
> I gave her a skirt and bodice,
> so that she would change
> my husband's condition.
>   And she, very secretively,
> gave me a heart of wax
> with needles on the outside,
> and it has had as much effect on him
> as if I had done nothing at all. (II, 257–58)[24]

Although Doña Murmuración uses Nahuatl expressions in her speech and worships a devil who resides in the volcano Popocatépetl, she actually practices her magic arts in much the same manner as the Celestina.[25] The remedy, which she gives to Ocasión in order to transform her husband into a loving person, is almost identical to the wax hearts full of broken needles mentioned by Pármeno, another of Rojas' characters, as a frequent fetish of his former employer. Calisto's servant also states that Celestina, like Doña Murmuración, often required a garment belonging to her client or the intended victim of her spells and that her customers were socially prominent, like Ocasión,[26] who claims to be the granddaughter of a conqueror (II, 255). The failure of sorcery to change her husband's temperament forces Ocasión to confess what she has done to Voluntad (Goodwill) and Templanza (Temperance). They chide her for having considered such indefensible actions and, as a prelude to González de Eslava's dramatization of the sacrament of marriage, they suggest that she pray, attend mass, and make pilgrimages to the Virgin of Guadalupe's shrine. The dramatist's reason for including a Celestinesque character in his *coloquio* and for preventing her from helping Ocasión is a didactic one designed to discredit native *curanderas* (medicine women). He seems to feel particular concern over the vulnerability of some women to these self-proclaimed practitioners and their dependence upon them to fulfill amorous desires, resolve marital problems, and alleviate other stressful conditions related to womanhood.

In both of González de Eslava's *entremeses,* he reiterates the stance taken by Fray Olmos and the author of the *Auto de la caída de Adán y Eva* regarding women and their position in society. Female characters are portrayed as easily succumbing to worldly temptations in all of these early plays. Marriage is presented as the most honorable state for a woman, and as a wife, she is generally expected to be submissive and subservient to her mate. González de Eslava's females, however, have more substance than their predecessors in the early *autos* and are intimately related to their New World setting. His portrayal of the daughters of Spaniards indicates that they were raised in a protected environment to continue life in the colonies just as it was in Spain and that their resistance to any change in this traditional pattern frequently made them critical of their American surroundings and intolerant of other residents.

Another late sixteenth-century interlude that places the behavior of women in a critical light was written by the American-born churchman, Cristóbal de Llerena.[27] The purpose of his skit, however, is not to teach women how to better themselves, like that of González de Eslava, but rather to expose them as a detriment to society. The political furor arising from the Corpus Christi celebration of 1588 is probably responsible for the preservation of the first known theatrical work in which women are overtly satirized. Female characters, however, do not actually appear in this farcical sketch. The controversial *entremés* performed in Santo Domingo identified several social ills which allegedly contributed to Hispaniola's decline.[28] Because civil authorities were primarily concerned with the economic and political implications of this brief piece, fearing the return of Sir Francis Drake to the Caribbean and angered by the charges of corruption within their own ranks, little attention was given at the time to the play's unmerciful attack on the city's female population.[29]

The action of this sketch centers around the unusual birth of a monster by the *bobo* (fool), Cordellate. Several of the simpleton's friends are called upon to explain the meaning of this freak's arrival, and their opinions vary mainly in the degree of blame that is placed on women. Edipo, jokingly reputed to be a famous interpreter of monsters, holds women entirely responsible for Santo Domingo's present problems:

. . . this monster has the round face of a woman, the neck of a horse, the body of a bird, the tail of a fish; that is to say the attributes of those animals encased in the woman, as is stated in this four-line verse, which will serve as an interpretation:

> The best woman is an unstable ball,
> the most discreet is a dumb, insane beast;
> she, who is more serious, is more frivolous,
> and finally all women are born with tails. (p. 126)

Proteo, on the other hand, believes that the behavior of certain female residents is only a partial explanation for this phenomenon and cites several other possible causes. Since the head of the monster is that of a woman, however, he appears to consider women the prime source of the city's difficulties and characterizes them as: "disorderly women, whose trappings, appetites, and licenses are outside all that is natural" (p. 127). After discussing the origins of this grotesque being, the comic characters contemplate its future significance for the island community, and all agree that it is a harbinger of portentous events and a warning of impending danger and disaster.

Llerena's reference to women in this sixteenth-century interlude containing social criticism not only reveals the adverse reaction of some residents of Hispaniola to their conduct but also demonstrates how ridicule of them was presented on the early colonial stage. Although current conditions in Santo Domingo no doubt prompted the author to write this dramatic piece, his basic attitude toward women is not un-

,on for a religious writer. His manner of expression, however, is active and must have drawn the disapproval of his superiors. He, like Motolinía, for example, sees no redemption from women's wickedness in spirituality and offers no guidance for their salvation. The consequences of their debauchery, he contends in a tone reminiscent of the Roman satirists, are not religious but political and only serve to undermine the stability of the empire. The vehemence with which he conveys his antagonism toward women, probably fostered by his asceticism, made an all-male cast not only his preference but also an absolute necessity, as few women would have debased themselves to this extent to perform the skit in public. The inappropriateness of dramatizations such as this one for Church sponsorship eventually resulted in the separation of religious and secular drama and the creation of an independent dramatic art form in the colonies.

During the seventeenth century, Spanish American women were generally overlooked as literary characters by colonial dramatists because of the strong influence of Golden Age drama; however, one of the period's greatest playwrights came from among their number. Sor Juana Inés de la Cruz demonstrated her exceptional talent in the entire gamut of dramatic art forms produced in the New World. Her *autos sacramentales* (sacramental plays), *comedias, loas, sainetes* (intermezzos), and *sarao* (soiree) are unequaled by the works of other dramatists writing in the colonies and mirror Spanish Golden Age drama both in style and in excellence. Although she follows the strict canons of the Peninsular theater, her dramatic pieces are not without individuality and subtly reveal her view of herself, other women, and the relationship between the sexes.

Los empeños de una casa [The Trials of a Noble House] is Sor Juana's best secular drama, and it was first performed to celebrate the viceroyship of Don Tomás Antonio de la Cerda in 1683. It is a typical *comedia de capa y espada* (comedy of manners) and is patterned after Calderón's *Los empeños de un acaso*.[30] The action of the play is set in Toledo, Spain, and centers around the amorous entanglements of Don Pedro de Arellano and his sister, Ana. He is in love with Doña Leonor Castro, but she is eloping with Don Carlos. Doña Ana loves Don Carlos but is being pursued by Don Juan. In order to have the woman of his dreams, Pedro has Leonor kidnapped by men posing as the police and placed under his sister Ana's protection. Carlos, who was accompanying his fiancée at the time, flees the scene with his servant, Castaño, and seeks asylum in the Arellano household. Ana, out of her deep feelings for him, agrees to shelter him, unaware that Don Juan has been let into the house by the maid and is hiding in her bedroom. The numerous encounters in the dark house as well as Pedro's return home, create a complex situation in which love, honor, jealousy, and vengeance emerge as the principal themes, and comedy abounds. Everything is resolved at the conclusion of the third act, however, when all are betrothed except Pedro, who must remain a bachelor for his irresponsible acts which set the events of the play in motion.

Three female characters appear in *Los empeños de una casa,* and their generally stylized portrayal makes them interchangeable with numerous counterparts who crossed the stage during Spain's Golden Age. Doña Ana and Doña Leonor, like the women generally described in courtly lyric poetry, are aristocratic *damas* (ladies) and are models of grace and charm. Their pristine elegance is enforced, however, by a strong sense of duty and honor. The *criada* (servant girl), Celia, on the other hand, comes from a humble background and lacks the propriety displayed by the two ladies. Although her behavior is generally mimicry of the *dama* whom she serves, her simplicity and expediency often lead her to make mistakes that have serious consequences for her mistress, Ana.

As the lady of the Arellano household, Doña Ana has certain obligations to her family and community which are inherent in her position. Her conduct not only determines her own reputation but also reflects upon her brother's honor. Family ties are stronger than the affinity she feels for other women, and she even aids Pedro in his efforts to bring about another woman's downfall. While she does not want to endanger the steadfast relationship with her elder sibling, her attention is temporarily diverted away from him by her affection for Don Carlos. His unexpected appearance at the house in her brother's absence as well as Don Juan's intrusion have grave implications for her, as she readily admits: ". . . if my brother finds you here, / my life and my honor are in danger."[31] In addition to jeopardizing her family's dignity and esteem, her feelings for Carlos nurture her jealousy toward Leonor and inspire her craftiness at keeping the two lovers apart. Despite her determination to fulfill her own desires, however, she is willing to compromise in the final moments of the play and marry Juan, thus preserving the good name of the Arellanos and upholding the most prized societal values of the time.

The character of Doña Leonor, who is an exceptionally bright and extraordinarily beautiful lady of the court, is of special significance both to the play and to its author.[32] She resembles the famous nun in her youth, and her statements about herself offer the first personal information regarding the colonial period's most distinguished literary figure. The introduction of these autobiographical elements into Leonor's speeches lends originality to the play yet corresponds harmoniously to the conventional courtly mold for female personages. A learned woman's appearance in a Golden Age drama was not new, and Sor Juana had spent several years at court as the vicereine's lady-in-waiting before entering the convent. A glance at Sor Juana's own portrait[33] and a reading of her *Respuesta a Sor Filotea de la Cruz [Reply to Sister Philotea of the Cross]* confirm the close relationship between the playwright and her dramatic creation, and Leonor's divulgence of her inner turmoil to Ana even portends the confessional tone of the Hieronymite's famed letter to the Bishop of Puebla to whom she defended her obsession with study.[34] Doña Leonor, like Sor Juana, is endowed with both beauty and wisdom, which cause her considerable disquietude.[35] Their incompatibility is later emphasized by Doña Ana when she chides her lovely guest:

> Leonor, your ingenuity and your face
> one hurts the other,
> for someone who is so prudent
> it is a pity that you are beautiful. (IV, 83)

Although this statement was made by Ana out of spite because Leonor has taken Carlos away from her, it also betrays the opposition of some women to the erudition of members of their own sex and Sor Juana's sensitivity to it. Leonor's desire for learning parallels that of the Mexican nun as well, and her accomplishments in the pursuit of knowledge lead to her recognition and fame.[36] Dissatisfaction with the artificiality of the court causes her to reflect upon the meaning of her life and results in her decision to leave such a frivolous and contrived environment: "I could not succeed in loving anyone / seeing myself loved by so many" (IV, 38).[37] At this juncture, however, Leonor's similarities with her creator end. Although she considers entering a convent, this option is averted in the play when she is able to redeem her honor by marrying *how is she (all) like Sor Juana*

Carlos.[38] In this way, Sor Juana makes her dramatic character conform to the feminine ideal and so meets the expectations of seventeenth-century audiences. Strict conventions governing the *comedia* would generally not allow the leading lady to withdraw into a religious community. Matrimony, considered to be the most proper state for a young woman, resolves the entanglements of all of Sor Juana's female characters as prescribed by the genre, and thus brings the play to a satisfying and joyous conclusion. Although Leonor, like the other *damas* in *Los empeños,* is patterned upon the masculine view of femininity, Sor Juana only imitates this stereotype in literature. In real life, she would reject it by leaving the viceregal retinue and going into monastic seclusion. By endowing Leonor with traits closely related to herself, Sor Juana may have hoped to give expression to a common dilemma facing female intellectuals in the colonies. Spanish plays in which unusually gifted female characters took part were considered to have served as a forum for possible change in women's status in Spain,[39] and the Mexican nun may have thought that her work might fulfill a similar purpose in Spanish America.

Although Sor Juana appears to accept the male vision of the aristocratic lady for literary purposes and uses it in her creation of Doña Ana and Doña Leonor, she voices some criticism of women who try to emulate this feminine type and of men who encourage it. This is no doubt a reflection of her own disapproval of her life at court as well as that of the behavior of other individuals there. Sor Juana pokes fun at women's customs and dress, especially those regarding a lady's outward appearance, by having the *gracioso* (buffoon) appear in drag. Appropriately this is a reversal of the dramatic device employed by Spanish dramatists in which women were often permitted to dress like men in order to achieve a specific goal, and it provides one of the highlights of the comedy. After dressing himself in Leonor's clothing in order to escape from Pedro's house, Castaño teasingly solicits approval for his stunning outfit from the ladies in the audience and remarks: "It is true that I am lovely. / God protect me, for I am beautiful" (IV, 137). To complete his disguise, he realizes that he must change his mannerisms as well and carefully recites the instructions on social behavior generally given to young girls by their elders. His greatest fear is not being unmasked but responding improperly to some passion-struck admirer. Castaño's reservations are not unfounded when Pedro, recognizing Leonor's attire, addresses the servant affectionately and beseeches him to accept his love. Here the head of the Arellano household is caught in his own trap because he is duped by the external show that he has helped to create. Sor Juana takes advantage of this situation to chide men for their superficiality, but her principal target is the patriarchal figure that Pedro represents. After hearing Pedro's overtures, which seem rather foolish, Castaño states that he now understands why women are so haughty (IV, 149).[40]

In addition to using the character of Leonor to express her own feelings about herself and her life at court and the *gracioso* to mock the artificial behavior of both men and women, Sor Juana employs the contradictory actions of the play's male characters to illustrate her ideas about men's injustices toward women. Again discretion and care are exercised by the playwright to follow the tradition established by Spain's Golden Age dramatists and to avoid jolting theatergoers with her outspokenness. Although the hypocrisy of the double standard of conduct is more directly and forcefully stated in her poem "Hombres necios que acusáis a la mujer sin razón" (I, 228–29) ["Stupid Men Who Accuse Women Without Any Reason"], it emerges in *Los empeños* when discrepancies between men's behavior and their expectations of women become known. After sneaking into Ana's room to force himself upon her, Juan is appalled to find Carlos hiding there. Concluding that Ana and Carlos are lovers, Juan wrongfully condemns Ana. Carlos, on the other hand, wonders why Ana is so willing to help him, and his speech reveals how men paradoxically judge women. Friendly, courteous females are viewed as frivolous and easy, and only those who remain aloof and insensitive are regarded as honorable (IV, 76–77).[41] Leonor's father, as well, believes that women's basic moral frailty has led to his family's disgrace, but he reconsiders his harsh judgment when he is made aware of the prestige and wealth his daughter's marriage to Pedro could mean to him. The height of duplicity, however, is Pedro's surprise and wrath at finding numerous uninvited guests in his house after depriving Doña Leonor and the Castro family of their good name.

Sor Juana's presentation of female characters in *Los empeños de una casa* is probably the best example of how Golden Age drama influenced their portrayal in the colonial theater and how Spanish models replaced Spanish American women in dramatic works written in the viceroyalties during the seventeenth and eighteenth centuries. This play is also important because Doña Ana and Doña Leonor are two of the first literary creations by a female author to appear in the literature of the time.

While Sor Juana relies upon stereotypes and dramatic convention, these technical recourses afford her the opportunity of registering her discontent on several issues regarding women without appearing to break with tradition. The pressures of a strict, unyielding society that neither anticipated nor truly accepted the emergence of such a gifted woman made the use of these artifices imperative. Such a perfect framework would be impossible to utilize in her reply to the Bishop of Puebla, and its absence may have resulted in grave consequences for the Mexican nun. Although her conformity with Peninsular dramatists may have served as a subterfuge in one sense, it assured her success as an artist in another. Men set the standards of literary excellence, and her ability to match the style of some of the best male writers of the time was extraordinarily consistent and a talent that brought enjoyment to her admirers.

Apart from using the image of the courtly lady in her dramatic works, Sor Juana also deals briefly with the theme of the woman warrior in another *comedia* entitled *Amor es más laberinto [Love, The Greater Labyrinth]*.[42] The source of the play is the myth of Theseus and the Minotaur, and during the hero's audience with King Minos, he recounts his most memorable adventures, which include his victory over the Amazons. According to him, however, their effectiveness as warriors should be attributed to their womanhood rather than to their demonstration of manly valor:

> . . .I believe
> that the conquest of a woman
> is the greatest victory;
> for how do you subdue
> an enemy who
> imprisons with her glance
> and fights with a sword at the same time?
> And even if she were not beautiful,
> it is enough that she is a woman, for being a woman
> is sufficient advantage;
> for besides her courage,
> my compassion and respect
> are on her side. (IV, 226)

While female warriors and other heroic women with similar characteristics were frequently portrayed in early Spanish American historical writings, Sor Juana's reference to the famous *viragos* in *Amor es más laberinto* is one of the few to be found in colonial drama. By the time the Spanish American theater had become secularized, the image of the woman as rugged and brave had lost much of its literary appeal, and the refined, courtly woman had taken its place. In Spain, however, elements of both of these idealized visions of womanhood were combined in the creation of the *mujer varonil* (manly woman). Her addition to the *dramatis personae* of Golden Age plays was a popular one, and she often represented New World women in the genre. This unusual female figure fulfilled all the requirements of the typical *dama*, but she possessed some outstanding trait or ability then demonstrated principally by men. This form of characterization is exemplified by Sor Juana's presentation of the Amazons as beautiful ladies[43] and reveals that she was influenced far more by the descriptions of women by Lope de Vega and Tirso de Molina than by those of Carvajal or Fernández de Oviedo.[44] She was also, no doubt, aware that realistic accounts of exceptional women would not be as well received by colonial audiences or attain the literary success of the *comedias*.

Although female characters appearing in seventeenth-century colonial drama usually represented the highest ideals of Spain's society, feminine satire is contained in several short dramatic works by Juan del Valle y Caviedes, whose poetry has already been examined. In his three brief skits, which resemble Spanish *bailes de oficios*, [45] he presents comic interpretations of the love he describes in his amorous verse and renews his attack on the courtly image of women found in lyric poetry and the *comedias* of the Golden Age.[46] Just as female characters do not appear in Llerena's sixteenth-century sketch, so too are they absent from Caviedes' pieces. His decision to limit the cast to men, however, was probably made to avoid offending actresses rather than out of hatred for the opposite sex as in the case of Llerena. Women's imperfections are disclosed indirectly through testimony by some of their admirers, and a whimsical framework detaches them from reality. The vision of women that Caviedes provides in these interludes reflects the critical approach of his satirical poetry directed at the *limeñas*, but its intensity has been greatly modified for their presentation before a mixed audience. Once again he pokes fun at women who are ugly, stupid, and old, and his tone becomes more disapproving when he refers to those who have debased love by commercializing it.[47]

In the first skit, *El amor alcalde [The Justice Love]*, Cupid poses as a judge who must determine the guilt or innocence of five male defendants accused of breaking love's laws. These men, who are now his prisoners, have all become enamored by their own design and not at the behest of the mischievous deity. Women have been banned from his jail because they are more interested in themselves and their own personal gain than in showing affection or concern for another individual.[48] The five females who are named as accomplices in the alleged crimes brought before Cupid's court become progressively more repugnant as the play advances. While the first three women possess physical or mental deficiencies, and the third suffers from both, the last two are immoral. The fourth woman continually demanded payment for her services, and the fifth robbed her client without delivering any of the agreed upon favors. The two men who succumbed to this low form of temptation have made a mockery of genuine emotion and deep sentiment, according to Caviedes, and therefore deserve the most severe penalties. The poet must have regarded any association with old crones as a particularly disgusting experience, since this is the punishment assigned to the prisoner who habitually put a price on love and is now destitute.

Caviedes briefly reiterates his belief that women have little regard for love and use it simply to suit their own purposes in the other two skits that compose his dramatic trilogy. The action of his *Bayle cantado del amor médico [Dance and Song of the Doctor Love]* centers around Amor as a doctor who diagnoses and prescribes treatment for five male patients afflicted by love. Although their lady friends have caused their condition, these men are distinguished by their particular symptoms and not by the types of women who attract them as in *El amor alcalde*. For this reason, criticism of women is a factor only in the case of the first patient, who, like the courtly lover, complains that he is burning with passion. Instead of recommending that he pursue his beloved no matter what the consequences, the physician advises him to put out the fire with the coldness of the lady's rejection. In the third skit, *Baile de el amor tahur [Dance of the Gambler Love]*, love is presented as a game of chance. At the beginning of the play, Amor provides a description of himself in which he warns those who are attracted to him. One piece of advice that he gives to participants is that fortunes are lost "by the placement of a single bet" (p. 332). The Spanish word "blanca" refers to the name of a commonly circulated coin in the colonies, but it may also be the nominalized adjective meaning white female. In Lima's racially conscious society this term was frequently applied to a fair-complexioned woman. Light-skinned women were most closely associated with the Spanish ideal of womanhood, and they were often thought to be responsible for the dwindling wealth of their suitors.

The theme of women and their romantic association with men was also used by several of Lima's dramatists who followed Caviedes in the eighteenth century. Women, however, do appear as characters in their works, and the purpose for including them in the cast is not always to criticize their behavior but to depict contemporary feminine customs and manners in an entertaining way. The ladies of Lima provide an element of local color in several short works by both Pedro Peralta Barnuevo, a Peruvian-born dramatist, and Jerónimo de Monforte y Vera, a Spanish resident of the viceroyalty. Their comic skits present women of varying ages and temperament who are either in love or who use love as a ploy to fulfill their selfish designs. *Criollas*, rather than Indian or Spanish women, are more frequently featured in these pieces, but their image has changed since González de Eslava's portrayal of them in his sixteenth-century colloquies. Time and circumstances now separated them from their Spanish heritage, and they, unlike the *indias* and the *mestizas*, were unencumbered by social or racial barriers. Although these dramatic characters still resemble their Spanish and Spanish American predecessors and may be used to reinforce or contradict previous imagery, they often represent specific New World types and embody a new freedom of movement and expression. The detachment of many Creole women from a traditionally overprotective environment and the relaxation of a number of strict social rules resulted in their changing attitudes and behavior and led to a transition away from Spanish stereotypes in these late works of the colonial theater.

In his *Entremés para la comedia La Rodoguna, [Interlude for the Play, La Rodoguna]*,[49] Peralta relates the amorous antics of four resourceful daughters who, together with their suitors, trick their father into approving of their casual relationships. Without prior parental consent and under the guise of practicing their trades, a sexton, a reading instructor, a peddler, and a dancing teacher visit the young *limeñas* in order to court them. Barely disguising their intentions with professional patter, the couples exchange expressions of love in the very presence of the girls' concerned father, Lorenzo. In answer to the dance master's lines comparing rhythmical movements to his own personal sentiments, Chanita replies:

> I will always be your most accomplished
> student of love,
> for seeing your gracefulness,
> you are making me
> leap with desire;
> and to see you nimbly dancing about,
> your light steps
> counterbalance my reluctance.[50]

Panchita as well is unpretentious in her declarations of affection and appears eager to proceed with the lovemaking. Addressing the peddler, she boldly directs him:

> Press your lips together
> because in exchange for your bundles
> you will have my embraces. (p. 239)

Although they are obviously infatuated by these young gentlemen and openly demonstrate their feelings for them, the girls are keenly aware that their conduct is questionable. As they congregate to evaluate the progress of their scheme, they express apprehension about their father's reaction. Lorenzo realizes what his headstrong daughters are up to, but he is aware also that reprimanding them would not be appropriate. Abandoning Old World conventions and perhaps any personal aspirations he may have had for his children, he yields to their wishes and welcomes the young gentlemen into his home. The skit concludes on a joyous note as Lorenzo sits down to enjoy the food and drink brought by the daughters' companions to celebrate the occasion. In this interlude, Peralta has portrayed contemporary Creole characters in a situation which reflects a new moral climate regarding love and courtship. He also parodies the patriarchal figure whose duty it is to protect his daughters and to assure their future by marrying them to well-to-do gentlemen from prominent families.[51] Peralta's portrayal of Lorenzo's daughters does not appear to be critical of the liberties taken by them but to demonstrate an awareness of the dramatic possibilities of their actions for use on the stage.

The portrayal of female characters in two of Peralta's other brief dramatic compositions, *Baile del Mercurio Galante [Dance of the Gallant Mercury]* and the *baile* included in his longer program of *Triunfos de amor y poder [Triumphs of Love and Power]* is notably less personal and precise than in the previous *entremés*. Due to his blending of fantasy and reality and his presentation of several nameless figures, these short works are somewhat removed from their colonial setting, although the characters have been drawn from Lima's society. The tone of the *bailes* also differs from that of his interlude in that it generally reflects the disapproval of women's conduct. In the *Baile del Mercurio Galante,* the mythological messenger of the gods, posing as a professor of mathematics at the University of San Marcos,[52] serves as the matchmaker for five young couples who seek his services. The superficial interviews that he conducts alternate between the sexes and are designed to uncover the negative character traits of each individual. By expressing their expectations in a mate, his clients reveal aspects of their own personalities as well.

Peralta's five female characters all share a significant flaw which is their view of marriage as a means of enhancing their own position in life. Although this complaint about the feminine gender is a common one, its manner of presentation is new because each woman expresses this as a goal in the skit and speaks with complete frankness about her situation. For example, the second woman, after introducing herself to Mercury, describes her obsession with material things using the same emotional and poetic vocabulary with which she might characterize a deeply meaningful human relationship:

> I am, flying divinity,
> a lady who has no other love
> than that of finery,
> for my only desire is my elegance.
> Lace is my passion,
> I flirt with lamé,
> I sigh for jewelry,
> and I pine for silver. (p. 199)

A similar fascination with wealth and a desire to maintain appearances are expressed by the fourth woman as she requests a matrimonial partner. Addressing Mercury, she asks for

> . . .a good sort
> who is rich, and a lover
> with a good body.   (p. 201)

While such portrayals of women reveal them to be exceedingly self-centered and often extravagant, Peralta's depiction of men is no less severe. All of the mortals of both sexes possess serious faults, and Mercury's task is to match the two people who have similar imperfections so that these negative traits may counterbalance each other and thus make for a harmonious union. The scheming woman is betrothed to the fraudulent gentleman from Quito, the greedy lady to the corrupt miner, the vain woman to the boastful man from Pisco, the foolish woman to the prissy fellow from Lima, and the woman who only wants men of the court is given in marriage to the crafty Spaniard.

While Peralta presents young women's views of love in *Baile del Mercurio Galante,* he divulges those of three female characters who represent various stages of a woman's life in the *baile* accompanying *Triunfos de amor y poder.* When they, together with four male figures, appeal to the boatman, Cupid, to permit them to board his vessel in order to enjoy the pleasures of true love, their speeches contain a systematic breakdown of the idealized images associated with the maiden, the married woman, and the widow. The young, unmarried woman is egotistical, overconfident, and vain and is, therefore, unable to comprehend the nature of such a delicate emotion as that of love. The deity is quick to see the drawbacks of having a person like this as a passenger and bluntly criticizes her before rejecting her completely. The request of the married woman is quite different from that of the single one, since she is seeking refuge from her husband. While Cupid states that he is not permitted to accept wives, his query concerning the status of her marriage leaves open the possibility for her to board and betrays the deviousness often attributed to his character. Although matrimony is supposed to be the ideal state for a woman, this *señora* complains adamantly about the incompatibility between her and her husband. When asked about how long the problem had existed, she abruptly responds with cynical candor:

> since my repentance,
> which was the first night,
> and the last one of desire. (p. 83)

Even the widow, who describes herself as a volcano "that shows off a headdress of snow / and hides a flame of love" (p. 83), indicates that being married is not always the perfect arrangement between a man and a woman. She too speaks out boldly concerning the relationship she had with her deceased spouse and expresses her intention of finding a new lover. While she is eager to enjoy a man's company again, she is not unhappy with her present situation and opposes a second marriage primarily for practical reasons:

> my status is the best
> in the world, because I have
> the freedom of a single girl,
> and the rights of a matron. (p. 83)

Her statement in this case appears to reflect the growing desire of women to have more independence in their lives but an unwillingness to sacrifice their respected social position to attain it. Widowhood, according to her, is the only way to achieve this easily. At the end of this short sketch, after each woman has presented her case, Cupid refuses to let any of them come aboard because he is afraid his boat will sink with so many opportunistic women.

Although the female faults exposed by Peralta in his *bailes* reflect former allegations against the opposite sex, they are unabashedly presented by the women themselves, and their testimony usually contains some insight into the cause of their particular condition. These female characters, like those of his *entremés* accompanying *La Rodogruna*, want to enjoy life and be free of the moral preoccupations expressed in sixteenth- and seventeenth-century colonial drama, and while he criticizes them, his tone is not condemnatory. Discourses on feminine virtue or the responsibilities of marriage are absent from his dramatic works, and he discloses the imperfections of men and women alike.

In Jerónimo Monforte y Vera's *El amor duende [The Ghost Love]*, Cupid again appears as the principal character, but this time he is a visitor to Lima in search of delinquent lovers. The *sainete's* most important prop is the opaque veil worn by the eighteenth-century *limeñas*, and its use creates the dramatic situation and the complications that follow. This garment was often criticized by contemporary satirists such as Terralla y Landa because of its ability to conceal a woman's identity while masking her misconduct. In this skit, however, the god of love uses it not only to deceive men but also to trick the *tapadas* themselves and to disclose what he believes to be the latter's true appearance and character. Amor, who assumes the guise of a farcical specter, and is, therefore, visible only to members of the audience, finds two cloaked women who are being pursued by a couple of young gallants out for a night on the town. Although both gentlemen have been warned about these notorious females, they are unable to resist the temptation of their veiled beauty. The ladies put up little resistence to their advances, since they look upon this encounter as an opportunity to fleece their victims. To thwart the intended mockery of love, Amor reveals the identity of one of the women, turns the men's gold into coal, and transforms both lovely *tapadas* into hideous figures. One becomes a duenna and the other a black woman. The elderly chaperon was despised as a symbol of traditional Spanish morality,[53] and blacks were viewed with suspicion because of superstitions associated with their color and their religious practices.[54] The turning point of the comedy occurs when the men discover that they have been duped. The *dueña*, who has no doubt aged considerably, still demands attention and favors from them, and the *negra* shocks one of the men so much that he is unable to contain his astonishment. Unveiling her, he exclaims:

> By God, what
> a dark night!
> (. . .) Bad nights are all that I have
> without my money and with your skin.

Although her color produces the dramatic effect that Monforte y Vera is seeking, he also attempts to emulate black diction in order to enhance his characterization of her.[55]

In addition to being an amusing sequence of events set in motion by the confusion over a piece of ladies' wearing apparel, Monforte y Vera's *El amor duende* outlines the social conditions regarding women during the latter part of the colonial period that were identified in other satirical works. Although his allusions to the effects of urbanization on women are made within a fantastic context, the fact that unaccompanied females were frequently seen out on city streets and that many were forced to make their living there by some illegal means is clear. The men who patronized them preferred Caucasian girls because of their conception of the ideal woman, and older and racially mixed women were customarily rejected. Playwrights in Peru such as Peralta and Monforte y Vera were not the only ones to reflect changes in the dramatic portrayal of women during the eighteenth century; those living in the viceroyalties of Río de la Plata and New Spain varied their female characters as well.

American themes and characters introduced into the Argentine theater of the 1700's reflect life in the provincial regions of southern South America. Women who appear in these plays range from brave pioneers to humorous rustics, and they are directly confronted by the remoteness and primitiveness of their natural surroundings. The contrast between these two distinct female types is indicative of the changing view of frontier women that had taken place after the conquest. In outlying areas of the empire, man's struggle against the Indians and the forces of nature was still being carried on, and courageous women of the past continued to draw the respect of male writers and provide role models for many female residents. Civilization was quickly encroaching upon this New World wilderness, nonetheless, and the appearance and behavior of women settlers soon became the subject of ridicule.

Lucía Miranda, the wife of the conqueror Sebastián Hurtado, is the heroine of the tragedy *Siripo* by Manuel de Lavardén. Unfortunately, no analysis of her portrayal can be made because the play has been lost; however, the fact that the playwright chose to focus on a Spanish woman's experiences among the Indians rather than those of a man makes this play an unusual one. According to Ruy Díaz de Guzmán's history of Argentina, the supposed source of the drama, Lucía Miranda accompanied her husband on a mission to explore the region surrounding the Paraná River and to establish a fort at Sancti Spiritu. When the settlement is attacked by Indians and destroyed, she is taken captive. During her captivity, she meets a young chief named Siripo, who falls in love with her. Although she constantly rejects him, he is not convinced that her refusal is final until her husband arrives, and the Indian leader sees the two of them together. In a fit of rage, he murders them both.[56]

From this brief resume of the play's action, it appears that Lavardén has captured the heroic spirit in the creation of his leading lady. *Siripo* is one of the few dramatic works in which a female character appears to have displayed the daring and fortitude of the female warrior types described in early colonial literature, although the development of the theme of love must have also influenced her characterization to some extent. Lucía Miranda upheld traditional societal values and conformed to the standards of feminine conduct of the first emigrants to Spanish America. As the wife of an army officer, she followed her husband into the wilds of the South American interior and was prepared to accept the consequences of this undertaking. She was determined to remain faithful to her spouse throughout her life and dies as a result of this commitment.

In a less serious vein, the *sainete, El amor de la estanciera [The Love of the Ranchwoman]* ascribed to another Argentine writer, Juan Bautista Maciel,[57] offers an amusing profile of two rural Argentine women amid preparations for a betrothal. Although a dilemma involving love and marriage might easily provide the situation for a Spanish *comedia*, this dramatic piece contrasts sharply with previous works of the Peninsular theater. Instead of noble ladies and gentlemen who play at the refined game of love, country bumpkins haggle over choosing a suitable husband for their daughter. According to tradition, the girl's father bears this responsibility; however, in the play, patriarchal authority is eroded by the women who protest his choice vehemently. Crude behavior and blunt language rather than courtly decorum characterize the performances of these two female characters who are portrayed as quite ordinary and often repugnant. In addition to mocking the image of the *dama*, the dramatist scoffs at the glorified vision of women of the countryside and the frontier.

Both Cancho and Pancha want to make the best possible arrangement for their daughter Chepa's future security and happiness, and they consider the social and economic status of her suitors to be the most important factor in their decision. Cancho has chosen Juancho, a neighboring rancher who owns considerable property, as his prospective son-in-law, but Pancha is impressed by the charm and breeding of a Portuguese merchant who is traveling in the area.[58] The tone of the couple's exchange reflects their uncivilized behavior, and their vulgarity and stridency contribute to the play's comedy.[59] Cancho treats his wife with little respect during their quarrel, and after upbraiding her as "an old loud mouth" (p. 99) who is stubborn and hellish, he even threatens her with violence if she does not obey him. Pancha appears undaunted by his remarks, however; and her retort reveals her dogged determination, volatile disposition, and capacity to equal him in name calling.

Chepa is much like her mother, and her forcefulness and independence lead her to defy her father. She is repelled by Juancho and repeatedly refers to him as a pig. Juancho, on the other hand, who professes his love for her, clearly admits that she is not his idea of the ideal woman. While talking to the other suitor, he confesses:

> There will be another ranchwoman
> with whom you could get married,
> one who is neater and has larger lips
> and who knows how to milk a cow. (p. 108)

After stating her preference for the salesman, Chepa changes her mind and decides to marry Juancho at the last minute thus breaking the stalemate between her parents. Later, when the Portuguese gentleman comes to call, he barely escapes being hung from the *ombú* tree outside the house and is forced to prepare an elaborate meal in honor of the betrothal. Pancha is the last to accept Juancho into the family, but she is finally persuaded by his gifts of meat and cheese.

The dramatist deliberately exaggerates both the actions and the dialogue of this *sainete*'s female characters in order to mock traditionally idealized visions of womanhood and to add humor to his dramatization. His assignment of such masculine traits as strength and boldness to these women is the basis for their derision, and their raucous behavior that parallels that of the men also betrays the naiveté and lack of refinement of Argentine countryfolk in general. Apart from his caricature of females, however, he records their response to changing times which is characteristic of Creole society. Chepa does not necessarily feel bound by the decisions of her elders, and Pancha, who initially hopes to add prestige and honor to her daughter's social standing through marriage, comes to the realization that a foreigner would not be welcome in their rural community. She, like Peralta's Lorenzo, reluctantly trades her ideals for the more practical and immediate needs of her family.

Although American women appeared more frequently in short dramatic works of the eighteenth century than they did in longer ones, they are not totally absent from colonial *comedias*. In *El apostolado en las Indias y martirio de un cacique [The Apostleship in the Indies and the Martyrdom of a Chief]*, written by New Spain's Eusebio Vela, two noble Indian women are portrayed as *damas*. These female characters, who are the wives of chief Axotencalt, play significant parts in the plot's development, which deals with the role of Fray Martín de Valencia in the conversion of the Indians in Mexico and the murder of the newly converted Indian boy, Cristóbal.[60] Symbolizing the forces of good and evil, the two women serve as catalysts of the action. Mihuazóchil, the loving and protective mother of Cristóbal, encourages him to attend Fray Martín de Valencia's school and to follow the Christian faith in defiance of her husband's wishes. She, like the mother of Christ, has brought her child up to be spiritually strong and sees him die as a result of his religious convictions. Xochipapalotl, motivated by jealousy because she wants her son to be the tribe's next leader, tells Axotencalt of Mihuazóchil's advice to Cristóbal. She knows this will anger him because he has already openly condemned the work of Christian missionaries among his people. When Cristóbal destroys several Indian idols and replaces them with the Virgin Mary's image, his father, the chief, becomes enraged, and at the insistence of the malevolent Xochipapalotl, kills the boy. According to historical accounts, Mihuazóchil was also murdered; however, in order to conform to conventions of the Golden Age *comedia*, Vela permits her to live and has the conqueror, Hernán Cortés, give her in marriage to the Indian nobleman, Iztlizúchil.[61] By becoming the only wife of another man, Mihuazóchil is then considered to be a Christian both in her beliefs and her practices. Polygamy among Indian chieftains was one of the major obstacles that the first friars encountered in their missionary work, and Vela alludes to it several times in his play.[62]

Although the tone of *El apostolado en las Indias* is generally serious, an episode involving an Indian *graciosa* (buffoon) named Malaguani contributes a comic element to the work. Communicating in broken Spanish, she tries to help a friar who claims that he is starving to death. When she finally understands what he wants, she brings him some stale *tamales*. He unwraps them and to his surprise finds a snake that bites him. The frightened friar then calls upon Fray Martín de Valencia to help him, but he ultimately considers this unpleasantness a just punishment for his lack of moderation.

Despite Vela's presentation of several Indian women involved in the conversion of New Spain's natives, Mihuazóchil, Xochipapalotl, and Malaguani, like the female characters in Sor Juana's *Los empeños*, have been patterned after idealized women from Spanish society. Even the historical facts of this true story have been changed by the dramatist in order to comply with the strict rules governing this Golden Age genre. Just as in earlier colonial dramas either written by churchmen or containing religious themes, some women are portrayed as succumbing to worldly temptations and causing man's destruction while others are recognized for their remarkable spirituality and their contribution to the conversion. Marriage is again presented as the most acceptable state for a woman, and a wife has important responsibilities to her family. Few native American women play significant roles in dramatic works after the evangelization of the Indians, and *El apostolado en las Indias y martirio de un cacique* is one of the rare exceptions.

In order to complete this study of the dramatic presentation of early Spanish American women, it is necessary to discuss several plays written in Spain during the sixteenth and seventeenth centuries. Peninsular playwrights were fascinated by the exceptional women portrayed in early colonial chronicles and epic poetry, and they cast them as principal characters in works of the Spanish Golden Age. Historical accuracy, just as in the characterizations of Sor Juana's Doña Leonor or Vela's Mihuazóchil, has been subordinated to artistic creation in order to follow the established guidelines which define the *comedia*. The female charracters portrayed in these works primarily follow the feminine ideal and are beautiful ladies with courtly customs and manners who become involved in various amorous entanglements. As a secondary characteristic, however, they demonstrate some trait that is generally associated with masculinity. In the case of the works to be considered in this section, *mujeres varoniles* are able leaders or warriors. Because of their leading roles, as well as their skillful portrayal, these women emerged as symbols of strength and independence who personify American adventure and conquest.

Fray Gaspar de Carvajal's account of Amazons on the South American continent, along with references to them in Ferdinand Magellan's diary and Gonzalo Fernández de Oviedo's history,[63] revived considerable interest in these ancient mythological women and inspired a number of plays by Spain's most outstanding dramatists. *Las justas de Tebas y reina de las amazonas, Las grandezas de Alejandro,* and *Las mujeres sin hombres*, written by Lope de Vega, all deal with this superior breed of women warriors who, it was thought, had established a stronghold in the New World. *Las mujeres sin hombres [Women without Men],* the best of the three works,[64] reveals the most about the existence of a matriarchal society and relates the inevitable consequences of the Amazons' extended contact with the outside world. Although these warring women were isolated from males and brought up to believe in their own self-sufficiency, they are, according to Lope, still attracted to men and subject to falling in love. The romantic rather than the military conquest of Queen Antiopía's legions provides the plot for the *comedia*. Theseus, Hercules, and Jason invade Amazon territory to subjugate it, but their hostile purpose is soon forgotten when they come face to face with its capable and beautiful leaders. The women, too, neglect their own defense as a result of this meeting with the illustrious warriors.

The lovely monarch and the attractive members of her court are awed by the heroic invaders, and their amazement stirs emotions of affection for the men and jealousy among themselves. Deyanira concludes that the exclusivity practiced by the Amazons is an unnatural state "Because life without men / Causes a thousand problems," and Menalipe senses a void in her life when she remarks: "A woman without a man / Is matter without form."[65] Even the *gracioso* Fineo, who had accompanied the invading army, questions their reasons for shunning men and concludes that they are demons without male companionship. When he hears that Theseus is betrothed to Antiopía, he pokes fun at one of their well-known customs and out of curiosity asks the prospective bridegroom:

> Ask her (after you are
> Married and relaxed),
> If they have the left tit,
> Which they say is cut off of
> The beautiful Amazons;
> Because I know of a woman
> Who has them hanging down to her waist. (p. 59)

In *Las mujeres sin hombres,* the Amazons are portrayed as capable rulers and fighters, but as Lope de Vega indicates in his dedication, they are not invincible precisely because of their own "naturaleza" or instinctive desire for love (p. 35). This, according to him, is a feminine trait common to all women, and lady warriors are no exception. While Lope demonstrates respect for their remarkable discipline, he comically chides them throughout the play. To resolve all differences among the characters and to conclude his *comedia* in the customary fashion, Lope joins Antiopía, Deyanira, and Menalipe in wedlock to Theseus, Hercules, and Jason.[66]

Amazons appear as secondary characters in part two of Tirso de Molina's Pizarro trilogy, *Las amazonas en las Indias [The Amazons in the Indies].* In this dramatic work, the Amazon queen and her sister meet and fall in love with Gonzalo Pizarro and his commander in chief, Francisco de Carvajal, who are exploring the interior of South America. As the two men are about to depart, the women plead with them to remain in their kingdom because they foresee the perils of civil conflict that lie ahead for Peru and the tragedy in store for the rebellious Spaniards.[67]

In addition to the Amazons, several female characters taken from Ercilla's *La Araucana* play prominent roles in Spanish Golden Age plays and are found in the dramatic works of Gaspar de Avila, Lope de Vega, and Ricardo de Turia.[68] Of the Spanish women mentioned in Ercilla's epic poem, Dona Mencía de Nidos is the most outstanding, and her courageous deeds during an Araucanian attack on Concepción are the subject of Turia's *comedia, La belígera española [The Belligerent Spanish Woman]*. In this *comedia*, Doña Mencía is portrayed as an unyielding leader and superb military strategist whose brave efforts win her the respect and recognition of Concepción's citizenry and also restore peace to the Chilean settlement.[69] She herself associates womanhood with weakness. Referring to an act of cowardice by an Indian warrior she says: "This confirms my first suspicion, / that that man was a woman."[70] Initially she denies her own emotions as a sign of femininity and rejects the love of her suitor, Don Pedro de Villagrán. By the end of the play, however, she is able to reconcile her deep affection for him with her power and position, and she does not regard her betrothal to him as an act of submission.[71] Another of Ercilla's characters, Lautaro's wife, Guacolda, is involved in the secondary plot of *La belígera española*. Although she is an Araucanian Indian woman, her portrayal follows that of the Spanish *dama*. She quarrels with Lautaro and, at one point, disguises herself as a Spaniard in order to escape him.[72] While their relationship is often stormy, her love and devotion for him are unquestionable, and she suffers greatly when he is killed in the last act of the play.[73]

The most unusual female figure to participate in the Spanish campaigns in the New World and then emerge as a literary character was Catalina de Erauso. Referred to as the nun ensign, she abandoned a convent in Spain as a young girl and in the early 1600's fled to America where she assumed the identity of a soldier. She drank, gambled, and fought her way across Peru and Chile, and only admitted her true sex when she was gravely wounded in a brawl in Guamanga. After her recovery, she decided to resume her religious duties because the military was closed to her, but she was granted special permission to remain dressed as a man by Pope Urban VIII.[74]

The New World exploits of Catalina de Erauso were widely known in Spain, and as a result of this popularity, her life became the subject of several Golden Age plays. The best dramatic work in which she is a major figure is Juan Pérez de Montalbán's *La monja alférez [The Nun Ensign]*.[75] Although the presentation of a lady in masculine attire was a common device of the Golden Age *comedia*, Catalina actually wanted to be a man and is regarded as a sex variant woman. Instead of portraying her as a *dama* with a multitude of manly characteristics, Montalbán introduces her as the gentleman, Guzmán. As a typical male character, she is romantically linked with Doña Ana, fights to preserve the lady's honor, and then escapes marriage when her femininity is revealed.

Montalbán employs both the expression of Guzmán's feelings about himself and the testimony of his companions to deny the existence of any womanly traits in his leading character's behavior. In the first act, Guzmán states clearly that his choice of a masculine pursuit was not one of personal preference but was his predetermined destiny (p. 154). When his secret is finally revealed, Guzmán openly declares his feelings about the inconsistency between his mind and his body and divulges his own self-hatred (pp. 259–60). The truth, that Guzmán is really a woman, is not easily accepted by his friends, who immediately recall his feats of courage and bravery. Even Catalina's brother is incredulous:

> How is it possible
> That such manly daring dwells
> In a woman's breast,
> If everyone who draws a sword
> In war and in peace attests,
> That fighting a duel
> Is the greatest act of courage? (pp. 186–87)

While Montalbán was aware of Catalina's uniqueness and includes one aspect of this in Guzmán's continual denial of femininity, he failed to portray her as the truly extraordinary figure she was in real life. By presenting Catalina as a stereotyped gentleman and by involving him in a fictitious love entanglement, the playwright placed more importance on following the conventions of the Golden Age theater than on exploring the dramatic possibilities of his central character. This lack of inspiration and originality in *La monja alférez*, together with the failure of any other contemporaries of Catalina to provide an adequate literary portrait of her, contributed to some extent to the relative obscurity of the adventuress after her death.

The dramatic portrayal of women who demonstrate behavioral patterns regarded as masculine by sixteenth- and seventeenth-century standards was popular during the Spanish Golden Age, and the appearance of Amazons, Doña Mencía de Nidos, and Catalina de Erauso as leading female characters indicates the importance of America in providing models for this theme. Because of the Spanish dramatists' concept of New World inhabitants and their demanding environment, these female characters are portrayed as leader-warrior types like their predecessors in early colonial literature. Although they were depicted in nonconventional roles, their womanliness is generally regarded as the essential part of their personality as required by the genre. The only exception to this, because of the well-known historical circumstances, is Catalina de Erauso, whose complete rejection of her sex left Montalbán no alternative but to cast her as a man.

The diverse views of womanhood expressed in the dramatic pieces considered in this chapter generally represent a continuance of those found in colonial prose and poetry. Positive images of women as warriors and as symbols of virtue and beauty generally appear in early Spanish American plays that follow the conventions of Spain's Golden Age theater. Although the *mujer varonil* associated with New World history and legend enjoyed considerable popularity in the Peninsula, dramatists in the colonies preferred to portray the idealized Spanish *dama*. Interest in heroic female types regarded as manly waned in Spanish America with its permanent settlement by the Spaniards although several examples of morally and spiritually strong women occur in eighteenth-century historical plays by Lavardén and Vela. From what is known about these characters, however, they do not demonstrate the vitality and ruggedness against the forces of nature that is characteristic of their precursors described in chronicles, and they, like Sor Juana's Amazons in *Amor es más laberinto*, resemble courtly figures rather than fearless individuals.

The favorable view of women presented in full-length colonial plays is counterbalanced by a critical, satirical one offered by numerous short theatrical works. Because many of the first dramas were written by churchmen or dealt with religious themes, the ecclesiastical attitude toward women as evil and inferior beings inevitably surfaced, and it influenced to some extent totally secular works which were to follow. Early *autos* and *coloquios* by Olmos, the author of *La caída de Adán y Eva,* and González de Eslava were all designed to dictate the conduct and morality of women and to dramatize their obligations as Christians. The manner in which these men held women responsible for their troubled world ranged considerably from inferences of wrongdoing to bold accusations of moral turpitude, and the consequences of their alleged malfeasance varied in gravity from the failure of a marriage to the collapse of the empire. Women continued to be satirized in later skits by laymen such as Caviedes, Peralta, Monforte y Vera, and Maciel, but their characterizations deviate from those in other forms of satire. Although these works echo the age-old complaints about women, greed and vanity rather than sexual excesses are stressed, and their tone is noticeably less harsh to enable them to be performed in public.

In addition to reflecting previous visions of womanhood, colonial drama reveals changes in the attitude toward women and in their portrayal as Spanish American society emerged from the conquest and conversion and gradually approached revolution. During the first one hundred years of Spain's presence in the New World, the Church controlled the development of the theater, and the dramatization of the relationship between the sexes in catechistic plays was often presented for the edification of women. Complications arising from love, courtship, and marriage continued to provide plots for colonial works even after the secularization of drama, but they proved to be a great source of entertainment and humor for generally sophisticated audiences rather than a means of indoctrination for native females. The austere moral climate and grave preoccupation with women's behavior that the Spaniards brought with them to the New World lessens measurably as the colonial period draws to a close, and matters of morality become more of a human concern to be approached with openness and frankness.

While Indian women were generally the focus of the earliest works written and performed in the Indies, their portrayal became less important as they were assimilated into Spanish American society. After the sixteenth century, *indias* only occasionally appear in plays, and then, as in Vela's *comedia, El apostolado en las Indias y martirio de un cacique*, they seem to be Spanish women with Indian names. Although native American females failed to maintain their popularity as dramatic subjects in colonial works, they continued to intrigue Spanish playwrights throughout the Golden Age. However, just as in their portrayal in colonial *comedias*, they retain few of their racial characteristics and little of their cultural heritage.

Because of economic and political circumstances created in the colonies by Spain's rule, the Creole element of society had forged its own identity and had become a formidable force within Spanish America during the seventeenth and eighteenth centuries. The emergence of this social sector is reflected to some degree in the theater as *criollas* received more recognition than ever before both as writers and as literary characters. Sor Juana Inés de la Cruz demonstrated her extraordinary artistic talent and skill in a wide range of plays and skits performed in the late 1600's, and although her female characters generally followed idealized Spanish women, Doña Leonor of *Los empeños de una casa* divulges the plight of a female intellectual in the colonies. Dramas by the Mexican nun provide a view of some of the first female characters created by a woman writer and a rare opportunity to observe her own reaction to the masculine concept of femininity. Her cleverly concealed criticism of literary trends and social customs regarding women was not meant to be a proclamation of women's rights, but it does portend a stronger statement of her feminism in her letter to the Bishop of Puebla. Shortly after Sor Juana's death, Creole women returned to the stage after a one-hundred-year hiatus, but they exhibited an unprecedented independence from both literary and social tradition. The *criolla* of the eighteenth century contrasted sharply with the overprotected daughters and granddaughters of conquerors who appeared in González de Eslava's sixteenth-century colloquies and with the aristocratic Creole woman whose standardized description appears throughout colonial lyric poetry. Regionalist influences led colonial dramatists such as Peralta, Monforte y Vera, and Maciel to avoid established models like Eve, the Celestina, and the *dama* and to introduce a unique literary figure into the theater that typified a society in flux. The growing awareness of their immediate surroundings expressed by such innovations displays a new consciousness germinating among American writers and serves not only as a preliminary step toward their artistic emancipation from Spain but also as a prelude to their search for truly American types to be portrayed in literature.

Notes

1. The secularization of drama increased opportunities for women to participate in the theater's development. By 1594, María Rodríguez and her husband, Francisco Morales, were managing a *corral de comedias* (playhouse) in Lima, and in 1599, the actress Isabel de los Angeles arrived there with the first

Spanish theater company. The period's most famous star was Micaela Villegas, better known as La Perricholi, who rose to prominence during the second half of the eighteenth century and continued to entertain Lima's audiences into the early 1800's. Although she enjoyed a long and prosperous career as the theater's leading lady, she is equally well known for the scandal she caused as the mistress of the Viceroy Manuel de Amat. Mérimée's *Carrosse du Saint Sacrément,* Offenbach's *La Perricholi,* and Wilder's *The Bridge of San Luis Rey* are all based on her life. Guillermo Lohmann Villena, *El arte dramático en Lima durante el virreinato* (Madrid: Estades, Artes Gráficas, 1945), p. 68. A.S.W. Rosenbach, "The First Theatrical Company in America," in *Proceedings of the American Antiquarian Society* (Worcester, Mass.: Published by the Society, 1939), XLVIII, ii, 303-5. Willis Knapp Jones, "Women in the Early Spanish American Theater," *Latin American Theater Review* 4, no. 1 (1970), pp. 29–30.

Women also engaged in puppetry. America's first female puppeteer, Leonor de Goromar, put on performances in Lima during the late seventeenth century. Paul McPharlin, *The Puppet Theater in America* (Boston: Plays, 1969), p. 7.

Ladies frequently attended the theater during the colonial period, and their presence there became a matter of concern for both church and state officials. With the women's welfare in mind, restrictions were announced in parts of the colonies regarding the content of the plays, the hours of presentation, and the seating arrangement within the theater. One of the most comprehensive documents regulating the operation of a theater was the 1783 *Instrucción [Order]* issued by the Viceroy of Río de la Plata, Juan José de Vértiz y Salcedo. These rules, devised for La Ranchería theater in Buenos Aires, reveal the code of conduct expected of women and certain precautionary measures taken for their protection. The members of the audience were separated according to their sex, social standing, and dress. Order was maintained both in and around the building by a number of guards, and particular care was taken for the safety of women. Actresses were obligated to appear in respectable attire and were forbidden to dress like a man except above the waist. José Torre Revello, "El teatro en la colonia," *Humanidades* 23 (1933), pp. 161–65.

2. Sor Juana is considered to be second only to Juan Ruiz de Alarcón who, although he was born in Mexico, spent much of his life in Spain and wrote his dramatic works there.

3. J. Luis Trenti Rocamora, *El teatro en la América colonial* (Buenos Aires: Editorial Huarpes, 1947), pp. 298–303.

4. Irving A. Leonard, "A Shipment of *Comedias* to the Indies," *Hispanic Review* 3, no. 1 (1934), p. 42. Lohmann Villena, *El arte dramático en Lima,* pp. 387–90.

5. Arnold G. Reichenberger, "The Uniqueness of the *Comedia,*" *Hispanic Review* 27, no. 3 (1959), pp. 304–5.

6. Otis H. Green, *Spain and the Western Tradition*, 4 vols. (Madison, Wisc.: University of Wisconsin Press, 1963), I, 236.

7. Sor Juana was not the only woman to write dramatic works. During the seventeenth century, the *limeña* Ana Morillo is also reported to have been an "autora de comedias" (playwright). Although nothing is known of her works, she may have been, according to Irving A. Leonard, the American admirer "Amarilis" who wrote a laudatory poem to Lope de Vega. This exceptional work, "Epístola a Belardo" ["Epistle to Belardo"], was published in 1621 along with Lope's reply. Irving A. Leonard, "More Conjectures Regarding the Identity of Lope de Vega's 'Amarilis Indiana'," *Hispania* 20, no. 2 (1937), pp. 113–20. In the eighteenth century, short religious pieces were written by the Peruvian nun, Josefa Francisca de Azaña y Llano. Lohmann Villena describes her *loa* (dramatic poem) about convent life as a brief piece whose style is fresh and open. She also wrote *Coloquio a la Natividad del Señor*. Lohmann Villena, *El arte dramático en Lima*, p. 428.

8. Anthony M. Pasquariello, "Two Eighteenth-Century Peruvian Interludes, Pioneer Pieces in Local Color," *Symposium* 6 (1952), pp. 386–87.

9. José Rojas Garcidueñas lists *El fin del mundo [The End of the World]*, a play presented in Santiago Tlaltelolco in 1533, as the first dramatic presentation performed in an Indian language. According to him, the work was anonymous. José Rojas Garcidueñas, "Piezas teatrales y representaciones en Nueva España en el siglo XVI," *Revista de literatura mexicana* 1, no. 1 (1940), p. 148.

10. Angel María Garibay K., *Historia de la literatura nahuatl* (México, D.F.: Editorial Porrúa, 1971), II, 131–32. Manuscripts of *El Juicio Final* or *El Juicio Universal* are in the Library of Congress in Washington and the Academy of History in Madrid.

11. Vern L. Bullough, *The Subordinate Sex: A History of Attitudes toward Women* (Urbana, Ill.: University of Illinois Press, 1973), pp. 119–20.

12. Willis Knapp Jones, *Behind Spanish American Footlights* (Austin, Tex.: University of Texas Press, 1966), p. 19.

13. Although women played traditional religious roles in the earliest performances, the characters themselves soon became Americanized. In the sixteenth-century *Desposorio espiritual entre el pastor Pedro y la Iglesia Mexicana [Spiritual Marriage between the Shepherd Peter and the Mexican Church]* by Juan Pérez Ramírez, the shepherdess Menga portrays the Mexican Church, and in Lima, the Coliseo Imponente put on a play shortly after its opening in 1662 based on the life of Santa Rosa de Lima. José Juan Arrom, *El teatro de Hispanoamérica en la época colonial* (Havana: Talleres de Ucar, García, 1956), p. 63. Jones, *Behind Spanish American Footlights*, p. 255.

14. While performances of this Spanish play were probably held in various areas of the Caribbean and the North American mainland, the first documented presentation of it took place in Mexico in 1526. According to Jones, an all-

female cast was often used to convey the purity of Christ's birth. However, all-male casts, as well, performed this piece, and even Gila was portrayed by a boy. Jones, *Behind Spanish American Footlights,* pp. 460–61. One of the modern versions of this play appears in both English and Spanish in *Memoirs of the American Folklore Society.* "*Los pastores,* a Mexican Play of the Nativity," trans. M. R. Cole in *Memoirs of the American Folklore Society* (Boston and New York: Houghton Mifflin and Company, 1907), IX, 1–175. See also Stanley L. Robe, ed., *Coloquios de pastores from Jalisco, México* (Berkeley and Los Angeles: University of California Press, 1954), pp. 4–11.

15. Fray Toribio de Benavente (Motolinía), *Historia de los indios de la Nueva España* (México, D.F.: Editorial Porrúa, 1969), p. 61. References to Motolinía's history have been taken from this edition and cited in the text of the chapter. For the English translation of his work, see *Motolinía's History of the Indians of New Spain,* trans. and ed. Elizabeth Andros Foster (Westport, Conn.: Greenwood Press, 1973), pp. 107–9.

16. Katherine M. Rogers, *The Troublesome Helpmate, A History of Misogyny in Literature* (Seattle, Wash.: University of Washington Press, 1966), pp. 3–7.

17. Alfonso Méndez Plancarte, *Poetas novohispanos, primer siglo (1521–1621),* 3 vols. (México, D.F.: Imprenta de la Universidad Nacional Autónoma de México, 1964), I, xviii.

18. Although the theater separated itself from the Church, the performance of works with religious themes continued throughout the entire colonial period.

19. Fernán González de Eslava, *Coloquios espirituales y sacramentales,* 2 vols. (México, D.F.: Editorial Porrúa, 1976), I, 228. Notations appearing in the text have been taken from this edition.

20. Francisco Santamaría defines *huipil,* which comes from the Nahuatl word *huipilli,* as a sleeveless cotton shirt worn by Aztec women. The garment was usually long and loose fitting and was elaborately embroidered. Francisco J. Santamaría, *Diccionario general de americanismos,* 3 vols. (México, D.F.: Editorial Pedro Robredo, 1942), II, 109. A description of this popular article of clothing is found in Motolinía's history, and Alonso Carrió de la Vandera reports in his journal that it was still worn by Mexican *mestizas* in the late eighteenth century. Toribio de Benavente, *Historia,* p. 182; Alonso Carrió de la Vandera ("Concolorcorvo"), *El lazarillo de ciegos caminantes* (Barcelona: Editorial Labor, 1973), pp. 451–52.

21. In her study *Lo cómico en el teatro de Fernán González de Eslava,* Frida Weber de Kurlat notes the dramatist's repetition of a marital dispute as a comic technique and cites this as an example of the low regard he expresses for women. She further documents this conclusion by quoting other instances from colloquies III, V, and XIV (I, 77, 159; II, 148) in which female characters receive prejudicial treatment. Frida Weber de Kurlat, *Lo cómico en el teatro de Fernán*

González de Eslava (Buenos Aires: La Imprenta de la Universidad de Buenos Aires, 1963), p. 217.

22. Julie Greer Johnson, "Three Celestinesque Figures of Colonial Spanish American Literature," *Celestinesca* 5, no. 1 (1981), pp. 42–43.

23. The cause of Ocasión's breach with her husband is attributed to the local busybody, Doña Chisme (Lady Gossip). She does not appear in the *coloquio* but is described by Ocasión as

> . . . my neighbor
> who has composed a thousand lies
> with her slanderous tongue. (II, 257)

24. Witchcraft was widely practiced among the Indians as Ocasión's recounting attests: "Another one thousand Indian women gave me herbs, ointments, and potions" (II, 258).

Motolinía also mentions the appearance of witches and the influence they had over some women in a play about Saint Francis: "Then the saint went on again with his sermon and there came some witches, very cleverly imitated, of the kind who with their native drugs very easily produce abortions." Toribio de Benavente, *Historia,* p. 74. Toribio de Benavente, *Motolinía's History,* p. 119.

25. Doña Murmuración appears as a character throughout *Coloquio XVI;* however, the previously cited passage provides the clearest example of Rojas' influence upon her. On page 217, she makes her first speech and mentions her ties to the underworld.

According to Frida Weber de Kurlat, the influence of *La Celestina* extends into González de Eslava's other *coloquios* as well and may be seen in his combination of serious and comic elements, his use of certain situations, and his presentation of several secondary characters. Weber de Kurlat, pp. 163–64, 171, 217–18.

26. Fernando de Rojas, *La Celestina,* ed. Bruno Mario Damiani (Madrid: Cátedra, 1976), p. 77. Fernando de Rojas, *The Celestina,* trans. Lesley Byrd Simpson (Berkeley and Los Angeles: University of California Press, 1955), p. 19.

27. Arrom, *El teatro de Hispanoamérica,* p. 64.

28. Francisco A. de Icaza, "Cristóbal de Llerena y los orígenes del teatro en la América española," *Revista de Filología Española* 8, no. 2 (1921), pp. 121–30. The author reprints the interlude in his article. Page numbers within the text refer to this reproduction.

29. Anthony M. Pasquariello, "The *Entremés* in Sixteenth-Century Spanish America," *Hispanic American Historical Review* 32, no. 1 (1952), pp. 55–57.

30. In her study of American elements in Sor Juana's plays, María Esther Pérez comments on the feminine perspective which the Mexican nun brings to

the opening scenes of her drama and contrasts the focus and the development of the action to those of Calderón's work. María Esther Pérez, *Lo americano en el teatro de Sor Juana Inés de la Cruz* (New York: Eliseo Torres and Sons, 1975), pp. 73–74.

31. Sor Juana Inés de la Cruz, *Obras completas*, 4 vols. eds. Alfonso Méndez Plancarte and Alberto G. Salceda (México, D.F.: Fondo de Cultura Económica, 1957), IV, 58. Other references to this edition have been included in the text.

32. Ezequiel A. Chávez, *Ensayo de psicología de Sor Juana Inés de la Cruz* (México, D.F.: Asociación "Ezequiel A. Chávez," 1970), pp. 204, 208. The character of Leonor may have been named for the vicereine, Doña Leonor de Carreto, who invited Sor Juana to be her lady-in-waiting at court. However, the *dama* in Calderón's *Los empeños de un acaso* is also named Leonor.

33. Her best known portrait was painted by Miguel Cabrera during the mid-1700's and hangs in the Museo de la Ciudad de México. Chávez, *Ensayo de psicología de Sor Juana*, p. 81.

34. A discussion of this letter is contained in chapter 5. See also Sor Juana's *Respuesta* in her *Obras completas* (IV, 440–75).

35. In his book, *Baroque Times in Old Mexico*, Leonard notes Sor Juana's comeliness, which adds an element of mystery to her personality. Irving A. Leonard, *Baroque Times in Old Mexico* (Ann Arbor, Mich.: University of Michigan Press, 1966), p. 173.

36. See Sor Juana's *Obras completas* (IV, 445) for the discussion of her "inclination" in the *Respuesta*.

37. Sor Juana's resentment of the superficiality of court life is succinctly reiterated in the intermezzo, *Sainete primero, De palacio [The First Skit about the Palace]*, which is part of the *comedia's* larger dramatic program. Anthony M. Pasquariello, "The Seventeenth-Century Interlude in the New World Secular Theater," in *Homage to Irving A. Leonard*, eds. Raquel Chang-Rodríguez and Donald A. Yates (East Lansing, Mich.: Latin American Studies Center of Michigan State University, 1977), p. 107.

38. Sor Juana mentions her reasons for entering a convent in her *Respuesta* (IV, 444–45).

39. Melveena McKendrick, *Woman and Society in the Spanish Drama of the Golden Age* (Cambridge: Cambridge University Press, 1974), p. 44.

40. Raquel Chang-Rodríguez, "Relectura de *Los empeños de una casa*," *Revista Iberoamericana* 44, nos. 104–5 (1978), pp. 414–15.

41. Chávez, *Ensayo de psicología de Sor Juana*, p. 211.

42. The first and third acts of the play were written by Sor Juana. Licenciado Juan de Guevara wrote the intervening one.

43. Gerald Flynn, *Sor Juana Inés de la Cruz* (New York: Twayne Publishers, 1971), pp. 49–51.

44. Lope's *Las mujeres sin hombres* and Tirso's *Las amazonas en las Indias* are discussed briefly at the conclusion of this chapter.

45. A *baile de oficio* is a musical dramatization in which a comic figure poses as a professional and receives clients who are in need of his services. Pasquariello, "The Seventeenth-Century Interlude," p. 109.

46. Julie Greer Johnson, "Three Dramatic Works by Juan del Valle y Caviedes," *Hispanic Journal* 3, no. 1 (1982), pp. 59–71.

47. Glen L. Kolb, *Juan del Valle y Caviedes: A Study of the Life, Times and Poetry of a Spanish Colonial Satirist* (New London, Conn.: Stonington Publishing Company, 1959), p. 34.

48. Rubén Vargas Ugarte, ed. *Obras de Don Juan del Valle y Caviedes* (Lima: Talleres Gráficos de la Tipografía Peruana, 1947), p. 323. References taken from this edition are noted in the text.

49. This *comedia* is based on Corneille's *Rodogune* in which a mother and daughter plot to kill each other. Another of Peralta's plays dealing with women, which also imitates a French work, is the finale of his *Afectos vencen finezas*. This short piece is quite similar to a portion of Molière's *Les femmes savantes*. Irving A. Leonard, "A Great Savant of Colonial Peru: Don Pedro de Peralta," *Philological Quarterly* 12, no. 1 (1933), p. 69.

50. Pedro de Peralta Barnuevo, *Obras dramáticas* (Santiago, Chile: Imprenta Universitaria, 1937), p. 240. Other references to this edition of Peralta Barnuevo's dramatic works appear in the text.

51. Pasquariello, "Two Eighteenth-Century Peruvian Interludes," p. 388.

52. Arrom, *El teatro de Hispanoamérica*, p. 149.

53. Regarded as an improper guardian of women, the duenna was also berated in Spanish literature, and Quevedo's portrait of Dueña Quintañona in "El sueño de la muerte" exemplifies this. Francisco de Quevedo y Villegas, *Obras completas*, 2 vols. (Madrid: Aguilar, 1958), I, 189–90.

54. Two blacks, for example, attempt to attack Glaura in *La Araucana,* and the black woman, Juana García, dabbles in witchcraft in *El carnero*. Alonso de Ercilla, *La Araucana* (México, D.F.: Editorial Porrúa, 1977), XXVIII, 391. Juan Rodríguez Freile, *El carnero* (Bogotá: Imprenta Nacional, 1963), pp. 132–39.

55. Lohmann Villena, *El arte dramático en Lima*, pp. 552–53. Pasquariello, "Two Eighteenth-Century Peruvian Interludes," p. 389.

56. Mariano Bosch, *Manuel de Lavardén, poeta y filósofo* (Buenos Aires: Los Talleres Gráficos de Guillermo Kraft, 1944), pp. 84–85. Ruy Díaz de Guzmán, *La Argentina* (Buenos Aires: Espasa-Calpe Argentina, 1945), pp. 55–61. This history also contains the novelistic episode of the Spanish woman called La Maldonada. She, like the biblical figure Daniel, aided a lion in pain and was later spared by the same lion when she was condemned to be thrown into a den of wild animals. Díaz de Guzmán, pp. 76–77, 81–82.

57. Arrom, *El teatro de Hispanoamérica*, p. 208.

58. Mariano Bosch, *Teatro antiguo de Buenos Aires* (Buenos Aires: Imprenta

El Comercio, 1904), p. 100. Other references to this work appear in the chapter proper.

59. In an effort to duplicate the language of country people, the author has included many crude expressions for authenticity as well as comic effect. Because of this coarseness, women usually left the theater before the interlude began, according to Bosch (p. 107). It is also his reason for presenting an abridged version of the work in his *Teatro antiguo*.

60. Motolinía tells this tragic story in chapter 14 of his history's third part.

61. Jefferson Rea Spell, "Three Manuscript Plays by Eusebio Vela," *Revista de Estudios Hispánicos* 1, no. 3 (1928), p. 272.

62. Jefferson Rea Spell and Francisco Monterde, *Tres comedias de Eusebio Vela* (México, D. F.: Imprenta Universitaria, 1948), pp. 6, 30, 49. The conversion of the Indians theoretically brought with it an end to their polygamous society. However, many chieftains were reluctant to disband their harems. Some of these chiefs had as many as two hundred wives, according to Motolinía, and these women contributed significantly to the economic well-being of their husbands by selling and trading their handicraft. The Franciscan cites some of the difficulties he and his companions encountered and charges that the number of illicit relationships carried on by the Spaniards added to their problems. Toribio de Benavente, *Historia,* p. 263.

63. Irving A. Leonard, *Books of the Brave* (New York: Gordian Press, 1964), p. 36.

64. McKendrick, *Woman and Society*, pp. 174–75.

65. Félix Lope de Vega, *Obras de Lope de Vega* (Madrid: Establecimiento Tipográfico "Sucesores de Rivadeneyra," 1896), p. 54. Other references to this edition are noted in the text.

66. McKendrick, *Woman and Society*, pp. 182–83.

67. Otis H. Green, "Notes on the Pizarro Trilogy of Tirso de Molina," *Hispanic Review* 4, no. 3 (1936), pp. 207–18. Women warriors also appear in *Las amazonas de Escitia* by Antonio de Solís, and another member of the Pizarro family, Francisco Pizarro, plays a leading role in Luis Vélez de Guevara's *Las palabras a los reyes y gloria de los Pizarros.* In the latter work, the Indian *cacica*, Tucapela, falls in love with the conqueror but tries to kill him. McKendrick, *Woman and Society*, pp. 176, 187.

68. In his prologue to *Dos comedias famosas y un auto sacramental*, José Toribio Medina discusses the appearance of Chilean historical figures in works of the Spanish theater and reprints the dramas to which he refers. The Indian women, Guacolda and Fresa, are included in the cast of Gaspar de Avila's *El gobernante prudente,* Fidelfa and Glitelda appear as *indias* in Lope's *auto, La Araucana,* and the last play is *La belígera española.* José Toribio Medina, *Dos comedias famosas y un auto sacramental* (Santiago-Valparaiso, Chile: Sociedad Imprenta-Litografía "Barcelona," 1915).

69. Ercilla's description of Doña Mencía is quite short and considerably different. Although he portrays her as a spirited woman, she is not the beautiful, physically strong person she is in *La belígera española*. Ercilla, VII, 102–4.

70. Medina, *Dos comedias famosas*, p. 218.

71. McKendrick, *Woman and Society*, pp. 163–64. Pedro de Villagrán is also a character in Ercilla's *La Araucana*; however, the poet never links him romantically with Doña Mencía.

72. This is a frequent device used by Golden Age dramatists. See Carmen Bravo-Villasante, *La mujer vestida de hombre en el teatro español* (Madrid: Artes Gráficas Clavileño, 1955) and B. B. Ashcom, ''Concerning 'La mujer en hábito de hombre' in the *Comedia*,'' *Hispanic Review* 28 (1960), pp. 45–62.

73. See Ercilla, XIII, 194–96.

74. Jeannette H. Foster, *Sex Variant Women in Literature* (London: Fredrick Muller, 1958), pp. 41–43. See also James Fitzmaurice-Kelly, *The Nun Ensign* (London: T. Fisher Unwin, 1908), pp. xvi-xxv, and Catalina's alleged autobiography. Catalina de Erauso, *Historia de la Monja Alférez Doña Catalina de Erauso, escrita por ella misma* (Paris: Impr. de Julio Didot, 1829).

75. Fitzmaurice-Kelly reprints Montalbán's play in his book, *The Nun Ensign*. Other references to this work appear in the text.

CHAPTER 5

THE FEMININE PERSPECTIVE

Because men dominated the writing of both history and literature, the image of women during the colonial period is largely based upon their vision. Illiteracy impeded the vast majority of the New World's females from documenting their daily lives and from recording personal feelings and responses to the quality of their existence. Those who possessed the requisite skill and talent were generally not encouraged to develop them, and a literary career was an unrealistic and an almost impossible goal for a woman. Sor Juana Inés de la Cruz and Madre Francisca Castillo, however, both of whom wrote literary works containing autobiographical elements, were able to overcome these obstacles, although their advancements in what was regarded as a male discipline were not unopposed.[1] Their presentation of themselves contributes significantly to existing information about women in colonial Spanish America and also reveals the influence that society's previously held images of womanhood had upon their lives. Although the perspective of these two women writers is different from that of the men, their perception of the colonial woman, like the masculine vision, is actually quite restricted. Literate Spanish American women were usually upper-class Creoles and members of religious orders, and this viewpoint is reflected in the writings of the Mexican nun and the Colombian prioress.

During the colonial period, women, especially those from aristocratic families, continually found themselves in a sheltered atmosphere and under the protection of some male authoritative figure. Domesticity was regarded as their most outstanding attribute, and the home and family, it was thought, delineated a woman's area of interest as well as her ability. Ironically, the Church, whose approach toward women was undoubtedly repressive, offered an alternative to both married and single women who wanted to escape the rigid pattern of secular society. Charity work relieved the tedium of traditional duties and brought fulfillment and satisfaction to many, and the convent provided a more permanent place of refuge for others. Becoming a member of a religious community was viewed as the only socially acceptable option for girls who did not wish to marry or who were unable to, and its isolation, organization, and resources were crucial to the intellectual development of women in colonial Spanish America. Nunneries were relatively free from male domination as well as outside social pressures, and the daily routine permitted time for reading and study in institutional libraries and archives. The colonial convent became an enclave for educated women, and virtually all information about Spanish America's female population written from a feminine point of view may be traced to the confines of its walls.

Although women living in the colonies who were members of religious orders enjoyed a degree of freedom denied to those who remained in secular society, they were also acutely aware of the Church's male orientation and the misogynic tendencies of its clergy. By taking their vows, they were forced to reconcile themselves to both of these factors and to resign themselves to the fact that these traditions were unlikely to change. Some nuns did so reluctantly and with considerable anger, and others simply accepted the role and image of womanhood assigned to them and endeavored to make amends for the past and to establish themselves as paragons of spirituality. For all of these women, however, who sought to live in harmony with the Church yet maintain a measure of individualism, Saint Teresa of Jesus, Spain's most famous female religious figure, provided the perfect role model. She was greatly admired in the viceroyalties, and her accomplishments touched the lives of Sor Juana, whose dramas have already been examined, and Madre Castillo, whose importance to colonial literature would not be recognized until after her death. During the sixteenth century, Saint Teresa reformed the Carmelite Order and established the Discalced branch of the community. Vitality was injected into its organization under her direction, and its network of convents was extended at her insistence. As a result of her intense religious experiences, she also changed the orientation of the society toward mysticism.[2] Both of Saint Teresa's exceptional New World disciples aspired to become members of the Discalced Carmelite sisterhood but were unable to join because of its rigorous requirements.

The dynamism of Saint Teresa inspired Sor Juana to achieve a greatness not previously attained by a woman in the colonies, although she channeled her talents in a different direction from that of the nun from Avila.[3] During the latter part of the seventeenth century, she was consciously forging a new image for a Spanish American woman that was not simply that of a learned woman but one of a truly outstanding intellectual of her time. The Church, suspicious of her motives, challenged this initiative, however, and ultimately forced her to abandon her dreams of a better destiny for women. God, she felt, should be the only one to judge her worthiness as a nun, and she found the task of defending herself to the Bishop of Puebla belittling and humiliating. Her resentment and bitterness are concealed to some degree by the baroque intricacies of her writings, but her stubborn resistance to limiting her role in life to that of an ordinary nun is quite clear. Madre Castillo, on the other hand, was attracted to the contemplative side of Saint Teresa's life, and she sought to emulate her spirituality and her introspection. At the behest of her confessor, Father Francisco de Herrera, she wrote accounts of her existence using the works of the Spanish mystic as literary models. Saint Teresa's influence upon her writing, however, was not limited to style alone but also affected her interpretation and presentation of her childhood, conventual experiences, and visions.[4] Madre Castillo hoped to follow in the footsteps of the canonized nun, and the fulfillment of her vows was paramount to her achievement of a perfect union with God.

The many works of Juana Inés de Asbaje y Ramírez de Santillana, which encompass all genres represented during the colonial period, received immediate acclaim from Mexico's cultural elite and circulated widely throughout the Spanish empire during her lifetime. One of the earliest and most sincere tributes to the Tenth Muse, as she was known among her contemporaries, is that of her close friend, Don Carlos Sigüenza y Góngora. In his *Teatro de virtudes políticas [Theater of Political Virtues]*, he praises her for her accomplishments and foresees the importance she will attain:

There is no pen that can rise to the eminence of hers, . . . I would like to overlook the appreciation I feel for her, the veneration that she has earned with her works, in order to let the world know how much is stored in her genius in terms of the comprehensiveness of her knowledge and the universality of her literary production, so that it might be known that in one single individual, Mexico enjoys what was divided by the Graces in past centuries among the many learned women who are the great wonders of history.

He closes his appraisal of her contributions to New Spain's culture by saying, "we should applaud the excellent works of the rare talent of Mother Juana Inés de la Cruz, whose fame and name will end only with the world."[5]

In spite of her renown, Sor Juana remained a very private person, and what little is known about her personal life is disclosed mostly in her own works. While aspects of her complex personality are evident in her theater and poetry, her *Respuesta a Sor Filotea de la Cruz [Reply to Sister Philotea of the Cross]*, a prose work described by Amado Nervo as "an extremely valuable document by all standards, in which we see her life and her great spirit through the most translucent and beautiful crystal,"[6] offers the clearest and most complete portrait of this enigmatic woman. Her *Respuesta* was written in response to a letter sent to her by the Bishop of Puebla, Don Manuel Fernández de Santa Cruz. His communication, dated November 25, 1690, regarded her eloquent and erudite challenge of a sermon delivered many years earlier by the Portuguese Jesuit, Antonio de Vieira.[7] While he praises her exceptional display of knowledge in her learned refutation, he admonishes her for not wholly dedicating her intellectual ability and energy to religious thought and practices. The bishop's letter, which he signed Sor Filotea de la Cruz, was published at his behest along with Sor Juana's rebuttal of Vieira's speech.[8]

In her *Respuesta* of March 1, 1691, Sor Juana responds to the bishop's criticism by tracing the development of her desire for truth and knowledge and by defending women's rights to intellectual freedom, and she does this within the literary artifice he set forth in his letter to her. His use of the pseudonym, Sor Filotea de la Cruz, softens the critical remarks from such a high-ranking official of New Spain's Church and enables him to present them as advice from a well-meaning friend. In order to answer the fictitious character created by the bishop and to clarify her position in this matter, Sor Juana invents a literary figure of her own based upon a male image of femininity and uses the form of a confession to structure her reply. She had employed various dramatic characters from her program of *Los empeños de una casa [The Trials of a Noble House]* in a similar fashion, and now, although she deeply resented it, she had to portray herself as an ordinary nun.

Sor Juana's irritation at having to make this defense is evident in the condescending tone of her letter and her expression of exaggerated amenities and false modesty. Women who possessed literary skills were expected to preface their work with an apology or declaration of humility, and Sor Juana mockingly does this. In answer to the bishop's letter, which she describes ironically as "extremely learned, discrete, holy, and affectionate" (IV, 440), she professes to be puzzled by Sor Filotea's interest in her work and includes several subtle but slyly barbed queries in the text of her reply: "Why, venerable lady, why are you so interested in me? By chance am I any more than a poor nun, the most unimportant creature in the world and the least worthy to be the object of your concern?" (IV, 440–41). As a humble cloistress, she feigns presumption in speaking out on sacred matters and denies having any aspirations for greatness:

What knowledge do I have, what preparation, what resources, or new information for that matter, but four superficial academic degrees? Leave that for someone who understands, for I do not want any trouble with the Inquisition, for I am ignorant and afraid of saying the wrong thing or misinterpreting a genuine bit of knowledge from somewhere. I do not study in order to write, much less to teach (for that would be unconscionable arrogance on my part), but only to see if by studying, I can be less ignorant. (IV, 444)

Obedience rather than egotism, Sor Juana contends, motivated her to write her many works: "I have only written because I have been forced and compelled to and only then to give pleasure to others" (IV, 444).[9] The only exception to this statement, as she mentions later, is a single poem entitled *Primero sueño [First Dream]*.[10] Her desire to please admirers does, in fact, partially explain her reason for writing so many secular compositions; however, her delight at creating intricate characters and plots and devising multitudes of complex, eloquent metaphors cannot be disregarded. While she declares that she felt obligated to comply with the requests of both church and state, she states also that she found the drafting of such pieces as her *Carta atenagórica [Athenagoric Letter]*, which she refers to as her "scribblings" (IV, 440), a rather unpleasant task "because it appeared that I wanted to criticize, something I find naturally abhorrent" (IV, 471). Here she makes use of the common misconception that women shrink from confrontation and conflict in order to mask her attempts to defy traditional social roles.

Although Sor Juana, with perhaps less than total candor, presents herself as a modest individual, an evaluation of her *Respuesta* or "simple narration" (IV, 460), as she calls it, reveals the work of a truly gifted intellectual. Writing in her own defense, Sor Juana subtly chides her prominent critic for his hasty and unfounded conclusions, and the manner in which she responds thoroughly refutes his accusations. Because the bishop criticizes her for not totally dedicating herself to her profession, she masterfully makes use of scholastic thought and methodology in her reply and displays her extensive knowledge of the Bible and of works by religious scholars in support of her own point of view. Her "natural impulse" to study, Sor Juana avers, was the result of her God-given love of the truth, which emerged during her childhood in Nepantla and Amecameca and quickly eclipsed all other worldly endeavors. Concerned by the importance this intellectual curiosity had assumed in her life, she begged God to relieve her of this passion for learning and to leave her with only a desire to serve Him. This would have been appropriate, she interjects sarcastically, because "the rest is superfluous in a woman, according to some people" (IV, 444). Her brief outline of the development of her studious nature, however, not only reveals her own persistence to learn but also illustrates that the capacity for acquiring and utilizing knowledge is a human capability and does not belong solely to one sex.

Sor Juana tells the bishop that she learned to read at the age of three simply by accompanying her older sister to school and by telling the teacher that her mother wanted her to be taught. Although she was too young to enroll formally, the teacher, who was not deceived by her childish prank, recognized her ability and determination and provided her instruction. After this triumph, she disciplined herself to learn other skills. Sor Juana even stopped eating cheese, which she was told would dull her wits, and sacrificed her long hair, considered so important to a girl's appearance, in order to accelerate the learning process:

. . .my hair grew quickly, and I was learning slowly, and in fact I cut it as punishment for my failure to acquire refinement: for I did not think it was right that my head be covered with hair and so lacking in information, which was the more desirable adornment. (IV, 446)

Although Sor Juana frequently resorted to trickery when her intellectual advancement was at stake, this particular ruse that she plays on herself betrays her early rejection of the traditional concept of femininity.[11]

Just as the threat of a spanking had not deterred Sor Juana's earlier efforts to learn, the thought that she would have to dress like a man to attend the University in Mexico City did not pose any real problem for her either. She realized even then that erudition was considered to be a masculine goal, and she was prepared to change her appearance in order to enjoy the freedom automatically accorded to boys. However, for a girl of six or seven, this was an impossibility. At her mother's insistence and in the absence of other reading materials, she was forced to occupy herself by exploring her grandfather's library. During these years, she began to compose poetry, and when she was only eight, she wrote her first eucharistic poem (I, xxviii).

In her late teens, Sor Juana vowed to dedicate her obsession for study to God and did so by choosing religion as her profession. Since she did not wish to marry, the convent offered her the only real opportunity to expend her mental energy. Apart from putting her abilities to use, she also sought to insure her salvation as well.[12] Her newly acquired religious state, however, did not bring her the stability and peace of mind that she had hoped for but only increased her yearning for knowledge. She realized then that her troubles were self-inflicted and that this was only the beginning of her difficulties:

I thought that I was running away from myself but, alas, I brought myself with me and so too my worst enemy in this inclination which I cannot tell if it was sent by Heaven as a gift or a punishment, for instead of dying down or going out in this religious environment, it exploded like gunpowder, and I myself proved that *privatio est causa appetitus*. (IV, 447)

Her immense library,[13] along with her many musical and scientific instruments, was housed in her cell at the convent. There she spent her free time preparing herself not only in the traditional disciplines but in the new areas of mathematics and science as well.[14] Knowledge for Sor Juana was an orderly body of information, which, she emphasizes to the bishop, naturally progressed in an ascending scale from a study of the humanities and the sciences to theology.

Although she wrote a number of works during her early years as a nun, life in the convent was not an ideal existence for her. Conventual duties proved to be tedious and time-consuming, and her sisters often disturbed her work and envied her for the attention that she received. Her account of their reaction to her extensive knowledge echoes Doña Ana's criticism of Doña Leonor's learning in Sor Juana's *comedia, Los empeños de una casa*, and discloses the intolerance of some women toward gifted members of their own sex. Unfortunately, many females actually believed that they were incapable of functioning in the roles reserved for men, and this attitude made the advancement of an exceptional woman like Sor Juana even more difficult. On several occasions, she was prohibited from studying, but this did not quench her desire or inhibit her ability to learn. When a well-meaning prioress forbade her to read books because she thought they were evil, Sor Juana used surreptitious observation and experimentation to investigate basic scientific principles. While she herself preferred to delve into disciplines formerly reserved for men, she does not belittle the domestic tasks in which most women engaged. She found cooking and caring for children to be especially informative and jokingly remarks: "If Aristotle had cooked, he would have written much more" (IV, 460). By alluding to the Greek philosopher in this instance, she not only scoffs at the scholastic method as the sole manner by which to determine the truth but also derides this commonly cited authority for his belief in the inferiority of women.[15]

Over the years, Sor Juana's extraordinary inclination toward study became a cause of controversy, and she found herself caught between what she wanted and what others wanted for her. In several love sonnets, she veils this internal struggle by portraying herself torn between two suitors, who seem to represent symbolically these distinct ways of life. Other poems such as "Finjamos que soy feliz" (I, 5) ["Let Us Pretend That I Am Happy"] and "En perseguirme, Mundo, ¿qué interesas?" (I, 277–78) ["Why, People, Do You Persecute Me So?"] contain expressions of protest against the pressures brought to bear upon her.[16] In her *Respuesta*, she identifies the cause of her predicament and concludes that she is destined for a martyrdom in which she serves as her own executioner. The opposition of both men and women to her studious nature was, she declares, a predictable reaction, and she was deluding herself to expect understanding: "the head in which knowledge is stored cannot expect any other crown than that of thorns" (IV, 455). Although she tried to deal with the criticism leveled against her, it undoubtedly had its effect upon her, and she began to question her own actions and thoughts: "I continually lack so much confidence in myself that I do not trust my own judgment on anything" (IV, 460).

After recounting such intimate personal details relating to her passion for knowledge and truth, Sor Juana broadens the scope of her *Respuesta* and considers the question of intellectual freedom for women in general.[17] By presenting some of the arguments for educating women, she hopes not only to gain acceptance for the main driving force in her life but to remove cultural barriers which restricted women's access to learning.[18] Among the authorities she cites in support of her case are the apostle Paul and the founder of her order, Saint Jerome. As representatives of the Church, they both recognized the spirituality of women, but they also believed that women had inherent weaknesses. While Saint Jerome avoided making strong assertions about the opposite sex by focusing his attention on innocent girls and widows, Saint Paul directly associated females with wickedness, and his views are often regarded as misogynistic.[19] Sor Juana, however, is undaunted by any reservations these Church fathers may have had, and knowing that their opinions were greatly respected, she cleverly counters their negative statements with positive aspects of their teachings. Although Saint Paul spoke out against women preaching in church, he was not opposed to their pursuit of studies in private, and Saint Jerome, as well, did not object to women acquiring knowledge; he supported education for young girls.

Scholarly endeavors should indeed be reserved for a select group of people, according to Sor Juana; however, females should be included in this minority. She boldly criticizes men who are granted the privilege of study by virtue of their sex but who possess only mediocre capabilities to carry out their goals.[20] Talented women, on the other hand, deserve the opportunity to develop their own potential, and she names a number of outstanding women who have contributed to world culture throughout the ages. In her brief history, she mentions such Christian women as Saint Catherine of Egypt, Saint Gertrude, and Saint Paula and cites Saint Teresa as an example of a woman who was able to achieve greatness under the auspices of the Church.

Sor Juana's readiness to identify and commend exceptional women of all walks of life is evident throughout her works, and although she praises women of antiquity such as Lucrecia, Portia, and Julia, she also honors several contemporary women of Mexico in a series of poems dedicated to "Laura" and "Lysi." The poetic name "Laura" was given by Sor Juana to Vicereine Doña Leonor María de Carreto, the wife of Don Antonio Sebastián de Toledo, the Marquis of Mancera, and "Lysi" refers to Doña María Luisa Gonzaga y Manrique de Lara, the wife of Viceroy Don Tomás Antonio de la Cerda y Aragón, the Count of Paredes and Marquis of La Laguna.

At the age of sixteen, Sor Juana was invited to the court of the Marquis of Mancera where she immediately became the vicereine's favorite lady-in-waiting and the official poetess of the court. The exposure that her literary works received there brought her much recognition and acclaim from the public, and Doña Leonor's continuous support assured her protégée's success. She genuinely cared for Sor Juana as she would her own daughter until the girl entered the convent, and even later, after ill health forced Sor Juana to leave the Carmelite monastery of Saint Joseph in 1667, she took her back into the palace.[21] When Sor Juana returned to court to convalesce, the viceroy arranged to have her examined by forty university professors to confirm officially the rumors of her brilliance.[22] Sor Juana does not mention her life at court in her *Respuesta*, but she does reflect upon what she considered to be an artificial environment through the female character, Leonor, in *Los empeños de una casa* (IV, 38–39).[23]

The vicereine was especially saddened by Juana's decision to continue her religious vocation by joining the Order of Saint Jerome in 1669, but she visited her daily at the convent. In 1673, the viceroy was recalled to Spain, but before he could depart from Mexico, Doña Leonor died on the way to the port of Vera Cruz.[24] Sor Juana was shocked and grieved at the news of her untimely death and in a masterful sonnet describes her passing poetically with visions of celestial light. The poetess, like Diego de Ribera in his portrait of her in his "Funerales pompas de D. Felipe IV y plausible aclamación de Carlos II" ["Funeral Ceremony of H. M., Philip IV and Plausible Acclamation of H. M., Charles II"], uses the conventional imagery generally ascribed to admirable women of prominence to portray Doña Leonor's former beauty and radiance.[25] For Sor Juana to have departed from this standardized description would have been inappropriate, and the vicereine undoubtedly represented the ideal woman of the time:

> The Heavens were in love with Laura's beauty,
> so they stole her and took her to their heights

because it was not right for her pure light
to enlighten these wretched valleys;

or because mortals, deceived
by the perfect architecture of her body,
and in awe of seeing such beauty
might think that they had fallen from grace.

She was born where the red veil of the east
opens up to the birth of the rubicund star,
and she died where, with burning desire,

the deep sea buries her light:
for it was essential to her divine flight
that she circle the earth like the sun. (I, 299–300)

In another sonnet, Sor Juana notes the profound effect this loss will have on her personally and describes her poetry as "black tears from my sad pen" (I, 300).

Several years later, Sor Juana again enjoyed the favors of the court when the Countess of Paredes became her patroness. During the reign of the Paredes from 1680 to 1686, Sor Juana experienced her greatest artistic activity. She wrote several dramatic programs to be presented at court, participated in poetic contests,[26] and composed her *Primero sueño*. Apart from the countess's personal encouragement, since she was a poetess herself,[27] she was instrumental in having Sor Juana's poetry published in Spain.[28] In response to the vicereine's kindness and generosity, Sor Juana wrote poems to celebrate her birthday, the baptism of her son, and other special occasions. She also endeavored to capture her exceptional features both on canvas[29] and on paper. The poetic language she uses to describe Doña María Luisa, however, is again typical of the love poetry of the Spanish Golden Age in that she refers to her as a divine spirit to denote her virtue and uses floral imagery to delineate her beauty:

You are the queen of the flowers
because Summer begs
for the carnations of your lips,
and the roses of your cheeks. (I, 52–53)

When the Count and Countess of Paredes returned to Spain, Sor Juana lost two of her greatest admirers and with them her considerable influence at court.[30]

Sor Juana at all times was very proud of her sex and believed that woman's potential should not be limited by society's traditional definition of her role. She may have sacrificed a great deal, however, to express this opinion so clearly in her *Respuesta*. The precise repercussions of the letter are not known, but certain changes in her life seem to have ensued. Her supporters at court dwindled, the archbishop, Francisco Aguiar y Seijas, was antagonistic toward her, and her confessor, the Jesuit Antonio Núñez de Miranda, who had encouraged her to leave the viceregal palace and join a religious order, abandoned her.[31] At this juncture she withdrew from secular life altogether and sold her most prized possessions to help the poor. On several occasions throughout her life, she had expressed a death wish in her poetry, and this desire may have taken on a new sense of urgency under these circumstances. In sonnets such as "Este, que ves, engaño colorido" ["This Colored Deception That You See"], "Rosa divina" ["Divine Rose"], and "Miró Celia una rosa" ["Celia Looked At a Rose"] (I, 277–79), she views life as a deception and expresses a desire to die young to avoid the indignities of old age. In 1694, she reaffirmed her religious vows and signed them: "I, the worst in the world."[32] When an epidemic struck the convent the following year, death was not long in coming for her, and she succumbed while ministering to the stricken members of her order.[33]

The limited account Sor Juana gives of her life in the *Respuesta* sheds considerable light upon the difficulties of a female intellectual in preparing herself and in pursuing her goals during the colonial period. She sought to expand the strict definition of the female role in society both in the way she conducted her life and the manner in which she wrote her works, and she faced opposition from members of her own sex as well as men. Knowing that her thoughts and ideas on women's advancement would generally not be favorably received, she only presented them in a few works and usually then within a carefully constructed literary framework. As a person who did not fit the mold that society had imposed upon her and later as the creator of literary characters, Sor Juana was well aware of the differences between fact and fiction and the intricacies of devising and projecting images. While she herself rejected male visions of femininity at an early age, she makes use of them as a façade in literary works to provide a semblance of conventionality for her liberal views. In *Los empeños de una casa*, Sor Juana speaks through stereotypical Spanish characters in order to express her criticism of the artificiality and hypocrisy of society at large, and she employs an idealized religious figure in her *Respuesta* to strike directly at the narrow-mindedness of the Church and its members. Although her letter is brilliantly written and outwardly follows the rules of polite correspondence, it does not afford Sor Juana the concealment that the structure of a Golden Age *comedia* provides, and her portrayal of herself as an ordinary nun is not one of her own choosing. Sor Juana, however, no doubt understood the risks posed by these factors, and having grown weary of elaborately disguising her opinions, she intentionally stated her position more clearly and forcefully than ever before. By doing this, she probably hoped to deter other people from such criticism and so provide the solitude that she desired. The Church, nonetheless, had not changed its approach toward women in centuries, and the bishop, as its representative, was unable or unwilling to understand Sor Juana's frustrating situation.

At the time of Sor Juana's death, Francisca Josefa Castillo y Guevara, who is second only to the Mexican nun among the women of colonial letters, had just been officially admitted to a religious community in New Granada and would soon begin composing her autobiographical works. She greatly admired Sor Juana's literary talent and was especially inspired by her poetry.[34] Like the famous poetess, she looked to outstanding women of the past to provide a suitable role model, and she too would be affected greatly by the male view of womanhood. Her reaction to the subordination of women, however, would not be one of defiance, as it was in Sor Juana's case, but one of resignation and compliance. Francisca accepted the Church's premise that females were easily tempted, and she constantly atoned for the guilt thrust upon her sex by the original sin. Since spirituality was considered by Church fathers to be one of the greatest assets of a woman, the attainment of complete spiritual harmony with God became her final destiny, and she sought to accomplish this by following in the footsteps of Saint Teresa of Avila.

Francisca's decision to become a member of Tunja's religious society was not surprising considering the atmosphere of the small Colombian town and her family ties to several of its convents and monasteries. Six religious orders had been established there, and their presence had encouraged the inscription of many of Tunja's citizens.[35] The convent of Santa Clara, which she entered at the age of eighteen, was founded in 1572 by Captain Francisco Salguero and his wife, Juana Macías de Figueroa, and Doña Juana, who was related to the young novice on her mother's side of the family, was its first prioress (I, xii, xxxii).[36] During Francisca's lifetime, her aunt and several nieces also were members of the convent, and her mother and sister, Catalina, took their vows as widows. Of the male members of the family, the two sons of her brother, Pedro, were ordained as Jesuits (I, xxxiv-xxxv). Imbued with the religious tradition of both the town and her family, she embarked upon a long career in the Church, and her life in the convent provided the necessary environment for her writing.

Madre Castillo's principal works, *Su vida [Her life]* and *Afectos espirituales [Spiritual Loves]*, represent two very distinct yet complementary aspects of the author's life and are the result of years of introspective analysis. *Su vida* is a factual account of her early life and her conventual experiences as she perceived them, and it further offers a composite of the negative factors which affected her life. It is both an open admission of her faults in order to clear her conscience and the documentation of her Christian virtues such as humility, endurance, obedience, perseverance, and patience. The pessimistic tone of *Su vida* is replaced by jubilation in her two-part *Afectos espirituales* as she recounts the spiritual progression of her soul toward God and their subsequent union. While her knowledge of mystical writings and the Bible obviously influenced this highly personal work, her own clear expression of a heightened sensory awareness and surge of basic emotions contributed significantly to her imaginative expression of the ineffable.[37] *Afectos espirituales* demonstrates the full extent of her creativity and talent as a writer.

According to Madre Castillo, persistent self-examination was an invaluable way of preparing the soul for life after death (II, 314), and this daily reflection loosely structures her writings. Culpability for real or imagined transgressions and the fear of losing God's love are expressed throughout her works and invariably caused her to judge herself and her situation quite harshly. Characterizations of herself as a "vile sinner, who is consistently wild and irresponsible" (I, 198) and one who has always been "a fabric of ignorance and guilt" (I, 190) are recurrent, and she constantly views herself as a person who is isolated from the mainstream of activity and continually shunned by almost everyone. The systematic enumeration of her faults[38] and her mention of a desire to escape from herself (I, 209) reveal not only her deep dissatisfaction with her own identity but a genuine obsession with these alleged inadequacies as well. Madre Castillo is constantly besieged by problems, which cause her both physical and psychological suffering and which create a dark, disturbing atmosphere around her (I, 138). Her attitude toward such an environment is, however, one of acceptance and "blind obedience" (II, 39), which only increases her desire to suffer and die in order to imitate Christ.

Following both the form and content of the first four chapters of Saint Teresa's *Vida*,[39] Madre Castillo recounts her early life in *Su vida* and traces the beginning of her lifelong problems to her difficult and dangerous delivery on October 6, 1671.[40] At the time, it was thought that the arrival of the baby Francisca into the world was so hopeless that her mother received the last rites just prior to the child's birth, and during the first month of her life, when she became seriously ill, preparations were again made for her burial. Poor health continued throughout her entire life (I, 4), and ailments such as fainting spells, allergies, psychoses, heart irregularities, gastric disorders, paralysis, and tumors interrupted her work almost daily and often lasted for extended periods of time (I, xliv, lxxxi).

Francisca did not receive a formal education but was taught to read by her mother, who introduced her to the works of Saint Teresa. Her exposure to the *Fundaciones* inspired her to follow a religious calling and to choose the Spanish mystic as a model of perfection for her own life (I, 5). In later years, she read Saint Teresa's *Vida, Las moradas*, and *Camino de perfección*, and they too influenced her not only spiritually but literarily as well. Although her interest in Saint Teresa encouraged her to read books by other mystical writers such as San Juan de la Cruz and Fray Francisco de Osuna (I, 75), she was especially drawn to those by churchwomen and found a common bond with female religious figures from both Europe and America. The lives and works of Santa Catalina de Sena, Santa María Magdalena de Pazzis, Santa Rosa de Lima, and Sor Juana Inés de la Cruz affected her character to varying degrees and are mentioned in her writings.[41] Apart from her serious reading, Madre Castillo found Spanish *comedias* a welcome relief from her dull, daily conventual routine, and she read them whenever she could (I, 7). Her fascination with this kind of light literature, however, produced pangs of guilt, and her misgivings about this diversion were compounded by her confessor, Father Pedro García. In response to her question about whether it was a sin to read fiction, he replied: "it is not a sin, but many people would not be in hell, if it were not for these plays" (I, 10).

Although Francisca was constantly instructed by members of the Church and reminded of the severe penalties for transgression and the horrors of perdition after she entered the convent, her indoctrination began much earlier. At that time, the blame placed upon women for the continuance of evil in the world was no doubt impressed upon her because the account of her childhood and adolescence documents her reaction to it. In an effort to rid herself of all worldly desires, she put on the habit of Santa Rosa de Lima and began a rigid program of self-denial (I, 6). Because of what she regarded as her lack of discipline, she wished to be blind in order to remove any threat of temptation (I, 29). She does, however, admit to having two brushes with love, which left her with such grave feelings of shame that she contemplated committing suicide on one occasion (I, 9): "I did not consider getting married because I wished and had decided to give myself to Our Lord, for it seemed the most perfect thing to do" (I, 17).

Dreams and visions of the supernatural, evidence of an active imagination and a tormented subconscious, also began during Francisca's youth, and although the appearance of benign spirits such as saints, the Virgin, and the Holy Trinity afforded her some consolation, vivid images of hell and purgatory only nurtured her fears. In the opening pages of *Su vida*, she recounts two of her nightmares, and her description of them, which is similar to Saint Teresa's graphic perception of the underworld in her *Vida*,[42] discloses Madre Castillo's impressionability and her confusion of fantasy with reality:

On one occasion, I seemed to walk over a floor made of bricks placed end to end, as if suspended in air; and being in great danger and looking down, I saw a horrible black river of fire inhabited by so many snakes, toads, and serpents, like the faces and arms of men that were sunken in that well or river; I woke up sobbing, and in the morning I saw evidence of the fire on the tips of my fingers and nails, although I do not know how this could be. Another time, I found myself in a huge and very deep valley, in frightful darkness which is difficult for me to describe or even think about, and at the bottom of the valley was a horrible well of dense black fire; around the edges of it malevolent spirits determined and carried out various forms of torture on a number of men according to their vices. (I, 5)

Satan, or the enemy as Madre Castillo often calls him, appears to her in many forms. As a human, he is seen as an old man, an Indian, a mulatto, and a black (I, 147, 150–51; II, 159–60), and he is also capable of transforming himself into an animal or a reptile (I, 143, 156). Frequent visions of this sinister force as a male may have been a subconscious rejection of the continual pressures placed upon her by confessors and other men with whom she was acquainted. Following the tendency of early colonial writers to perceive the conflict between good and evil as a clash between opposing armies, Madre Castillo describes the devil in her *Afectos espirituales* as an armed invader who commands demonic legions: "I saw this enemy as a scary figure, like a giant in bronze armor riding a horse or beast of bronze who, as he walked, produced a horrifying and extraordinary noise with his joints" (II, 227). On another occasion, Madre Castillo reports that Satan calls his warriors to battle by roaring like a lion and spewing black smoke from his mouth (II, 444).

In her early years, Francisca Castillo y Guevara sought solitude in order to read and to meditate, but gradually she began to withdraw even more from the outside world. Although she longed to retire from society, the thought of entering the convent was actually repugnant to her at first just as it was to Saint Teresa: "I remember that I was so scared that even the convent bells, which were heard in my room, upset me so much that I could not tolerate it, and I would go to my mother's room to avoid listening to them" (I, 15–16). But, in spite of her own fears and her parents' opposition, she became affiliated with a religious community in 1689 (I, xlii), and the next fifty-three years of her life were spent in the Santa Clara Convent, which she regarded as an "inferno" and a "jail of the Inquisition."

Francisca was formally admitted into the order and began her novitiate in 1694. Among her conventual duties over the years were those of door keeper, nurse, sacristan, and instructor of the novices (I, 119, 53, 46, 67). She was elected abbess in 1715, 1729, and 1738 (I, lviii) but lost the election by a narrow margin on another occasion (I, 158).[43] During one of her terms as the convent's director, she and her brother saved it from financial ruin (I, xciii). The many confessors that Madre Castillo had during her cloistered life were supportive but exigent, and they urged her to record her daily experiences. When she found the task of expressing her thoughts too difficult or too dull, she occasionally incorporated previously composed *afectos* (expressions of love) into *Su vida* in order to satisfy demands for continual progress (I, lviii, cxli). Her work was also hampered by her concern that the devil, not God, was providing the inspiration (I, 41). At various stages of their preparation, she considered burning her papers, (I, 122, 162; II, 110), but her confessors were able to dissuade her from destroying them (I, 164).[44]

Many pages of Madre Castillo's *Su vida* recount the daily ordeals that she endured. In addition to her multitude of illnesses, which nearly resulted in her discharge from the Santa Clara Convent (I, 91), she engaged in a routine of self-punishment, a practice that she had begun as a young girl:

I used to torture myself with different instruments until I was bleeding profusely. I would wear hair shirts and iron chains until my flesh swelled over the links. I would sleep without undressing or stretched out on boards. I prayed for hours and practiced mortification in everything that I did. (I, 11)

Physical abuse of herself was not her only source of pain nor were her confessors her only self-appointed judges. Female superiors as well as her sisters treated her harshly on a number of occasions: "The nuns would reprimand me, and one took nettles to the chorus to threaten me; others laughed and made fun of me" (I, 76). Aware of her innermost fears and anxieties, they often terrorized her by their insults probably as a protest to any claim that she might have as a chosen woman of God. Rumors that the abbess thought that she was possessed and that demons were coming to take away her soul had devastating psychological effects upon such a sensitive, impressionable individual and intensified her internal turmoil (I, 90). Her associates accused her of pretending to be sick (I, 119) and failed to show even the slightest sign of concern or understanding during her incapacitation. When her teeth mysteriously fell out, members of the Santa Clara Order shunned her as if her illness were contagious (I, 193).

Although Madre Castillo was momentarily discouraged, "when even the stones were growing thorns and weeds against me" (I, 119), she always minimized her personal conflicts by referring to them as "tiny insults" (I, 73)[45] and by remembering how much Christ had endured (I, 120). She felt that suffering was the manner in which God taught and tested the faithful and that it was the only means of achieving salvation: "I understood that I had to be dead in order to live, and I exist only to suffer" (I, 134).[46] Such tribulations often resulted in the discovery of new strength and always seemed to increase her desire to see and commune with God (I, 76).

While music and art offered some relief from her bleak surroundings, Madre Castillo's spiritual life, which she affectionately referred to as her "nest of repose" (II, 7), brought her hope and joy. *Afectos espirituales* is an account of her escape from daily existence and her soul's courtship and marriage to God. Following Saint Teresa's *Las moradas*, in which she recounts her spiritual progression toward the divine,[47] together with the biblical *Song of Songs*, Madre Castillo presents Christ as her lover and husband and describes his presence by using simple sensorial imagery:

. . . show me your face to delight my sight because it is so beautiful and majestic. Speak to me because your voice is like soothing music to my ears. Your garments are to my sense of smell like the greatest fragrance of all. How soft you are and how beautiful, oh most beloved! You are as sweet to my tongue and throat as honeycomb, and your lips are full of honey. . . . The husband's communication with the innermost part of the soul is a soft touch that exceeds all softness; it is a force greater than all strength; cleaner and purer than purity itself. And in the same way that the hand softly strums the *vihuela* and plays the chords that it desires, so too the chaste, sweet, and strong love is diffused throughout the soul. And it tastes, sees, hears, touches, and perceives the greatest of all goodness; a beauty that is not subjected to forms; a taste, a smell, a penetrating voice like holy oil, that is soft and delicate like a whistle, powerful like fire that seizes and consumes all combustible matter and even transforms iron. (II, 98–99)[48]

In 1742, Madre Castillo died after being isolated from the outside world and totally immersed in religion for most of her life. Her autobiographical works serve as testimony of her many years of secret suffering in an environment that was even more restrictive than that faced by Sor Juana. Determined to relive the experiences of a sixteenth-century mystic in a convent in New Granada nearly two hundred years later, she encountered continual pressure from male superiors to document the extent of her spiritual strength and intolerance from her sisters because of this exceptional inner power and her ability to express it. Madre Castillo openly acknowledged the influence of Saint Teresa upon her works, which constitute the lengthiest and most detailed outpouring of feminine sentiment written during the colonial period, and she has carefully preserved the canonized nun's extraordinary lucidity and sensibility in the adaptation of her literary image. Although New World mystics such as Santa Rosa de Lima attained great religious prominence, Madre Castillo's fame is derived from her skill and talent as a writer. She never thought of herself as an author but continually revised her writings because of her desire for perfection. *Su vida* was first published in Philadelphia in 1817, and a Colombian edition of her *Afectos espirituales* did not appear until 1843 (I, cxcvii). Madre Castillo was never recognized for her achievements during her lifetime, and a scholarly assessment of her importance to early Spanish American literature was not made before the nineteenth century.

Because of their predisposition to remain single and their desire for solitude, both Sor Juana and Madre Castillo committed themselves to the Church in return for a lifetime of protection. Disenchanted with the convent, yet not prepared to leave the profession, both women looked for new channels of awareness and unexplored dimensions. Each chose a different way to relieve the tedium of daily routine and one which seemed appropriate to the nature they revealed in their works. Surrounded by the affluence and sophistication of New Spain's capital, Sor Juana emerged as a knowledgeable, assertive young woman, who advocated change in the established patterns of conduct. Undaunted by social tradition which barred women from certain areas of endeavor, she extended her spheres of influence into all fields in which she felt capable and was the first pioneer of women's liberation in the Americas. By using the accomplishments of outstanding women of the past as a point of departure, she reached unprecedented levels of achievement for her sex and successfully challenged men in their own areas of expertise. Her ingenuity and enterprise at expressing her feminism, however, incensed and frightened Church officials, and they ultimately forced Sor Juana to abandon the new image for women that she represented and to conform to the conservative role of an urban nun. Just as she envisioned the advent of an age of reason in her studies of mathematics and science, so too she anticipated a movement of social reform in which women were granted the opportunities customarily given to men. Unfortunately, she would not live to see either of these changes.

Madre Castillo, on the other hand, had been brought up in a remote part of Spain's possessions in a provincial town that had remained poor and backward. The people of Tunja had relied upon their faith for years, and it provided a refuge for Francisca from the intolerable living conditions within her convent. She was a simple girl who looked to others for guidance and support all her life, and the development of an inner world in which she could express herself freely was the only option open to her. Burdened with the guilt heaped upon women for centuries, she lived in continual penance and used her suffering to strengthen her spiritually. Because she sought the approval and respect of her superiors, she fashioned herself as much as possible after the most positive image she knew, that of Saint Teresa of Jesus. Madre Castillo was not a saint, but she aspired to be one.

Both Sor Juana and Madre Castillo relied to some extent upon the adaptation of idealized religious figures in their autobiographical works, and they did so at the insistence of men. Sor Juana was a master of character portrayal, and she cleverly manipulates this stereotype to disclose only a certain amount of information about herself while exposing the obvious faults of her male adversary. She knew how to placate the bishop by following the advice in his letter, but instead she begrudgingly portrayed herself as a humble, obedient servant of God in answering his criticism. Madre Castillo was also aware of the importance of previous literary images; however, she used them to provide guidance for her life and followed them directly in her writings. Her emulation of Saint Teresa is a sincere tribute to the Spanish nun, who offered one of the few female role models for colonial women to follow. Neither Sor Juana nor Madre Castillo, however, was able to conform completely with the image imposed upon her or to reach the goal that she had established for herself, and life became increasingly frustrating and difficult for the two women to carry on. Although adversity and suffering no doubt served as a source of their creativity, death was the only way out of their situation, and they both longed for its arrival.

Notes

1. Very little is known about the personal lives or the extent of the literary production of minor female writers of the colonial period, and in numerous cases, even their names are unknown. Although they must have written about a wide variety of subjects, the works that have been preserved were generally written either to honor a famous person or to commemorate an important church or state event. Many of these pieces were prize-winning entries in the literary competitions of the time and were compiled as official records of the occasion.

Among the lesser known female writers of Mexico is the niece of the six-teenth-century dramatist, Fernán González de Eslava. Catalina de Eslava pays tribute to her uncle's fame in "El sagrado laurel ciña tu frente" ["The Sacred Wreath Crowns Your Head"], and her sonnet serves as partial preface to his *Coloquios espirituales y sacramentales [Spiritual and Sacramental Colloquies]*. Fernán González de Eslava, *Coloquios espirituales y sacramentales y poesías sagradas* (México, D.F.: Imprenta de Francisco Díaz de León, 1877), p. 3.

Catalina de Eslava was followed by María de Estrada Medinilla, who is considered by Méndez Plancarte to be Sor Juana's rightful precursor. Her poetic letter to her cousin describing the triumphant arrival of the new viceroy was written in 1640. Alfonso Méndez Plancarte, *Poetas novohispanos, segundo siglo (1621–1721)* primera parte, 3 vols. (México, D.F.: Imprenta Universitaria, 1944), II, xxxix, 43–46.

During the eighteenth century, several Mexican poetesses celebrated the canonization of Saint John of the Cross and the proclamation of new Spanish monarchs, according to José María Vigil. One woman, Doña Clementa, may have written her poem to prove that a woman is not as frivolous or superficial as men think, since she prefaces her verses with an expression of feminine protest: "Women do not always / have to think about trinkets and jewelry." José María Vigil, *Poetisas mexicanas, siglos XVI, XVII, XVIII y XIX,* Edición facsimilar (1893; rpt. México, D.F.: Imprenta Universitaria, 1977), p. 48. Another poetess, who is mentioned by Méndez Plancarte but about whom little is known, is Sor Teresa Magdalena de Cristo. In 1700, she wrote *décimas* (ten-line stanzas) in celebration of Saint John's feast day. Alfonso Méndez Plancarte, *Poetas novohispanos, segundo siglo (1621–1721)* pt. 2, 3 vols. (México, D.F.: Imprenta Universitaria, 1945), III, 150–51.

Considerable attention has been given to Peru's first poetess, Amarilis, because Lope de Vega regarded her verses so highly that he had them published in a 1621 volume of his works. Her "Epístola a Belardo" ["Letter to Belardo"] is a laudatory poem which she wrote to the famous dramatist asking him to compose a rhymed life history about Saint Dorothea. Her poetic request contains a brief profile of her background, and scholars have used this to suggest that María de Alvarado, María Tello de Lara, or Ana Morillo, a resident of Lima who wrote plays, may have been the mysterious Amarilis. Luis Alberto Sánchez, *Los poetas de la colonia y de la revolución* (Lima: Editorial Universo, 1974), pp. 139–49. Irving A. Leonard, "More Conjectures Regarding the Identity of Lope de Vega's 'Amarilis Indiana'," *Hispania* 20, no. 2 (1937), pp. 113–20.

Amarilis may have been preceded by the anonymous author of a history of poetry written in tercets. The "Discurso en loor de la poesía" ["Discourse in Praise of Poetry"] appears in Diego Mexía de Fernangil's *Primera parte del parnaso antártico* published in 1608 and is often attributed to Clarinda. Although the poet claims to be a woman, Sánchez concludes, after a close analysis of the lengthy poem, that this was a device used to conceal a masculine identity. Sánchez, *Los poetas de la colonia y de la revolución*, pp. 71–76. By claiming to be a woman, the poet no doubt drew more attention to his work.

Another religious woman, who wrote at approximately the same time as Amarilis, was Santa Rosa de Lima. She was the daughter of María de Oliva, a native of Lima, and Gaspar de Flores, who had come to Peru with President La Gasca's forces to quell Gonzalo Pizarro's rebellion. While living in the convent, she wrote religious poetry, and some of her verses describe her mystical encounters. The quality of these pieces, however, does not compare to the works of other outstanding religious writers of her time. Rosa led quite a remarkable life, and hardly fifty years after her death in 1617, she was proclaimed Patroness of America and was canonized by the pope. Frances Parkinson Keyes, *The Rose and the Lily, the Lives of Two South American Saints* (New York: Hawthorn Books, 1961), pp. 79, 85, 89. Keyes also presents a biographical sketch of Quito's Mariana de Jesús (1618–1645). Luis A. Getino reproduces several of Santa Rosa's verses in his essay and reports that she borrowed fragments of poetry from other sources. According to him, she would sing several lines from *La Celestina* when her lover (Jesus) failed to arrive on time:

> It is after twelve
> My lover is not coming
> Who could be the lucky one
> Who is keeping him?

Luis A. Getino, *Santa Rosa de Lima, su personalidad intelectual* (n.p.: Talleres Gráficos de la Penitenciaría, n.d.), pp. 41–42. Sánchez, *Los poetas de la colonia y de la revolución*, p. 139. José Luis Trenti Rocamora, *Grandes mujeres de América* (Buenos Aires: Editorial Huarpes, 1945), pp. 107–10.

2. Edgar Allison Peers, *El misticismo español* (Buenos Aires: Espasa-Calpe Argentina, 1947), pp. 36–39.

Because of her outstanding strength and courage, Saint Teresa is referred to as "the Christian Amazon" by Fray Bartolomé de Segura in his biography of her. M. Ruth Lundelius, "The *Mujer Varonil* in the Theater of the *Siglo de Oro*," (dissertation, University of Pennsylvania, 1969), p. 62.

The Spanish saint was dismayed by the Church's lack of regard for its female leaders and appealed to God to treat the virtuous souls of women just like He did those of men. Mary Daly, *The Church and the Second Sex* (New York: Harper and Row, 1975), pp. 98–99.

3. Alfonso Méndez Plancarte and Alberto G. Salceda, eds., 4 vols. *Obras completas de Sor Juana Inés de la Cruz* (México, D.F.: Imprenta Nuevo Mundo, 1955), IV, 453–54, 467. References to Sor Juana's works have been taken from this four-volume edition and are cited hereafter in the text of the chapter.

4. Darío Achury Valenzuela compares the writings of these two religious women in his edition of Madre Castillo's works. Darío Achury Valenzuela, ed., *Obras completas de la Madre Josefa de la Concepción de Castillo*, 2 vols.

(Bogotá: Talleres Gráficos del Banco de la República, 1968), I, ci, clxxix-clxxxiv. This edition also contains a number of Achury Valenzuela's previously published articles on Madre Castillo. References regarding these articles and Madre Castillo's works have been taken from this two-volume set and are cited hereafter in the text of the chapter.

5. Carlos Sigüenza y Góngora, *Obras* (México, D.F.: Sociedad de Bibliófilos Mexicanos, 1928), pp. 23–24, 38. Irving A. Leonard, *Baroque Times in Old Mexico* (Ann Arbor, Mich.: University of Michigan Press, 1966), pp. 191–92.

6. Amado Nervo, *Juana de Asbaje,* vol. 8 of *Obras completas* (Madrid: La Imprenta de Juan Pueyo, 1910), p. 167.

7. Sor Juana's discourse, in which she questions Vieira's sermon, is known as the *Carta atenagórica* because it is considered to be a work worthy of the goddess Athena. Méndez Plancarte, *Obras completas*, IV, 694–97.

8. Méndez Plancarte reprints the bishop's letter in his *Obras completas*, IV, 694–97.

9. Sor Juana also presents this same reason for writing through the character, Religion, in a short dramatic poem in which she introduces the religious play *El divino Narciso [The Divine Narcissus]*. Méndez Plancarte, *Obras completas*, III, 19.

10. *Primero sueño* is considered by Karl Vossler to be Sor Juana's masterpiece. Karl Vossler, "El mundo en el sueño" in *Primero sueño* by Sor Juana Inés de la Cruz (Buenos Aires: Imprenta de la Universidad, 1953), pp. 7–17. In this Gongoristic poem, Sor Juana narrates her soul's journey after it leaves her sleeping body and rises to commune with the universe.

11. Santa Rosa de Lima, imitating Santa Catalina de Sena, cut her hair as well in order to discourage young men who were attracted by her beauty. Trenti Rocamora, *Grandes mujeres de América*, p. 107; Keyes, *The Rose and the Lily*, p. 93.

12. Another reason she may have entered the convent was to conceal her illegitimate birth. Leonard, *Baroque Times*, p. 173. Sor Juana was born in 1648 to Isabel Ramírez Santillana and the Basque, Pedro Manuel de Asbaje y Vargas. Her childhood was spent with her mother and her grandfather, and little is known about her father except his name and his nationality. Anita Arroyo, *Razón y pasión de Sor Juana* (México, D.F.: Gráfica Panamericana, 1952), pp. 26–27, 35.

13. Although the exact size of her library, once placed at four thousand volumes, has been questioned, Ermilo Abreu Gómez enumerates some of the known subjects and authors of Sor Juana's many books. Ermilo Abreu Gómez, *Sor Juana Inés de la Cruz, bibliografía y biblioteca* (México, D.F.: Imprenta de la Secretaría de Relaciones Exteriores, 1934), pp. 331–46. The length of his list is an indication of the amount of personal property a nun was permitted

to retain upon entering the convent and of the relative comfort of some of the cells.

14. Sor Juana probably became interested in mathematics and science as a result of her discussions with Sigüenza y Góngora, who was a professor of mathematics at the University of Mexico. Leonard, *Baroque Times*, pp. 182–83.

15. Vern L. Bullough, *The Subordinate Sex: A History of Attitudes toward Women* (Urbana, Ill.: University of Illinois Press, 1973), pp. 61–64.

16. Leonard, *Baroque Times*, pp. 177–88. Although some scholars have conjectured that her love poems relate to some romantic attachment, which she may have had before entering the convent, Leonard feels this is unlikely.

17. Sor Juana reflects a general social consciousness in her works, which encompasses not only women but blacks as well. In her church carols, she endearingly portrays two princesses of Guinea who think of the Virgin Mary ("Señola Malía") as a black slave and describe her ascension into heaven as her manumission. Méndez Plancarte, *Obras completas*, II, 72–73. Sor Juana's description of these women contrasts sharply with the prejudicial treatment they receive in *El carnero* by Rodríguez Freile and *Lima por dentro y fuera* by Terralla y Landa.

18. Changes in women's education do not take place until the latter part of the eighteenth century. A literary work specifically about the education of women does not appear until 1818, when José Joaquín Fernández de Lizardi publishes his novel, *La quijotita y su prima*. See Asunción Lavrin's article "In Search of the Colonial Woman in Mexico: The Seventeenth and Eighteenth Centuries," in her *Latin American Women* (Westport, Conn.: Greenwood Press, 1978), pp. 28–29.

19. Bullough, *The Subordinate Sex,* pp. 116, 103–4.

20. Sor Juana also speaks out against men in the poem "Hombres necios que acusáis a la mujer sin razón" ["Stupid Men Who Accuse Women Without Reason"], in which she protests against the double standard of morality and chides men for the antithetical demands they place upon women. Méndez Plancarte, *Obras completas*, I, 228–29.

21. Arroyo, *Razón y pasión de Sor Juana*, pp. 61–62, 71.

22. Leonard, *Baroque Times*, p. 173.

23. Ezequiel A. Chávez, *Ensayo de psicología de Sor Juana Inés de la Cruz* (México, D.F.: Asociación "Ezequiel A. Chávez," 1971), p. 204. Sor Juana's criticism of life in the viceregal court is also evident in her *Sainete primero, De palacio [First Skit about the Palace]* that accompanies *Los empeños de una casa*. Méndez Plancarte, *Obras completas*, IV, 65–74.

24. Arroyo, *Razón y pasión de Sor Juana*, pp. 75, 95, 106–7.

25. For my discussion of Diego de Ribera's description of Doña Leonor, see chapter 2.

26. Two of her poems appear in Sigüenza's *Triunfo parthénico* as prize winners. Playfully she entered them under pseudonyms. Sigüenza divulged her masquerade as Bachiller Felipe de Salaizes Gutiérrez, and Juan Sáenz del Cauri is an anagram for Sor Juana. Arroyo, *Razón y pasión de Sor Juana,* p. 116.

27. Julio Jiménez Rueda, *Sor Juana Inés de la Cruz en su época* (México, D.F.: Editorial Porrúa, 1951), p. 82.

28. Marcelino Menéndez y Pelayo, *Obras completas* (Madrid: Imprenta Fortanet, 1911), II, 82–83. This volume of her poetry appeared in 1689.

29. Arroyo, *Razón y pasión de Sor Juana,* p. 112.

30. Doña Elvira de Toledo, the wife of Don Gaspar de Sandoval Silva y Mendoza, who was viceroy from 1668 to 1695, took some interest in Sor Juana's work but not to the extent of the other vicereines. She, however, enjoyed her *El divino Narciso* so much that she had a 1690 edition of it published in Mexico by Bernardo Calderón's widow. Jiménez Rueda, *Sor Juana Inés de la Cruz,* p. 95. Sor Juana also wrote several poems honoring Doña Elvira. Her description of the Countess of Galve, in conventional imagery, is contained in "El soberano Gaspar" (I, 119–20) ["The Sovereign Gaspar"].

31. Dorothy Schons, "Some Obscure Points in the Life of Sor Juana Inés de la Cruz," *Modern Philology* 24, no. 2 (1926), pp. 151–59.

32. Nervo includes a photostatic copy of her signature in his volume on Sor Juana. The document is presently in the Benson Collection at the University of Texas at Austin. Nervo, *Juana de Asbaje,* pp. 176–77.

33. Leonard, *Baroque Times,* p. 191.

34. Francisca had copied fragments of Sor Juana's poetry into a book belonging to her family. When these poetic pieces were first discovered, they were mistakenly attributed to the prioress herself. Achury Valenzuela, *Obras completas,* I, cxcii–cxciv.

35. Ibid., I, xi.

The seventeenth-century chronicler Lucas Fernández de Piedrahita noted the importance of religion to the declining township and the relatively large number of daughters of prominent families that entered the convents. Lucas Fernández de Piedrahita, *Noticia historial de las conquistas del Nuevo Reino de Granada* (Bogotá: Ediciones de la Revista Ximénez de Quesada, 1973), p. 332.

36. In *Canto III* of the second part of his *Elegías de varones ilustres de Indias,* Juan de Castellanos praises Doña Juana Macías for her commitment to the Church. Juan de Castellanos, *Elegías de varones ilustres de Indias,* vol. 4 of *Biblioteca de Autores Españoles* (Madrid: Imprenta de Aribau y Compañía, 1874), p. 203.

37. In examining the mysticism of Saint Teresa of Jesus and Marie de l'Incarnación, Helmut Hatzfeld notes that women, who have not received previous theological training, are more creative in relating their spiritual experiences than the men, who tend to rely upon the opinions of theologians and

philosophers to explain them. Helmut Hatzfeld, "Mística femenina clásica en España y Francia" in his *Estudios literarios sobre mística española* (Madrid: Editorial Gredos, 1955), p. 254.

38. In her *Afectos espirituales,* she creatively presents her vices and passions as three little old ladies who follow her (II, 359).

39. In the opening segment of her autobiography, the saint describes her family, expresses a desire to be a hermit, and remembers the pleasure that she got from reading works of fiction. According to her own testimony, she resisted entering a convent at an early age, but as prayer became increasingly significant in her life, she was drawn toward a religious profession. She also recounts that she suffered from a number of maladies during her lifetime. Santa Teresa de Jesús, *Obras completas* (Madrid: Imprenta Fareso, 1979), pp. 28–37.

40. Madre Castillo was the daughter of Francisco Ventura de Castillo y Toledo, who had come to New Granada as a royal official, and María de Guevara Niño y Rojas, who was a native of Tunja and was descended from the Marquises of Poza and Albentos. Achury Valenzuela, *Obras completas,* I, xxxiii. She attests in *Su vida* that they provided a loving, Christian home for the family (I, 4, 6).

41. Madre Castillo wrote at the end of an era in which a number of religious women wrote autobiographies. Santa Catalina de Sena was a fourteenth-century Italian mystic of the Dominican Order, and Santa María Magdalena de Pazzis (1566–1607) was a Carmelite of Italian origin. María Teresa Morales Borrero, *La Madre Castillo, su espiritualidad y su estilo* (Bogotá: La Imprenta Patriótica del Instituto Caro y Cuervo, 1968), pp. 15–20, 50–51.

42. Santa Teresa de Jesús, *Obras completas,* p. 143.

43. When Madre Castillo becomes abbess, she asks to be removed because she feels she is unable to carry out the duties properly (I, 185).

44. She also wanted to leave the Santa Clara Convent to join the stricter Carmelite Order, but her confessor prevented her because of ill health (I, lii).

45. Madre Castillo, like Saint Teresa, uses diminutives throughout her works. Achury Valenzuela considers the frequent use of this form to be a feminine trait and a sign of her tenderness and affection. Achury Valenzuela, *Obras completas,* I, cxxvii-cxxviii.

46. The oxymoron life-death is used by Madre Castillo a number of times in her works, and it probably reflects Saint Teresa's influence. Morales Borrero, *La Madre Castillo,* p. 357; Achury Valenzuela, *Obras completas,* I, xciii.

47. The Spanish mystic's explanation of spiritual betrothal and marriage is contained in her description of the seventh mansion. Santa Teresa de Jesús, *Obras completas,* pp. 438–50.

48. Madre Castillo's tendency to view the opposite sex in terms of stereotypes follows that of many male writers during the period. Her descriptions of men as either perfect or demonic reflect the same love-fear relationship between the sexes.

CONCLUSION

Although the literary images of women changed throughout the three hundred years of Spain's domination of America, they continually represented types rather than individuals and generally perpetuated the traditional attitudes toward women inherent in Western culture. Because of their reliance upon previous female imagery devised by men, colonial writers reaffirmed the view of woman as a symbol of sexual desire or a paragon of spiritual strength and continued to define her role in terms of her relationship to man. As a result, therefore, many questions about the lives and feelings of actual women remain unanswered. However, from an artistic standpoint, the variety of well-wrought female characters in colonial literature is exceptional and demonstrates the extensive knowledge of Spain's literary heritage possessed by writers in the colonies and their skill at adapting aspects of it for their own creative purposes.

The original blend of elements from Spanish literature with American historical reality, while obscuring the individual identities of colonial women, reveals some general information about their status and the factors that determined it. Females residing in the New World were respected, feared, hated, and adored, and the selection of literary imagery used to express these sentiments depended upon the cultural, political, religious, and social environment of the time. As Spain's American colonies were transformed from frontier settlements into imperial viceroyalties, and later into centers of revolutionary activity, female types and their characteristics changed. The courageous female warrior was replaced by the beautiful courtly lady as the feminine ideal, and from the opposite perspective, increased racial discrimination and the growth of crime and vice in the cities adversely affected the descriptions of women. The female subjects of literary works also shifted as the centuries progressed, and women of Creole backgrounds became the focus of attention rather than those of native or Spanish origin. The most continuously influential component in the creation and transmission of attitudes toward women, however, was the Catholic Church, and its tradition not only dictated specific images but controlled the lives and destinies of the learned sector of the female population as well.

Besides mirroring Spain's literary trends and general historical developments in its colonies, female images projected by early Spanish American writers also served to influence the behavior of women and the view they had of themselves. Many females were unaware of the nature of the restrictions imposed upon them, and they readily accepted these standards as a system by which society at large rewarded or punished them. Ignorant of the fact that such requirements were created by men in order to maintain women's subservience, most women openly espoused these attitudes and judged members of their own sex by their ability to conform to the male conception of femininity. Women who were dutiful, elegant, or saintly met men's expectations, while those who lacked or failed to display these qualities were often criticized severely. Gifted women, however, who did not fit this pattern and who aspired to make their mark on society, were forced to consider adopting certain masculine customs and modes of thinking in order to be what was regarded as the norm for a human being and to enjoy the freedoms that went with it. The fact that such a genius as Sor Juana Inés de la Cruz was able to overcome some of these obstacles and effectively challenge men's image of women as well as their position of superiority over them, leads scholars to conjecture about how many women could have made outstanding contributions to colonial culture had they been given the opportunities granted to men.

Although female characters in colonial literature may be criticized for their lack of authenticity in reflecting the feminine experience and for reinforcing restrictive and repressive patterns upon society, their appearance serves as a tribute to the art of character portrayal in Peninsular literature, especially to the uniquely Spanish types such as the

Celestina, the women of the picaresque novel, the *dama* of the *comedia*, and the mystic, Saint Teresa of Jesus. Their adaptation to a New World context by colonial writers adds a new freshness and vitality to these literary figures of the past and is indicative of the authors' talents as successful creators. Bernal Díaz' portrayal of the native American heroine, Doña Marina, Ercilla's poetic presentation of Araucanian women, Caviedes' scathing descriptions of Lima's prostitutes, Sor Juana's dramatic interpretation of Spanish ladies, and Madre Castillo's self-portrait are some of the many remarkable characterizations of women, and their preservation has contributed to the generally high quality of colonial letters. This strong tradition not only establishes a solid foundation for the creation of future female figures in Spanish American literature but also anticipates the increase of characters whose roots are American and whose presentation is made from the feminine perspective.

SELECTED BIBLIOGRAPHY

Primary Sources—Spanish Texts

Balbuena, Bernardo de, *La grandeza mexicana*. México, D.F.: Editorial Porrúa, 1971.

————. *Siglo de Oro en las selvas de Erífile*. Madrid: Ibarra, Impresor de Cámara de S. M., 1821.

Benavente, Fray Toribio de (Motolinía). *Memoriales e Historia de los indios de la Nueva España*. Vol. 240 of *Biblioteca de Autores Españoles*. Madrid: Ediciones Atlas, 1970.

Carrió de la Vandera, Alonso, (Concolorcorvo). *El lazarillo de ciegos caminantes*, ed. Emilio Carilla. Barcelona: Editorial Labor, 1973.

Carvajal, Fray Gaspar de. *Relación del nuevo descubrimiento del famoso río Grande de las Amazonas*. México, D.F.: Fondo de Cultura Económica, 1955.

Castellanos, Juan de. *Elegías de varones ilustres de Indias*. Vol. 4 of *Biblioteca de Autores Españoles*. Madrid: Imprenta de Aribau y Compañía, 1874.

Castillo y Guevara, Francisca Josefa. *Obras completas*, ed. Darío Achury Valenzuela. 2 vols. Bogotá: Talleres Gráficos del Banco de la República, 1968.

Caviedes, Juan del Valle y. *Obras*, ed. Rubén Vargas Ugarte. Lima: Talleres Gráficos de la Tipografía Peruana, 1947.

El Conquistador anónimo. *Relación de algunas cosas de la Nueva España y de la gran ciudad de Temestitan México, hecha por un gentilhombre del señor Fernando Cortés*. México, D.F.: José Porrúa e Hijos, 1961.

Cortés, Hernán. *Cartas de relación*. México, D.F.: Editorial Porrúa, 1970.

Díaz de Guzmán, Ruy. *La Argentina*. Buenos Aires: Espasa-Calpe Argentina, 1945.

Díaz del Castillo, Bernal. *Historia verdadera de la conquista de la Nueva España*. México, D.F.: Editorial Porrúa, 1970.

Erauso, Catalina de. *Historia de la Monja Alférez Doña Catalina de Erauso, escrita por ella misma*. Paris: Imprenta de Julio Didot, 1829.

Ercilla, Alonso de. *La Araucana*. México, D.F.: Editorial Porrúa, 1977.

Espinosa Pólit, Aurelio, ed. *Los dos primeros poetas coloniales ecuatorianos*. Puebla, Méx.: Editorial J. M. Cajica, Jr., 1960.

Fernández, Diego. *Historia del Perú*. Vols. 164–165 of *Biblioteca de Autores Españoles*. Madrid: Ediciones Atlas, 1963.

Fernández de Oviedo, Gonzalo. *Historia general y natural de las Indias*. Vols. 17–21 of *Biblioteca de Autores Españoles*. Madrid: Ediciones Atlas, 1959.

González de Eslava, Fernán. *Coloquios espirituales y sacramentales*. 2 vols. México, D.F.: Editorial Porrúa, 1976.

Gutiérrez de Santa Clara, Pedro. *Quinquenarios*. Vols. 165–167 of *Biblioteca de Autores Españoles*. Madrid: Ediciones Atlas, 1963.

El Inca Garcilaso de la Vega. *Obras completas*. Vols. 132–135 of *Biblioteca de Autores Españoles*. Madrid: Ediciones Atlas, 1960.

Sor Juana Inés de la Cruz. *Fama, y obras pósthumas del fénix de México*. Madrid: La Imprenta de Antonio Gonçalez de Reyes, 1714.

———. *Obras completas*, eds. Alfonso Méndez Plancarte and Alberto G. Salceda. 4 vols. México, D.F.: Imprenta Nuevo Mundo, 1955; Fondo de Cultura Económica, 1957.

Las Casas, Bartolomé de. *Historia de las Indias*. 3 vols. México, D.F.: Fondo de Cultura Económica, 1951.

———. *Brevísima relación de la destrucción de la Indias*. Paris and Buenos Aires: Sociedad de Ediciones Louis-Michaud, 1957.

Medina, José Toribio. *Dos comedias famosas y un auto sacramental*. Santiago–Valparaiso, Chile: Sociedad Imprenta-Litografía "Barcelona," 1915.

Méndez Plancarte, Alfonso, ed. *Poetas novohispanos*. 3 vols. México, D.F.: Ediciones de la Universidad Nacional Autónoma, 1964, 1943, 1945.

Monterde, Francisco, ed. *Poesías profanas*. México, D.F.: Ediciones de la Universidad Nacional Autónoma, 1939.

Navarrete, Manuel. *Entretenimientos poéticos*. 2 vols. México, D.F.: Imprenta de Valdés, 1823.

Núñez de Pineda y Bascuñán, Francisco. *El cautiverio feliz*, ed. Angel C. González. Segunda Edición (Abreviada). Santiago, Chile: Empresa Editora Zig-Zag, 1967.

Oña, Pedro de. *Arauco domado*. Santiago, Chile: Imprenta Universitaria, 1917.

Palma, Ricardo, ed. *Flor de Academias, y Diente del Parnaso*. Lima: Oficina Tipográfica de El Tiempo por L. H. Jiménez, 1899.

Paz y Melia, A. "Cartapacio de diferentes versos a diversos asuntos compuestos ó recogidos por Mateo Rosas de Oquendo." *Bulletin Hispanique* 8 (1906): 255–78.

Peralta Barnuevo, Pedro de. *Obras dramáticas*. Santiago, Chile: Imprenta Universitaria, 1937.

Rodríguez Freile, Juan. *El carnero*, ed. Miguel Aguilera. Bogotá: Imprenta Nacional, 1963.

Sigüenza y Góngora, Carlos. *Obras*. México, D.F.: Sociedad de Bibliófilos Mexicanos, 1928.

——. *Triunfo parthénico*. México, D.F.: Ediciones Xochitl, 1945.

Spell, Jefferson Rea, and Francisco Monterde. *Tres comedias de Eusebio Vela*. México, D.F.: Imprenta Universitaria, 1948.

Terralla y Landa, Esteban. *Lima por dentro y fuera*, ed. Alan Soons. Exeter, England: Exeter University Printing Unit, 1978.

Terrazas, Francisco de. *Poesías,* ed. Antonio Castro Leal. México, D.F.: Librería de Porrúa Hnos. y Cía., 1941.

Primary Sources—English Translations

Beckett, Samuel, trans. *Anthology of Mexican Poetry,* ed. Octavio Paz. Bloomington, Ind.: Indiana University Press, 1958.

Benavente, Friar Toribio de (Motolinía). *History of the Indians of New Spain*. Trans. and ed. Elizabeth Andros Foster. Westport, Conn.: Greenwood Press, 1973.

Carrió de la Vandera, Alonso (Concolorcorvo). *El lazarillo: A Guide for Inexperienced Travelers Between Buenos Aires and Lima*. Trans. Walter D. Kline. Bloomington, Ind.: Indiana University Press, 1965.

Carvajal, Friar Gaspar de. *The Discovery of the Amazons*. Trans. H. C. Heaton. New York: American Geographical Society, 1934.

Cieza de León, Pedro. *The War of Chupas*. Trans. Sir Clements R. Markham. London: Chiswick Press, 1917.

Cole, M. R., trans. "*Los pastores*, a Mexican Play of the Nativity." In *Memoirs of the American Folklore Society*. Boston and New York: Houghton Mifflin and Company, 1907.

Díaz del Castillo, Bernal. *The Discovery and Conquest of Mexico*. Trans. A. P. Maudslay. Ed. Genaro García. New York: Farrar, Straus and Cudahy, 1956.

Ercilla, Alonso de. *The Araucaniad*. Trans. Charles Maxwell Lancaster and Paul Thomas Manchester. Nashville, Tenn.: Vanderbilt University Press, 1945.

El Inca Garcilaso de la Vega. *The Florida of the Inca.*Trans. and eds. John Grier Varner and Jeanette Johnson Varner. Austin, Tex.: University of Texas Press, 1951.

————. *Royal Commentaries of the Incas and General History of Peru.* Trans. Harold V. Livermore. 2 vols. Austin, Tex.: University of Texas Press, 1966.

Núñez de Pineda y Bascuñán, Francisco. *The Happy Captive.* Trans. William C. Atkinson. London: The Folio Society, 1977.

Oña, Pedro de. *Arauco Tamed.* Trans. Charles Maxwell Lancaster and Paul Thomas Manchester. Albuquerque, N.M.: University of New Mexico Press, 1948.

Rodríguez Freile, Juan. *The Conquest of New Granada.* Trans. William C. Atkinson. London: Folio Society, 1961.

Secondary Sources—Books

Abreu Gómez, Emilio. *Sor Juana Inés de la Cruz, bibliografía y biblioteca.* México, D.F.: Imprenta de la Secretaría de Relaciones Exteriores, 1934.

Alvar López, Manuel. *Americanismos en la "Historia" de Bernal Díaz del Castillo.* Madrid: Imprenta Márquez, 1970.

Anadón, José. *Pineda y Bascuñán, defensor del araucano.* Santiago, Chile: Editorial Universitaria Seminario de Filología Hispánica, 1977.

Arrom, José Juan. *El teatro de Hispanoamérica en la época colonial.* Havana: Talleres de Ucar, García, 1956.

Arroyo, Anita. *Razón y pasión de Sor Juana.* México, D.F.: Gráfica Panamericana, 1952.

Barrera, Isaac J. *Literatura ecuatoriana.* Quito: Editorial Ecuatoriana, 1939.

Bosch, Mariano. *Manuel de Lavardén, poeta y filósofo.* Buenos Aires: Los Talleres Gráficos de Guillermo Kraft Ltda., 1944.

————. *Teatro antiguo de Buenos Aires.* Buenos Aires: Imprenta El Comercio, 1904.

Caillet-Bois, Julio. *Análisis de La Araucana.* Buenos Aires: Centro Editor de América Latina, 1967.

Carilla, Emilio. *Un olvidado poeta colonial.* Buenos Aires: Imprenta de la Universidad, 1943.

Chang-Rodríguez, Raquel, and Donald A. Yates, eds. *Homage to Irving A. Leonard.* East Lansing, Mich.: Latin American Studies Center of Michigan State University, 1977.

Chávez, Ezequiel A. *Ensayo de psicología de Sor Juana Inés de la Cruz.* México, D.F.: Asociación "Ezequiel A. Chávez," 1970.

Dauster, Frank. *Breve historia de la poesía mexicana.* México, D.F.: Ediciones de Andrea, 1956.

Dinamarca, Salvador. *Estudio del "Arauco domado" de Pedro de Oña.* New York: Hispanic Institute in the United States, 1952.

Fitzmaurice-Kelly, James. *The Nun Ensign.* London: T. Fisher Unwin, 1908.

Flynn, Gerald. *Sor Juana Inés de la Cruz.* New York: Twayne Publishers, 1971.

García Calderón, Ventura. *Costumbristas y satíricos.* Paris: Desclée de Brouwer, 1938.

García Icazbalceta, Joaquín. *Francisco Terrazas y otros poetas del siglo XVI.* Madrid: Ediciones José Porrúa Turanzas, 1962.

Garibay K., Angel María. *Historia de la literatura nahuatl,* México, D.F.: Editorial Porrúa, 1971.

Getino, Luis A. *Santa Rosa de Lima, su personalidad intelectual.* N.p.: Talleres Gráficos de la Penitenciaría, n.d.

González Peña, Carlos. *Historia de la literatura mexicana.* México, D.F.: Editorial Porrúa, 1975.

Hanke, Lewis, ed. *History of Latin American Civilization,* 2nd ed. 2 vols. Boston: Little, Brown and Company, 1973.

Jiménez Rueda, Julio. *Sor Juana Inés de la Cruz en su época.* México, D.F.: Editorial Porrúa, 1951.

Jones, Willis Knapp. *Behind Spanish American Footlights.* Austin, Tex.: University of Texas Press, 1966.

Keyes, Frances Parkinson. *The Rose and the Lily, the Lives of Two South American Saints.* New York: Hawthorne Books, 1961.

Kolb, Glen L. *Juan del Valle y Caviedes: A Study of the Life, Times and Poetry of a Spanish Colonial Satirist.* New London, Conn.: Stonington Publishing Company, 1959.

Leonard, Irving A. *Baroque Times in Old Mexico.* Ann Arbor, Mich.: University of Michigan Press, 1966.

———. *Books of the Brave.* New York: Gordian Press, 1964.

———. *Don Carlos Sigüenza y Góngora: A Savant of the Seventeenth Century.* Berkeley, Calif.: University of California Press, 1929.

———. *Romances of Chivalry in the Spanish Indies.* Berkeley, Calif.: University of California Press, 1933.

Lohmann Villena, Guillermo. *El arte dramático en Lima durante el virreinato.* Madrid: Estades, Artes Gráficas, 1945.

Madariaga, Salvador de. *Hernán Cortés, Conqueror of Mexico.* Chicago: Henry Regnery Company, 1955.

McPharlin, Paul. *The Puppet Theater in America.* Boston: Plays, 1969.

Medina, José Toribio. *Vida de Ercilla.* México, D.F.: Fondo de Cultura Económica, 1948.

Miró Quesada, Aurelio. *El Inca Garcilaso y otros estudios garcilasistas.* Madrid: Ediciones Cultural Hispánica, 1971.

Morales Borrero, María Teresa. *La Madre Castillo, su espiritualidad y su estilo*. Bogotá: La Imprenta Patriótica del Instituto Caro y Cuervo, 1968.

Nervo, Amado. *Juana de Asbaje*. Vol. 8 of *Obras completas*. Madrid: La Imprenta de Juan Pueyo, 1910.

O'Sullivan-Beare, Nancy. *Las mujeres de los conquistadores*. Madrid: Compañía Bibliográfica Española, 1956.

Pérez, María Esther. *Lo americano en el teatro de Sor Juana Inés de la Cruz*. New York: Eliseo Torres and Sons, 1975.

Reedy, Daniel R. *The Poetic Art of Juan del Valle Caviedes*. Chapel Hill, N.C.: University of North Carolina Press, 1964.

Reyes, Alfonso. *Obras completas*. 19 vols. México, D.F.: Fondo de Cultura Económica, 1960.

Robe, Stanley L., ed. *Coloquios de pastores from Jalisco, México*. Berkeley and Los Angeles: University of California Press, 1954.

Rojas Garcidueñas, José. *Bernardo de Balbuena: la vida y la obra*. México, D.F.: Imprenta Universitaria, 1958.

Sánchez, Luis Alberto. *Los poetas de la colonia y de la revolución*. Lima: Editorial Universo, 1974.

Trenti Rocamora, José Luis. *Grandes mujeres de América*. Buenos Aires: Editorial Huarpes, 1945.

———. *El teatro en la América colonial*. Buenos Aires: Editorial Huarpes, 1947.

Van Horne, John. *Bernardo de Balbuena: biografía y crítica*. Guadalajara, Méx.: Imprenta Font, 1940.

Vargas Ugarte, Rubén. *Rosas de Oquendo y otros*. Lima: Clásicos Peruanos, 1955.

Vigil, José María. *Poetisas mexicanas, siglos XVI, XVII, XVIII y XIX*. Edición facsimilar. 1893: Rpt. México, D.F.: Imprenta Universitaria, 1977.

Weber de Kurlat, Frida. *Lo cómico en el teatro de Fernán González de Eslava*. Buenos Aires: La Imprenta de la Universidad de Buenos Aires, 1963.

Secondary Sources—Articles

Aubrun, Charles. "Poesía épica y novela: El episodio de Glaura en *La Araucana* de Ercilla." *Revista Iberoamericana* 21, nos. 41–42 (1956): 261–73.

Bataillon, Marcel. "Gutiérrez de Santa Clara, escritor mexicano." *Nueva Revista de Filología Hispánica* 15, nos. 3–4 (1961): 405–40.

———. "Introducción a Concolorcorvo y a su itinerario de Buenos Aires a Lima." *Cuadernos Americanos* 19 (1960): 197–216.

Benso, Silvia. "Técnica narrativa de Rodríguez Freyle." *Thesaurus* 32, no. 1 (1977): 95–165.

Chang-Rodríguez, Raquel. "El 'Prólogo al lector' de *El carnero.*" *Thesaurus* 29 (1974): 73–76.

———. 'El propósito de *Cautiverio feliz* y la crítica." *Cuadernos Hispano-americanos* 297 (1975): 657–63.

———. "Relectura de *Los empeños de una casa.*" *Revista Iberoamericana* 44, nos. 104–5 (1978): 409–19.

———. "Tapadas limeñas en un cancionerillo peruano del siglo XVII." *Revista Interamericana de Bibliografía* 28, no. 1 (1978): 57–62.

Durand, José. "Los silencios del Inca Garcilaso." *Mundo Nuevo* 5 (1966): 66–72.

Gilman, Stephen. "Bernal Díaz del Castillo and *Amadís de Gaula.*" Vol. 2 of *Studia Philologica, Homenaje a Dámaso Alonso.* Madrid: Editorial Gredos, 1961.

Giménez Fernández, Manuel. "Fray Bartolomé de Las Casas: A Biographical Sketch" in *Bartolomé de Las Casas in History.* Eds. Juan Friede and Benjamin Keen. DeKalb, Ill.: Northern Illinois University Press, 1971.

Giraldo Jaramillo, Gabriel. "Don Juan Rodríguez Freyle y *La Celestina.*" *Boletín de Historia y Antigüedades* 27, nos. 308–9 (1940): 582–86.

Hatzfeld, Helmut. "Mística femenina clásica en España y Francia." In his *Estudios literarios sobre mística española.* Madrid: Editorial Gredos, 1955, pp. 253–90.

Icaza, Francisco A. de. "Cristóbal de Llerena y los orígenes del teatro en la América española." *Revista de Filología Española* 8, no. 2 (1921): 121–30.

Johnson, Julie Greer. "Bernal Díaz and the Women of the Conquest." *Hispanófila* 82 (1984).

———. "A Caricature of Spanish Women in the New World by the Inca Garcilaso de la Vega." *Latin American Literary Review* 9, no. 18 (1981): 47–51.

———. "Feminine Satire in Concolorcorvo's *El lazarillo de ciegos caminantes.*" *South Atlantic Bulletin* 45, no. 1 (1980): 11–20.

———. "Three Celestinesque Figures of Colonial Spanish American Literature." *Celestinesca* 5, no. 1 (1981): 41–46.

———. "Three Dramatic Works by Juan del Valle y Caviedes." *Hispanic Journal* 3, no. 1 (1982): 59–71.

Jones, Willis Knapp. "Women in Early Spanish American Theater." *Latin American Theater Review* 4, no. 1 (1970): 23–34.

Leonard, Irving A. "A Great Savant of Colonial Peru: Don Pedro de Peralta." *Philological Quarterly* 12, no. 1 (1933): 54–72.

———. "More Conjectures Regarding the Identity of Lope de Vega's 'Amarilis Indiana'." *Hispania* 20, no. 2 (1937): 113–20.

———. "A Shipment of *Comedias* to the Indies." *Hispanic Review* 3, no. 1 (1934): 39–50.

Lerner, Lía Schwartz. "Tradición literaria y heroínas indias en *La Araucana*." *Revista Iberoamericana* 38, no. 81 (1972): 615–26.

Mazzara, Richard A. "Some Picaresque Elements in Concolorcorvo's *El lazarillo de ciegos caminantes*." *Hispania* 46, no. 2 (1963): 323–27.

Medina, José Toribio. "Las mujeres de *La Araucana*." *Hispania* 11 (1928): 1–12.

Pasquariello, Anthony M. "The *Entremés* in Sixteenth-Century Spanish America." *Hispanic American Historical Review* 32, no. 1 (1952): 44–58.

———. "Two Eighteenth-Century Peruvian Interludes, Pioneer Pieces in Local Color." *Symposium* 6 (1952): 385–90.

Pupo-Walker, Enrique. "La reconstrucción imaginativa del pasado en *El carnero* de Rodríguez Freyle." *Nueva Revista de Filología Hispánica* 27, no. 2 (1978): 346–58.

———. "Sobre la configuración narrativa de los *Comentarios reales*." *Revista Hispánica Moderna* 39 (1976–1977): 123–35.

Reedy, Daniel R. "Poesías inéditas de Juan del Valle Caviedes." *Revista Iberoamericana* 29, no. 55 (1963): 157–90.

Rojas Garcidueñas, José. "Piezas teatrales y representaciones en Nueva España en el siglo XVI." *Revista de Literatura Mexicana* 1, no. 1 (1940): 148–54.

Rosenbach, A.S.W. "The First Theatrical Company in America." In *Proceedings of the American Antiquarian Society*. Worcester, Mass.: Published by the Society, 1939, pp. 300–310.

Schons, Dorothy. "Some Obscure Points in the Life of Sor Juana Inés de la Cruz." *Modern Philology* 24, no. 2 (1926): 141–62.

Spell, Jefferson Rea. "Three Manuscript Plays by Eusebio Vela." *Revista de Estudios Hispánicos* 1, no. 3 (1928): 268–73.

Torre Revello, José. "El teatro en la colonia." *Humanidades* 23 (1933): 145–65.

Toussaint, Manuel. "Nuevos aspectos en la biografía de Fray Manuel Navarrete." *Revista de Literatura Mexicana* 1, no. 2 (1940): 226–34.

Vossler, Karl. "El mundo en el sueño." In *Primero sueño* by Sor Juana Inés de la Cruz. Buenos Aires: Imprenta de la Universidad, 1953, pp. 7–17.

Weckmann, Luis. "The Middle Ages in the Conquest of America." *Speculum* 26 (1951): 130–41.

Other Works Consulted

Boxer, Charles R. *Women in Iberian Expansion Overseas, 1415–1815*. New York: Oxford University Press, 1975.

Bullough, Vern L. *The Subordinate Sex: A History of Attitudes toward Women*. Urbana, Ill.: University of Illinois Press, 1973.

Daly, Mary. *The Church and the Second Sex*. New York: Harper and Row, 1975.

Donovan, Josephine, ed. *Feminist Literary Criticism: Explorations in Theory*. Lexington, Ky.: University Press of Kentucky, 1975.

Figes, Eva. *Patriarchal Attitudes*. New York: Stein and Day, 1970.

Foster, Jeannette H. *Sex Variant Women in Literature*. London: Fredrick Muller, 1958.

Green, Otis H. *Spain and the Western Tradition*. 4 vols. Madison, Wisc.: University of Wisconsin Press, 1963.

Knaster, Meri. *Women in Spanish America: An Annotated Bibliography from Pre-Conquest to Contemporary Times*. Boston: G. K. Hall, 1977.

Lavrin, Asunción, ed. *Latin American Women: Historical Perspectives*. Westport, Conn.: Greenwood Press, 1978.

Mora, Gabriela, and Karen S. Van Hooft, eds. *Theory and Practice of Feminist Literary Criticism*. Ipsilanti, Mich.: Bilingual Press/Editorial Bilingüe, 1982.

Pescatello, Ann M. *Power and Pawn: The Female in Iberian Families, Societies, and Cultures*. Westport, Conn.: Greenwood Press, 1976.

Rogers, Katherine M. *The Troublesome Helpmate: A History of Misogyny in Literature*. Seattle, Wash.: University of Washington Press, 1966.

Santamaría, Francisco J. *Diccionario general de americanismos*, 3 vols. México, D.F.: Editorial Pedro Robredo, 1942.

Schurz, William Lytle. *This New World*. New York: E. P. Dutton and Co., 1964.

Torre Revello, José. *El libro, la imprenta y el periodismo en América durante la dominación española*. Buenos Aires: Talleres S. A. Casa Jacobo Peuse, 1940.

INDEX